Eurocentrism and Development in Korea

Under the global hegemony of the West, societies have interpreted the world and defined their identities through the frameworks of Eurocentric discourses. Since the mid-twentieth century, Eurocentrism has tended to be associated with economic developmentalism. The discourse of *seonjinguk* (developed country) has been a dominant Eurocentric developmental discourse in Korea.

However, in what historical contexts have the Koreans set *seonjinguk* as their national goal and yardstick to judge nations? What roles have been played by the concept of *seonjinguk* in Korea? What discursive frameworks did the Koreans use for their national identities and worldviews before the developmental era? *Eurocentrism and Development in Korea* is the first scholarly approach to those questions. Through a chronological analysis of Korea's dominant discourses from the late nineteenth century to the present, Kim demonstrates the historical nature of developmentalism and *seonjinguk* discourse for Korea's developmental era, and traces their genealogy to *gaehwa* (enlightenment) and *munmyeong* (civilization) discourses from a sociological-historical perspective.

Providing essential knowledge about Korea's history of Eurocentrism, developmentalism and national change, this enlightening monograph will appeal to undergraduate and postgraduate students, as well as postdoctoral researchers, interested in fields such as Korean Studies, Development Studies and Global Sociology.

Jongtae Kim is Humanities Korea (HK) Research Professor in the Asiatic Research Institute at Korea University, Seoul, Korea.

Routledge Studies in Emerging Societies

Series editor: Jan Nederveen Pieterse, University of California, Santa Barbara

The baton of driving the world economy is passing to emerging economies. This is not just an economic change, but a social change, with migration flows changing direction towards surplus economies; a political change, as in the shift from the G7 to G20; and over time, cultural changes. This also means that the problems of emerging societies will increasingly become world problems. This series addresses the growing importance of BRIC (Brazil Russia India China) and rising societies such as South Korea, Taiwan, Singapore, Indonesia, South Africa, Turkey, the UAE and Mexico. It focuses on problems generated by emergence, such as social inequality, cultural change, media, ethnic and religious strife, ecological constraints, relations with advanced and developing societies, and new regionalism, with a particular interest in addressing debates and social reflexivity in emerging societies.

1 Global Modernity, Development, and Contemporary Civilization
Towards a Renewal of Critical Theory
José Maurício Domingues

2 Globalization and Development in East Asia
Edited by Jan Nederveen Pieterse and Jongtae Kim

3 Brazil Emerging
Inequality and Emancipation
Edited by Jan Nederveen Pieterse and Adalberto Cardoso

4 Higher Education in the Global Age
Policy, Practice and Promise in Emerging Societies
Edited by Daniel Araya and Peter Marber

5 Critical Theory After the Rise of the Global South
Kaleidoscopic Dialectic
Boike Rehbein

6 Changing Constellations of Southeast Asia
From Northeast Asia to China
Edited by Jan Nederveen Pieterse, Abdul Rahman Embong, Siew Yean Tham

7 Eurocentrism and Development in Korea
Jongtae Kim

Eurocentrism and Development in Korea

Jongtae Kim

Routledge
Taylor & Francis Group
LONDON AND NEW YORK

First published 2018 by Routledge

2 Park Square, Milton Park, Abingdon, Oxfordshire OX14 4RN
52 Vanderbilt Avenue, New York, NY 10017

Routledge is an imprint of the Taylor & Francis Group, an informa business

First issued in paperback 2019

British Library Cataloguing-in-Publication Data
A catalogue record for this book is available from the British Library

Library of Congress Cataloging-in-Publication Data
Names: Kim, Jongtae, author.
Title: Eurocentrism and development in Korea / Jongtae Kim.
Description: 1 Edition. | New York, NY : Routledge, 2017. | Series: Routledge studies in emerging societies | Includes bibliographical references and index.
Identifiers: LCCN 2017050643 | ISBN 9781138234079 (hardback)
Subjects: LCSH: Korea (South)--Economic policy. | Economic development--Korea (South)
Classification: LCC HC467 .K 2017 | DDC 338.95195--dc23
LC record available at https://lccn.loc.gov/2017050643

ISBN: 978-1-138-23407-9 (hbk)
ISBN: 978-0-367-35994-2 (pbk)

Typeset in Times New Roman
by Taylor & Francis Books

Contents

Illustrations

Figures

Tables

Preface

I take a walk around the Han River Park in free evening time. Beneath the lonely high shining Seoul Tower is the calmly flowing Han River reflecting various colors of city lights. Lazily watching people cycling, dating, or playing with pets, I sometimes wonder if this is *seonjinguk* (an advanced country). In fact, not many metropolitan cities in the world, with sizes comparable to Seoul, have popular spaces like the Han River Park where people can enjoy their leisure time late into the night. Nonetheless, in many Seoulites' minds is a vague yearning for New York's Central Park, which turns into a dangerous zone at night.

A Korean visitor to the University of Illinois, whom I met in my doctoral years, came to the U.S. to study the U.S. subprime mortgage system. Shortly after his return to Korea, the U.S. underwent a severe financial crisis because of the subprime mortgage. This incident reflects a reality of Korean society that any kind of financial institution in the U.S. can be a research topic for Korea as an "advanced" case. In fact, is it not that Korean society has lost much of its critical and independent thinking ability in regard to the U.S. and the West, while settling under U.S. hegemony amidst the extreme intranational conflict with North Korea?

Studying in the U.S., I could not help but sometimes question if the U.S. was really a more desirable country than Korea, given that the U.S. had lots of its own domestic and international problems which it lacked the wisdom to solve for itself. In fact, there is a big difference between the "reality" of the U.S. and the U.S. in Koreans' imagination. Why is this? Why do the Koreans aspire to the U.S. and the West with a deficient self-identity? What justifies the epistemic hierarchy between Korea and the West?

To answer these questions, I try to find answers in the discourse of *seonjinguk*. Within this discursive framework, Koreans idealize the West while marginalizing the non-West including themselves. Insofar as the U.S. is *seonjinguk*, the Koreans tend to imagine it far better than its reality, longing for its every aspect. In this situation, the U.S. and the West easily enjoy their intellectual and moral leadership over Korea.

This book is the first sociological inquiry into the origin and unfolding of Korea's vague longing for and "deficient identity" to the West, and the effects of this on historical changes and developments in Korean society. To do this, it investigates the traces of dominant Eurocentric discourses in Korea from the late nineteenth century to the present.

As the research on this book started in my doctoral years, I am now humbly presenting its results to readers ten years later. My work thus far would be greatly rewarded if this book could contribute to deepening the understanding of Korean society, and ultimately enhancing people's imagination of the post-Eurocentric and post-developmental world. The book is based on my doctoral dissertation and its chapters include revisions of my journal publications, as follows:

Chapter 1: "South Korea's Developmentalist Worldview: Representations and Identities in the Discourse of *Seonjinguk*." *Asian Journal of Social Science* 42(3–4), 2014.

Chapter 2: "The Origins of Korea's Eurocentrism: A Study of Discourses on Gaehwa and Munmyeong." *Seoul Journal of Korean Studies* 25(1), 2012.

Chapter 3: "Geundae munmyeong damron-eui jeongchiseong yeongu" [A Study on the Politics of the Modern Discourse of Civilization]. *Hangukhak yeongu* [*The Journal of Korean Studies*] 60, 2017.

Chapter 4: "Rhee Syngman jeongbu sigi munmyeong damron-gwa *seonjinguk* damron-e natanan gukga jeongcheseong-gwa seogugwan" [National Identity and the Image of the West in Munmyeong and *Seonjinguk* Discourses during the Rhee Syngman Administration]. *Hanguk sahwoehak* [*Korean Journal of Sociology*] 46(2), 2012; "Baljeon sidae ijeon baljeon damron-eui wisang" [The Status of Developmental Discourse in the Pre-developmental Era]. *Hanguk sahwoehak* [*Korean Journal of Sociology*] 49(4), 2015.

Chapter 5: "Park Chung-Hee jeongbu sigi *seonjinguk* damron-eui busang-gwa baljeonjueui-jeok gukga jeongcheseong-eui hyeongseong" [The Rise of *Seonjinguk* Discourse and the Formation of Developmental National Identity during the Park Chung-Hee Era]. *Hanguk sahwoehak* [*Korean Journal of Sociology*] 47(1), 2013.

Chapter 6: "South Korea's Historical Constructions of 'Advanced Country': The Discourse of *Seonjinguk* from the 1980s to the Present." *Sahwoe-wa Iron* [*Society and Theory*] 18(1), 2011.

Chapter 7: "Hanguk baljeonjueui-eui damron gujo" [The Structure of Korea's Developmentalism]. *Gyeongjewa Sahwoe* [*Economy and Society*] 103, 2014.

Chapter 8: "Hanguk eonrone natanan hanguk, jungguk, ilbon-eui jeongche-seong-gwa pyosang" [The Identities and Images of Korea, China, and Japan in Korean Newspapers]. *Sahwoe gwahak yeonggu* [*Social Science Studies*] 22(1), 2014; "Hanguk, jungguk, ilbon-eui baljeon damron soge natanan gukga jeongcheseong-gwa sangho insik bigyo" [Comparative Study of National Identities and Mutual Perceptions in the Development Discourses of Korea, China, and Japan]. *Gyeongje•inmun sahwoe yeon-guhwoe inmun jeongchaek yeongu chongseo* [*Report for the National Research Council for Economics, Humanities and Social Sciences*] 2015–22,

2015, co-authored with Jeong Il-Jun, Park Jeong-Hyeon, and Song Byeong-Gwon.

Chapter 9: "Dongbuga-wa Europe jiyeok jeongcheseong bigyo" [A Comparison of Regional Identities between Northeast Asia and Europe]. *The Journal of Asiatic Studies* 59(3), 2016.

This book owes much to many people. Above all, I am greatly indebted to Prof. Jan Nederveen Pieterse, my doctoral advisor. An eminent global sociologist envisioning a multipolar world, Prof. Nederveen Pieterse has opened my eyes to post-Eurocentric and post-developmental worlds. I will never forget his great teachings about both studies and life at the University of Illinois, which sometimes took place in his nice wine-equipped house in Urbana. Already in his seventies, the Professor is still very active in researching and writing, awakening the laziness of his student. I sincerely hope that his scholarly activities provide the world with great insights for a long, long time, and would like to dedicate this book to him.

I am also thankful to the late Prof. Hong Seung-Chik, Prof. Park Gil-Sung, and Prof. Sohn Seok-Chun. Profs. Hong and Park at Korea University gladly wrote letters for me when I decided to study in the U.S. more than a decade after graduation. Prof. Sohn, then my senior reporter at the *Hankyoreh Daily News*, secretly supported my new plan and gave important help.

My thanks also to teachers at Arizona State University, especially to Profs. George Thomas, Mary Benin, and Karen Miller-Loessi. By virtue of their consideration, I was able to settle smoothly in the new study environment to successfully finish my Master's program. I am also grateful to Profs. Norman Denzin, Tim Liao, James Hay, and Brian Dill at the University of Illinois at Urbana-Champaign. Without their helpful advice and criticism, my doctoral dissertation might have taken far longer.

Profs. Cho Dae-Yeop and Kim Jong-Kil have offered various favors for my settling into Korean academia. I am truly grateful to them and, at the same time, feel sorry if I have not yet met their expectations. Conversations with Profs. Park Jeong-Hyeon and Lee Dong-Jun, which sometimes occurred over *makgeolli*, have provided essential nourishment for this book. I am especially thankful for their reminders of the importance of this study.

Since my return to Korea in 2011 with a fresh doctoral degree, the Asiatic Research Institute (ARI) at Korea University has provided me with a wonderful research environment. Without the ARI, the researching of this book might have been far more difficult. I am greatly thankful to colleagues in the ARI, especially to Profs. Lee Nae-Young, Yoon In-Jin, Song Gyu-Jin, and Lee Jeong-Nam.

The research on *seonjinguk* discourse and developmentalism is now expanding its scope to Northeast Asia, e.g., China, Japan, and Taiwan. I am grateful to Profs. Jeong Il-Jun, Yoon Eun-Ja, Song Byeong-Gwon, and Wang Eun-Mi, who have gladly collaborated with me on the international comparative research.

This book is a result of the Korea Research Foundation's funding for book writing from 2013 to 2016. I am greatly thankful to the blind reviewers of my book proposal and the people at the Korea Research Foundation, who agreed on the importance of this research which might have been somewhat unfamiliar to Korean society at the time.

I also give special thanks to those at Routledge who have effectively enabled this research to reach a wide range of readers around the world. I would like to draw readers' attention to the Korean version of this book, published by Dolbegae in 2018.

Finally, I would like to thank my family. I am grateful to my parents, who are always wishing for their eldest son's happiness. My wife, Young-Mi, an artist, is a person I can always lean on emotionally. I especially thank my son Wonjun, who has grown up wise in changing environments in the U.S. and Korea. I truly wish that this book contributes to making the world for Wonjun's generation more mature, humane, and peaceful.

Winter 2017 in Seoul
Kim Jongtae

Acknowledgements

This work was supported by the National Research Foundation of Korea Grant, funded by the Korean Government (NRF-2013S1A6A4017561).

1 Introduction

What is the Discourse of *Seonjinguk*?

South Korean society is trapped in the discourse of *seonjinguk* (an advanced country).[1] In November 2010, the leader of the then ruling Grand National Party (*Hannaradang*) delivered a speech to his party members as below. This speech used the term "*seonjinguk*" as many as eight times. It demonstrates well the importance of the concept of "*seonjinguk*" and its socio-political roles in Korean society.

> What is the political party that will lead our fatherland to *seonjinhwa* and *seonjinguk*, following the wish of President Park Chung-Hee? Isn't it the Grand National Party? In order for the Grand National Party to lead our country to *seonjinguk*, President Lee Myung-Bak should make a success [...] I think that it is the calling of our times that the Grand National Party put South Korea up to the level of *seonjinguk* by re-taking power for the next term, and also think that there is no other political party than the Grand National Party in South Korea able to do it [...] I think that if such a power as the Roh Moo-Hyun government is established again, or if the Democratic Party, leftist party, takes power, our country would eventually fail in entering into the rank of *seonjinguk*. It is my idea that President Lee Myung-Bak should make the basic framework for our country to enter into *seonjinguk* and, then, it should be done by the next president from our Grand National Party to complete the achievement of *seonjinguk*. In this way, if we make [gross domestic product (GDP) per capita] above $30,000, then it is unlikely to drop below $30,000. However, in our times of $20,000, we are unable to enter into the rank of full *seonjinguk* because we are up and down around $15,000 and $20,000 [...] Isn't it that our Grand National Party should re-take power for the next term if it is to upgrade our country to the level of *seonjinguk*, following the competent Lee Myung-Bak administration? Isn't it that it should be able to achieve the era of $30,000 in GDP per capita? For this, we should re-take power for the next term.[2]

Above all, the concept of "*seonjinguk*" presents a national goal for South Korea (Korea hereafter). The speech above emphasizes that it is a historical mission for the nation to go up or "enter" into the rank of "*seonjinguk*," and that there is no one but the Grand National Party that can achieve this mission. This speech seeks legitimacy for the political party from its ability to make the nation "enter into the rank of *seonjinguk*." It argues that the Grand National Party is the very political power that is capable of enhancing Korea to the level of "*seonjinguk*," while criticizing that a "leftist regime" like the former Roh Moo-Hyun government will take the nation to failure. As for the cause for then President Lee Myung-Bak's success, the speech insists that it is to lead the nation to the rank of *seonjinguk*. It claims that the creation of another government of his party after President Lee is a historical mission in this regard.

The speech above shows a self-identity of Korea. That is, it implies that Korea is not *seonjinguk* yet, but is in the process of entering into this rank. As for the reason why Korea has not "entered into" the rank of *seonjinguk* yet, the speech contends that Korea's per capita income is oscillating just between US$15,000 and $20,000. It presents $30,000 as a condition for *seonjinguk*.

The speech also suggests the nation's future plan for *seonjinguk*. It is that President Lee creates a basic ground for entering into *seonjinguk*, and the next government of the Grand National Party accomplishes the entry. In retrospect, the Grand National Party had to change its name to the *Saenuri* Party about three months after this speech to overcome its low popularity and, fortunately, succeeded in recreating its government by winning the 18th presidential election in 2012. However, later in 2016, it had to suffer again from people's harsh criticism as an accomplice to President Park Geun-Hye who was the first impeached in Korean constitutional history, instead of achieving the "historical mission" of the nation's entry into the rank of *seonjinguk*.

In fact, the impeached President Park Geun-Hye had presented a vision of "achieving the status of *seonjinguk* in five years" in 2007 when she was in the race to become the Grand National Party's presidential candidate. Her supporters trumpeted her qualifications for national leader to achieve the mission of *seonjinguk*, with such slogans as "*seonjinguk* in five years, Park Geun-Hye can do it," "let's go to *seonjinguk* with Park Geun-Hye," and so forth. Would Park Geun-Hye truly have had the ability to accomplish that, given her political career was totally reliant on her late father Pak Chung-Hee's reputation, without any notable self-achievement?

Despite Park's slogans for the achievement of *seonjinguk*, the Grand National Party chose Lee Myung-Bak for its presidential candidate, who had been called the "legend of salaried man," and Lee was elected as president, earning 48.7% of the vote in the 17th presidential election on 19 December 2007. The Koreans who had historically experienced the achievements of developmentalism might have expected that Lee Myung-Bak would lead the nation to *seonjinguk* by accomplishing his election pledges, such as "747" (7% annual economic growth, $40,000 per capita income, and seventh greatest nation in the world), given his notable achievements as a successful businessman in "bulldozer style" during the past industrializing era of Korea.

In office, President Lee constantly suggested the "entry into *seonjinguk*" as a national goal, promoting the slogan of "*seonjinhwa*" (becoming advanced). The supporters of the so-called "Project for Four Rivers," which President Lee carried forward in bulldozer style with the national budget of as much as ₩22,000 billion (about $20 billion), justified the project in such terms as the "way to *seonjinguk*," "making the momentum for advance to *seonjinguk*," etc.

The discourse of *seonjinguk* is widely used not only in the political sphere but in the mass media. For instance, in December 2016, when the whole nation was acutely embarrassed over the so-called "Park Geun-Hye – Choi Sun-Sil gate," an internet journal published an article entitled "The *seonjinguk*-style growth model is possible if the Park Geun-Hye gate is cleared." However, what would have been the exact causal relationship between the "clearance of the Park Geun-Hye gate" and the "*seonjinguk*-style growth model," which was argued in this article? Would this perhaps not have been an argument as vague as Park Geun-Hye's slogan of the "accomplishment of *seonjinguk* in five years?"

A firm fact is that the discourse of *seonjinguk* is widely used by opinion leaders in Korea, such as politicians, journalists, or even scholars, in a wide range of contexts regardless of the accuracy and validity of its contents. However, as the contents of *seonjinguk* discourse are vague, the Koreans, who are the very users of the discourse, are cautious about "what *seonjinguk* is." They seem generally to consider Western countries, such as the U.S. and Western European countries, as *seonjinguk*, but there are controversies over the criteria by which they are judged to be *seonjinguk*.

Some ask whether Korea is *seonjinguk* or not. On a Korean website in 2015, a question was posted with the title of "Do you think of Korea as *seonjinguk*?"

> While talking with my friends today, I said that Korea was yet a developing country and the like, but two friends quizzically responded that a country like Korea could be *seonjinguk*. And, we had words with one another to become somewhat awkward with one another … I haven't ever thought that Korea is *seonjinguk* but I am now wondering if there are many who think of Korea as *seonjinguk*, like my friends today. I don't like it, but I think that *seonjinguk* in the East is just Japan … The criteria for *seonjinguk* I think are that it is to be recognized in a good image by most people in foreign countries, and that its people are sensible with the consciousness of community and the like, and that it has a good welfare system … But, I think that Korea is not *seonjinguk* as it is quite lacking in the first and third points … And, is China a developing country too?[3]

To this question, various answers were posted, such as that "Korea is *hujinguk* while Japan is *seonjinguk*," or that "our country is sometimes categorized into *seonjinguk*, sometimes into a developing country, or sometimes into a newly industrialized country that is in-between."

This kind of discussion occurs out of curiosity, but some utilize the discourse of *seonjinguk* for their own interests, for example to appear knowledgeable. For instance, referring to the case of *seonjinguk* is a good conversational method to persuade others in Korean society. The "conversational method of mentioning *seonjinguk*" gives authority to the speaker regardless of the accuracy of information that the speaker delivers about *seonjinguk*, because the knowledge of *seonjinguk* cases itself tends to be the source of authority. However, information about *seonjinguk*, exchanged in the public space, is often vague and uncertain because of the ambiguity of the concept of *seonjinguk*.

If two people from the countryside – one who has visited Seoul and another who has not – were to argue with each other about Seoul, who would win? The answer would be the louder. Both Seoul for the countryperson and *seonjinguk* for Korean society can be the unknown world to be aspired to. In this respect, there are commonalities between those from the countryside talking about Seoul and Korean society mentioning *seonjinguk*.

The discourse of *seonjinguk* is a dominant interpretive framework in the current Korean society. Then, what is *seonjinguk* to the Koreans? From when have they set *seonjinguk* as their national goal and yardstick to judge nations? What roles are played by the concept of *seonjinguk* in Korean society? Is Korea *seonjinguk* or not? If not, how can it be *seonjinguk*?

This book is the first scholarly approach to the Koreans' discourse of *seonjinguk*. It aims to give answers to those questions about *seonjinguk*, by revealing the characteristics of *seonjinguk* discourse prevalent in the political and public spaces of Korean society, and tracing its historical genealogy as a Eurocentric discourse from a sociological perspective.

The Concept of *Seonjinguk*: Referents and Social Roles

What Seonjinguk *Refers to*

The term *seonjinguk* literally means "ahead-going country," with the syllables "*seon*," "*jin*," and "*guk*" denoting "ahead," "go," and "country," respectively. In a similar vein, the term *hujinguk* means "behind-going country" with the syllable "*hu*" meaning "behind" or "backward."[4] The standard Korean dictionary (*pyojun gugeo daesajeon*) defines *seonjinguk* as "the country that is ahead in the development of politics, economy, culture, etc."[5] Historically, it was the year 1938 when the term *seonjinguk* first appeared in the Korean dictionary. *Joseoneo sajeon* (Korean Dictionary], written by Mun Se-Young (1938), defined *seonjinguk* as "a country whose cultures and materials are developed ahead of a certain country."

The term *seonjinguk* began to popularize with the rise of developmentalism in Korea. Reflecting the transition of global discursive focus from "civilization" to "development" in evaluating progress, Korea's discursive focus moved from "*munmyeong*" (civilization) to "*baljeon*" (development) in the 1960s with the rise of the Korean developmental regime led by Park Chung-Hee. In the early developmental era of Korea, the discourse of *seonjinguk* emerged as a representative developmental discourse, which was based on a distinction between *seonjinguk* and *hujinguk* according to the degree of the country's economic development. In this context, the term *seonjinguk* popularized and gradually replaced the term *munmyeong-guk* (civilized country) in referring to an "advanced country."

Since its popularization, however, the term *seonjinguk* has been used in highly ambiguous and arbitrary ways. Despite its popularity, there has been no consensus on what *seonjinguk* is, and its referents have been largely dependent on the user's intentions and interpretations. In the contemporary context, the use of the term *seonjinguk* is analytically discerned by two types: the concrete and the abstract. The concrete type of *seonjinguk* is the case in which referents are specified in the message, while *seonjinguk* of the abstract type is that whose referents are not clearly mentioned in it.

As for the concrete type, *seonjinguk* frequently refers to certain countries. In my newspaper data,[6] 18 countries are explicitly designated as *seonjinguk* in various contexts, such as: the U.S. (66 cases), Japan (33), Britain (10), Germany (9), France (7), Korea (6), Australia (3), Sweden (3), Russia (2), and Finland, the Netherlands, Denmark, Belgium, Norway, Italy, Spain, Switzerland, and Ireland (1 case each).[7] As such, countries in the West are referred to as *seonjinguk*.[8] In some cases, the term *seonjinguk* refers to countries in certain international groups: For instance, the Organisation for Economic Co-operation and Development (OECD) is the group most frequently referred to of *seonjinguk*, and the Group of 7 (G-7) and the Group of 8 (G-8) are often mentioned as such.

However, the term *seonjinguk* is far more frequently used in abstract ways. As its referents are not specified in the message, they are to be inferred from the context. In this regard, *seonjinguk* most commonly means an abstract country or countries. For instance, an editorial of the *Dong-a* (25 March 2008) argues that "*seonjinhwa* [becoming advanced] is far to go unless people could consume foods without concern. This is a reason why *seonjinguk* strengthens regulation on food safety and the environment […]" As in this example, the referent of the term *seonjinguk* is not specified in the text, and the term is conventionally used as if there is a general consensus on what it refers to. However, as there is actually no consensus on it, the interpretation of *seonjinguk* becomes dependent on its users' imagination. In this case, countries categorized into *seonjinguk* are imagined as having similar enough social conditions to be homogenized into that category.

Another frequent abstract use of *seonjinguk* implies a national goal to achieve. The *Hankyoreh* (12 January 2006), for instance, mentions that "these are problems to be solved on the way for the harmonious mature community and true *seonjinguk*." This suggests that Korea is not true *seonjinguk* yet and that achieving true *seonjinguk* is a goal to be pursued at the national level. The term of this type often accompanies certain words related to achievement and goals, such as "*jinip*" (entry), "*doyak*" (leap), "*ggum*" (dream), "*hyanghada*" (head for), "*doeda*" (become), and "*naagada*" (go forward).

Third, it implies a national status. For instance, the *Chosun* (13 April 2005) argues that "this is the reason why the more a country is *seonjinguk*, the more it gives weight on sports in education curriculum [...]" In this case, *seonjinguk* is used in reference to a country's position in the world, which is supposed to have certain (positive) characteristics. Here *seonjinguk* is assumed to have desirable social conditions that other countries should emulate. In relation to this, the term *seonjinguk* is often combined with such words as "*sujun*" (level) or "*hyeong*" (type) to mean commendable levels or types of social aspects. Something referred to as *seonjinguk sujun* (*seonjinguk*-level) or *seonjinguk-hyeong* (*seonjinguk*-type) implies that it is of high quality, which characterizes the social conditions of *seonjinguk*.

Seonjinguk*'s Socio-political Roles*

Since its global expansion, the West has been identified as one of the most significant others by many non-Western societies in their modernization processes. Encountering the threat from outside in the "age of empire" (Hobsbawm, 1987), non-Western societies faced a paradoxical situation in which they had to participate in the game set by the West in order to resist it (Sakai, 1989). With the rise of development discourse, many non-Western countries realized that they were far behind the West to set it as a positive reference to "catch up" through their modernization projects. For many, national development projects were perceived as a way to attain economic independence and decolonization (Ndlovu-Gatsheni, 2012). In this process, the West played a significant role in providing criteria in various social dimensions by which non-Western countries evaluated their positions. In regard to this, Hall (1996: 186) notes the four main roles of the West:

> First, it allows us to characterize and classify societies into different categories – i.e. "western," "non-western" [...] Secondly, [...] [i]t functions as part of a language, a "system of representation" [...] for example, "western" = urban = developed; or "non-western" = non-industrial = rural = agricultural = under-developed [...] Thirdly, it provides a standard or model of comparison [...] Fourthly, it provides criteria of evaluation against which other societies are ranked and around which powerful positive and negative feelings cluster.

In Korea, the referential roles of the West are well reflected in the discourse of *seonjinguk*. As an ideal model of development, the concept of *seonjinguk* has played diverse roles in Korea's modernization process. In the contemporary context, some are notable as follows.

First, it suggests a direction for the country. The *Chosun* (22 August 2007), for instance, argues that "Korea should go forward to become *seonjinguk*, a leading part of the world [...]" In this example, the concept of *seonjinguk* as a national goal provides a point where the country should head. As such, it prescribes the direction of national change, which is premised upon an assumption that *seonjinguk* goes ahead on the linear path of development. In fact, it is considered advanced in various areas, such as technology, economy, welfare, and so forth. The *Dong-a* (9 December 2008), for instance, argues that Korea "took 13 years to have its export amount to reach $400 billion from $100 billion (FY [financial year] 1995), which was more than four years short of the average period taken by *seonjinguk* (17.2 years) that had reached the height of $400 billion ahead of us." As such, *seonjinguk* is represented as a group of countries that have already passed a developmental point where Korea is currently standing. In this respect, *seonjinguk* as an advanced entity shows a direction for Korea to head for. On these grounds, Korea's national identity is defined as a country pursuing *seonjinguk*.

Second, it provides a standard of comparison. In this regard, the *Chosun* (16 November 2007) mentions that "our country's percentage of health insurance coverage [...] is short of *seonjinguk*'s 70–80 percent." Here, the concept of *seonjinguk* is used in reference to abstract countries with no specific ones referred to as *seonjinguk*, and it suggests a referential point of health insurance coverage by which the Korean one is to be evaluated. In this way, *seonjinguk*, either abstract or specific, implies referential social conditions, which non-*seonjinguk* should refer to in their development processes. In relation to this, *seonjinguk* also suggests a comparable point of normality: That is, what is assumed as common in *seonjinguk* tends to be regarded as normal and common sense, by which others' degree of "normality" is to be assessed.

Third, it proposes a desirable model. The *Hankyoreh* (1 May 2008), for instance, argues that "the secret of the success of Finland, which is regarded as the best *seonjinguk* of education, lies in its policies on teachers." In this case, *seonjinguk* is specified as Finland and plays a role in providing a desirable educational model for Korea. When the concept is mentioned in such phrases as "*seonjinguk sujun*" or "*seonjinguk-hyeong*," it also implies a model that should be pursued in various fields of society. As such, desirability is an important characteristic of *seonjinguk*.

Fourth, it sometimes provides a simple referential case. In this case, it does not clearly connote desirability. With regard to Amnesty International's criticism of the Korean government's suppression of civil demonstrations, for instance, the *Dong-a* (21 July 2008) argues that Amnesty International "does not seem to know how the police in *seonjinguk*, such as the U.S. and Japan, treat demonstrators [...]" In this case, a legal practice in *seonjinguk* provides a point of reference for Korea, but is not necessarily regarded as desirable.

Last, it suggests a global trend. When assumed as common in *seonjinguk*, a certain phenomenon tends to be regarded as an inevitable tendency that countries should follow to keep abreast of the times. Neoliberal policy, for instance, is frequently referred to as a global trend in relation to globalization in recent decades, which is putatively adopted by *seonjinguk* and, thus, should also be accepted by Korea.

Representation of Seonjinguk

Setting *seonjinguk* as an advanced entity, the Koreans have endeavored to "catch up" with it in their national development. In this process, they have created an ideal image of *seonjinguk* by projecting their desired values onto it. Thus, *seonjinguk* is generally represented as a country that already has the national features that the Koreans aspire to attain in their development process.

As the discourse of *seonjinguk* is a development discourse, the economic dimension is the most important criterion to define a country as *seonjinguk* or not. In regard to this, *seonjinguk* is described as having high income, advanced technology, and large, competitive companies. These are the basic preconditions for *seonjinguk* as one cannot be *seonjinguk* without high income and technology. However, these are not sufficient conditions for *seonjinguk*'s economy as it requires some important qualitative aspects.

Above all, it is supposed to be fair and transparent. Freedom from corruption, for instance, counts as a main secret of the strong and competitive economy of *seonjinguk*. Thus, to become *seonjinguk* is not just a matter of raising national income, but of establishing an honest economic system. This gives legitimacy to *seonjinguk*'s wealth and bestows a status of respectability on it. An editorial states in this regard that "*seonjinguk* is not one which has a lot of money, large territory, or large population" but "is one that is respected in the international system" (*Chosun*, 26 February 2007). In this discursive practice, there is hardly a perception reflecting that "the achievement of development in the Euro-American zone was entwined with overseas conquest of the non-Western zones" (Ndlovu-Gatsheni, 2012: 19).[9]

In terms of economic ideology, *seonjinguk* is represented by conservative voices as a country on the principles of "liberal market economy" and "liberal democracy." For them, there is no *seonjinguk* that is not based on "free-market" ideology. Under the headline "We will defend liberty and market," for instance, the *Dong-a* (1 April 2006) argues that "one cannot be *seonjinguk* with anti-market ideologies." The conservatives' support of market ideology leads to further assumption that *seonjinguk* actively adopts neoliberalism and accommodates neoliberal globalization. Under the headline "2006 *seonjinguk* trend," the *Dong-a* (26 December 2006) argues that some keywords are found in the trend of *seonjinguk* policies, such as downsizing the government, privatizing public enterprise, deregulation, pro-business policy, and the open market. Then it adds that this "world trend" is summarized in a phrase of "small government, big market."

In regard to social aspects, *seonjinguk* is generally represented as a mature society, which has positive material and spiritual characteristics, such as an efficient disaster prevention system, transparent decision-making process, high awareness of human rights, civil consciousness, and tolerance towards differences. The following criticism of Chinese society well demonstrates the image of the *seonjinguk* society:

> It is not a first-class nation just because it has the largest amount of U.S. dollars and launches satellites into the air. When it is the situation in which a foreigner goes to the [Chinese] hospital, risking his/her life, who would respect China as a leading country of the world? [...] Regardless of its size, [China] would not be regarded as *seonjinguk* if it does not have the national consciousness of valuing human life and frankness, and a social system that punishes dishonesty and the evasion of the law.
>
> (*Chosun*, 22 August 2007)

This argues that China is not *seonjinguk* because of its disregard for human life, lack of frankness, and unjust social system, which conversely implies that *seonjinguk* has human-valuing, frank, and just social systems. The law is considered as a fair mechanism that maintains social trust among people in *seonjinguk*. In this regard, the *Chosun* (16 October 2003) argues that "the degree of respect for laws and systems" is "the most important thing to distinguish between *seonjinguk* and *hujinguk*."

In the credible social system, people in *seonjinguk* are supposed to behave responsibly and appropriately according to their social roles. Its ruling class, in particular, is regarded as the fitting leader of the mature society. As for this, the *Chosun* (2 May 2007) argues that "the power supporting the *seonjinguk* society is said to be '*noblesse oblige*.'" People in *seonjinguk* are also considered to be generous towards the weak, e.g., immigrants and foreign laborers, and, thus, its level of social tolerance is assumed high (*Dong-a*, 4 October 2008).

Like the other aforementioned spheres, *seonjinguk* politics is generally assumed as normal, mature, rational, and transparent. It is portrayed as far from corruption, which is often attributed to its stable and well-managed legal system. This reflects the assumption that *seonjinguk* is under the leadership of the mature and responsible ruling class.

Seonjinguk is also represented as having advanced, high-quality, and attractive cultural properties. These broadly range from a national brand and scientific knowledge to the ability to enjoy high culture. This perception becomes an important ground for *seonjinguk*'s cultural hegemony in Korea and for giving justification to the opening of Korea's cultural areas, such as education, to *seonjinguk*.

Represented as an ideal being in various fields, the concept of *seonjinguk* becomes a source of "auto-Orientalism" for the Koreans.[10] Compared with *seonjinguk*, Korea loses its attractiveness. In this regard, the Koreans tend to consider that something desired by Korean society is already existent in *seonjinguk* and, by contrast, some negative things existent in Korean society are absent in *seonjinguk*.

In relation to this, this study finds two main contexts in which the ideal representation of *seonjinguk* is used in Korean society. First, it is most frequently employed in the context of criticizing Korean society. Compared with *seonjinguk*, various aspects of Korea become unsatisfactory, and are considered as a reason why Korea is not full *seonjinguk* yet. In regard to what is considered as negative in Korea, the editorials tend to argue that "there is no such thing in *seonjinguk* [but just in Korea]." In this way, the supposedly negative aspects of Korean society raise internal shame for the Koreans vis-à-vis *seonjinguk* and are regarded as something to be corrected as soon as possible.

Second, the concept of *seonjinguk* is employed in the context of justifying one's argument. As an ideal representation, *seonjinguk* is a source of cultural authority in Korea and, thus, newspapers tend to rely on it to legitimize their arguments. That is to say, when they promote a policy or event, an easy way to give authority to their arguments is to imply that it is "common in *seonjinguk*."

Concept of *Hujinguk*: Referents and Attributes

By its hierarchical nature, the discourse of *seonjinguk* manifestly shows the operation of binary opposition between the concepts of *seonjinguk* and *hujinguk*. On this principle, the image of *seonjinguk* is constructed in the oppositional relation to the image of *hujinguk* in a similar way to how the Occident is constructed as the opposite image of the Orient in Orientalistic discourse (Said, 1979). In *seonjinguk* discourse, the hierarchy between *seonjinguk* and *hujinguk* has naturally appeared through the process in which the Koreans project their positive developmental values into *seonjinguk* while attributing negative ones to *hujinguk*. In this way, *hujinguk* is created as the marginalized "other" of *seonjinguk* and, thus, both concepts are constitutively interrelated in the discourse.

As with *seonjinguk*, the concept of *hujinguk* is highly ambiguous as there is no consensus on it. Thus, it is used somewhat arbitrarily according to the users' intention and interpretation. Like *seonjinguk*, two types can be discerned in regard to the referents of *hujinguk*: Concrete and abstract ones. In regard to the concrete type, certain countries are designated as *hujinguk*, such as: Korea (23 cases), Bangladesh (2 cases), China, Southeast Asia, Guatemala, Suriname, and past Ireland (1 case each).[11] In general, those designated as *hujinguk* are economically poor in terms of certain economic criteria, such as GDP per capita, and are geographically located in Africa, Latin America, and Asia – the non-West.

In regard to the abstract type, *hujinguk* implies an abstract country (or countries), without any real country or group specified. Thus, it exists as an abstract form of representation. In this case, *hujinguk* is assumed as a country (or countries) that has various negative and undesirable attributes, such as: Anti-human rights; backwardness; unhygienic conditions; risk and insensibility to safety; incapacity and irresponsibility; corruption; low women's status; confusion; conflict; anti-trend; disorder; fault; poverty; lack of principle; short-sightedness; nonsense; and inefficiency.

The way *hujinguk* is represented in the discourse is comparable to the way development studies construct the images of Africa by the practice of "reductive repetition," that is, repetitively reducing its cultures to "a set of essential deficiencies" (Andreasson, 2005: 981). This discursive practice underlies the Eurocentric discourse's tendency of "consignment of 'non-Western world' to 'static backwardness'" (Ndlovu-Gatsheni, 2012: 19). As such, the Eurocentric disposition to problematize the non-West is implicit in the concept of *hujinguk*.[12]

With those undesirable features, the concept of *hujinguk* functions as a negative referent that Korea should not resemble. In terms of Korea's development history, *hujinguk* is considered as the past status of Korea, from which Korea escaped through its successful development and modernization project. When the term *hujinguk* is used in "*hujinguk-hyeong*" (*hujinguk*-type) or "*hujinguk sujun*" (*hujinguk*-level), it implies an undesirable type or level, which Korea should not employ on its way towards *seonjinguk*.

Representation of Hujinguk

The negative attributes of *hujinguk* are well shown in the ways it is represented in regard to various fields. In the political area, *hujinguk* is characterized as having an unreliable political system, which is "confusing," "unpredictable," "corrupt," "inefficient," "irresponsible," or "incapable." Criticizing the Korean National Assembly's way of dealing with the Free Trade Agreement with the U.S., for instance, the *Dong-a* (9 May 2008) designates Korea as a "*hujinguk* of politics," deploring that Korean politics' "short-sightedness and ignorance are surprising and pitiful." Denouncing a political scandal in Korea, another editorial in the *Dong-a* (2 December 2008) questions "until when this kind of *hujinguk*-style corruption should be repeated."

In regard to the economy, *hujinguk* is generally perceived as a low-income country whose economic system is noncompetitive, backward, and unreliable. The *Chosun* (22 February 2007), for instance, defines *hujinguk* as a country that does not have many competitive global corporations. Thus, its economy is considered as lagging behind the global competition and trend, which is a main cause of poverty for *hujinguk*. In contrast with the transparent, fair economy of *seonjinguk*, *hujinguk*'s poor economy is often attributed to its own internal corruption and inefficiency. It is argued that Korea could roll back to the status of *hujinguk* if it does not overcome its economic problem, nor keep abreast of the "global trend."

In terms of the social dimension, *hujinguk* is portrayed as an immature, dangerous country struggling with disorder, dangerousness, irresponsibility, incapacity, nonsense, and unsanitary conditions. In this way, *hujinguk* society is considered as one that seriously lacks general conditions for decent living. As for its disorderly situation, the *Chosun* (7 August 2001) argues that:

> The whole land of Korea is a dumping ground [...] The solutions are the education of order and manner [...] and strict regulations on the scene of

> disorder [...] Or, we will not get out of "spiritual *hujinguk*" regardless of the income level.

As for the safety issue, *hujinguk* is regarded as incapable of preventing natural or man-made disasters. In regard to a deadly explosive accident in Korea, the *Dong-a* (9 January 2008) cynically argues that it is a "tragedy of the *hujinguk* of safety awareness and prevention system." A hierarchy appears even among diseases – that is, there are "*seonjinguk*-type" and "*hujinguk*-type" diseases. For instance, the *Chosun* (8 January 2001, 17 December 2001) designates certain epidemics as "*hujinguk*-type," such as dysentery, cholera, malaria, and the measles. The Koreans find the occurrence of those "*hujinguk*-type" diseases more frustrating and humiliating than others.

In regard to culture and knowledge, *hujinguk* is also regarded as backward. The *Chosun* (24 February 2007), for instance, argues that backwardness in mathematics and science is "not knowing world common sense," and adds that "Korea should not be rolled back to the ignorance of *hujinguk*" by ignoring mathematics and science. As such, traditional and indigenous knowledge is not much appreciated in the discourse.

As a marginalized referent, *hujinguk* is used in diverse contexts and, in this sense, it also plays significant roles in Korean society. It is most frequently used in the context of criticizing domestic affairs. Korea is most frequently and sarcastically designated as *hujinguk* in regard to what the Koreans themselves think is undesirable in their country. If a certain domestic circumstance is labeled as *hujinguk*, the Koreans tend to feel both a great shame of it and an urgent need to change it. In relation to this, the concept of *hujinguk* is also used in the context of supporting an argument. For instance, an easy way to raise a need for changing something in the country is to designate it as a characteristic of *hujinguk*.

Overall, *hujinguk* functions in diverse roles as a negative referent that Korea should not resemble in its path of development. In comparison with its positive other, *seonjinguk*, the contexts in which the term *hujinguk* is used are somewhat parallel to those for *seonjinguk* but in inverse ways in terms of contents.

Korea's Identity in the Discourse of *Seonjinguk*

Identity is defined as "the images of individuality and distinctiveness ('selfhood') held and projected by an actor [...]" (Jepperson et al., 1996: 59). In this respect, constructing an identity is a cognitive process that delineates a boundary between self and others, which is strongly affected by one's "significant others." Insofar as development is representation (Tripathy and Mohapatra, 2011), it provides a framework in which various developmental identities are constructed and negotiated.

In the discourse of *seonjinguk*, Korea's identity is mainly dependent upon two significant others, *seonjinguk* (the positive one) and *hujinguk* (the negative one), and is underlain by both senses of inferiority over the former and of superiority over the latter. This is related to a perception that Korea has rapidly progressed from *hujinguk* to almost *seonjinguk* today on a supposedly universal path of development. In this respect, *hujinguk* tends to be regarded as the past of Korea and *seonjinguk* as its future.

In the early and mid-twentieth century, Korea's national identity was mainly defined as a *munmyeong-guk* (civilized country – especially in ethical and spiritual terms) within the framework of *munmyeong* (civilization). It was with the rise of developmentalism and a developmental regime in the early 1960s that Korea's national identity began to be defined along the developmental line. In this discursive change, Korea underwent a notable change in its self-identity from a *munmyeong-guk* to a *hujinguk*. In this identity, Korea's deficiency in material condition, rather than spiritual affluence, was emphasized, and the country's poverty and low level of industrialization were identified as the urgent problems to overcome in the near future. Under such a slogan as *joguk geundaehwa* (the modernization of the fatherland), the most urgent national goal was set as the escape from the status of *hujinguk*, which became an important discursive basis for Korea's aggressive national modernization project. In terms of domestic politics, the aggressive projects for national development and modernization were good causes for the Park Chung-Hee regime's legitimacy, which rose to power through a military coup.

Due to its successful implementation of the national development project, Korea witnessed rapid economic growth in the 1970s. Reflecting this was a perception that the country had become a kind of *jungjinguk*, an intermediate status between *hujinguk* and *seonjinguk*. When it came to the late 1970s, Korean developmentalists started to designate the country as located in the top tier of *jungjinguk*, just in front of joining the group of *seonjinguk*.

Currently, Korea is sometimes claimed as *seonjinguk*, but is more frequently identified as "nearly *seonjinguk*," as is conveyed in such a phrase as "*seonjinguk munteok*" (on the threshold of *seonjinguk*). This is also an intermediate identity that generates both senses of superiority over *hujinguk* (or *jungjinguk*) and inferiority to *seonjinguk*. While a way to overcome the sense of inferiority may be to claim Korea as *seonjinguk*, there is considerable resistance to this within the country. For instance, a chief presidential secretary was criticized by the *Chosun Ilbo* for his argument that "Korea is already *seonjinguk*." As for this, the *Chosun* (26 November 2005) argued that an important criterion for judging *seonjinguk* was per capita income of $20,000, and that the number of countries above this level was 35. Thus, according to the *Chosun*, it was nonsense to argue that a country whose per capita income rank was 48th (i.e., Korea) was *seonjinguk*.

This debate well demonstrates the ambiguity of the concept of *seonjinguk*. For instance, a *Dong-a* (15 August 2008) editorial suggested $30,000 as a criterion for *seonjinguk*, which was $10,000 higher than the criterion suggested by the *Chosun Ilbo* just a few years before. The current dominant idea seems to be the criterion of $30,000.

Historically, President Park Chung-Hee in the late 1970s and President Chun Doo-Hwan in the 1980s frequently mentioned that Korea was approaching *seonjinguk* and the goal of *seonjinguk* was "just over there." National identities claimed by them in those periods are more or less akin to the identity of today's "*seonjinguk munteok*." In terms of the mobilization of developmental resources, the status of "near *seonjinguk*" might be better than that of *seonjinguk*. This is because "for development to proceed potential resources must be mobilized," which involves "ideas, inspiration, leadership, and the unquantifiable qualities that motivate people to believe and to act" (Sikkink, 1991: 25). In this sense, it is notable that Korea in *seonjinguk* discourse has been on the threshold of the group of *seonjinguk* for nearly 40 years, since the late 1970s, a status advantageous for the "mobilization of resources" under the cause of entering into the rank of *seonjinguk*.

It is argued that Korea's contemporary status, "near *seonjinguk*," has not been easily achieved. Rather, it is considered a status to which "ex-generations have climbed up, getting bloody bruises on their knees" (*Chosun*, 1 July 2005). The Koreans feel a sense of pride in their achievement of the status of "almost *seonjinguk*" in such a short period of modernization, which is assumed as having taken hundreds of years for the West. However, it also brings up an awareness of crisis. It is sometimes perceived that Korea is now in between the running-away *seonjinguk* and rapidly chasing "developing" countries, and that there is a possibility that Korea will never be able to cross the threshold of *seonjinguk*. This is a ground on which conservative newspapers argue that Korea's current status is due to the previous generations' blood, sweat, and tears, and that it is our generation's responsibility to make Korea a full-fledged *seonjinguk*. The national strategy for "moving forward," rather than "rolling back," is vigorously promoted in this regard. For this, the *Dong-a* (22 October 2008) argues that Korea is "on a forked road to the progress or to the retreat of 'national rank.'"

Theoretical Background of the Book

Sociological Understanding of "Discourse"

Discourse is understood in a variety of ways in different contexts (Mills, 1997). Among others, three main ways are discerned to conceptualize it: Utterance, knowledge, and totality of social relations. When used as utterance, discourse implies various forms of communication through which meanings are exchanged and constructed. Dant (1991: 7) explains discourse in this sense as "the material content of utterances exchanged in social contexts that are imbued with meaning by the intention of utterers and treated as meaningful by other participants." As such, discourse in this use is considered as forms of utterance and communication, or material contents delivered through them. Here discourse is not necessarily a systemic idea, and is distinguished from knowledge.

Second, discourse is not just forms or contents of utterance, but knowledge itself. Foucault (1972), for instance, does not distinguish discourse from knowledge in the sense that both are a formation of regularities among various dispersed elements constitutive of them. For Foucault (1972: 49), discourses should be treated not just as "groups of signs" but as "practices that systematically form the objects of which they speak." In this respect, he considers discourse as something more than utterance, noting that discourses are "irreducible to the language (*langue*) and to speech" (Foucault, 1972: 49). For Foucault, various disciplines of knowledge system, such as political economy, biology, psychopathology, etc., are rather identified with "discursive formation" (Foucault, 1972: ch. 2).

For Foucault, dispersed elements become discursive elements through a regularity they obtain. It is the rules of formation that render regularity to those elements. As for the rules of formation, Foucault (1972: 38) states that "[t]he conditions to which the elements of this division (objects, mode of statement, concepts, thematic choices) are subjected we shall call the *rules of formation*" (emphasis in the original). Without these rules there is no discourse but dispersed elements. In this respect, the rules are the very conditions for the existence of the elements of discourse. In this regard, he adds that "[t]he rules of formation are conditions of existence [...] in a given discursive division" (*ibid.*). Thus, there occurs a discursive formation when dispersed elements take on regularity by being arranged and organized according to certain rules of formation. As a system of rules of formation is not universally applicable, but is specific to a certain discourse, it is a constitutive factor of a totality of discursive system.

In this way, Foucault's concept of discourse focuses on a practice of formation that renders a unity to dispersed elements by setting a system of relations among them according to a certain rule of formation. Discourse becomes an interpretive totality that forms discursive objects and determines the positions of subjects whose subjectivities are dispersed too. There are no inherent attributes in discursive objects and subjects, but they are determined by relations among them that are set by a certain system of formation. As the system of formation is "a complex group of relations that function as a rule," Foucault (1972: 74) states that "[t]o define a system of formation in its specific individuality is therefore to characterize a discourse"

Third, discourse is understood as virtually equivalent to a system of social relations as no social activity is possible without being grounded upon it. Laclau and Mouffe (1987: 82), for instance, consider discourse as "totality which includes within itself the linguistic and the non-linguistics [...]" Hence, for them, discourse is not "a combination of speech and writing," but rather "speech and writing are themselves but internal components of discursive totalities" (*ibid.*). Somewhat similar to Foucault, they conceptualize a discourse as an interpretive totality, or a "systematic set of relations," which makes both linguistic and non-linguistic social activities possible.

However, their focus of discourse is not just on knowledge, but on general social relations. For them, no social relation or activity is possible without discourse. Therefore, every social activity is discursive and "every subject [and object] position is a discursive position" (Laclau and Mouffe, 2001: 115). As Laclau and Mouffe (1987: 82) mention, the meaning of a round object that is kicked arbitrarily in the street differs from that kicked according to a certain rule in the playground, and the latter situation is required for the object to be identified as a football. That is, the round object becomes a football when it is kicked in the system of relations called football and, in this situation, the kicker becomes identified as a football player. In this respect, we can say that the attributes and identities of the object to be perceived or the subject to perceive are defined in a specific system of relations or a discursive system to which it belongs. As such, Laclau and Mouffe (1987, 2001) do not distinguish between discursive and non-discursive practices on the grounds that every social relation is basically discursive. This notion of discourse supposes a far broader range of relations than do the other definitions.

I consider all three definitions of discourse as not only respectively valid in different contexts, but also closely interrelated with one another. In this book, I pay attention to the aspect of discourse that carries more systemic meanings than are delivered in simple utterance. Thus, I understand discourse as "a system of knowledge or of interpretive framework to interpret and construct the object (the world) and the subject, which is conveyed through various forms of utterances." In this respect, discourse is an arbitrary system that is coherent just internally, as a system consists of various discursive elements combined according to a certain rule of regularity.

In regard to its social roles, discourse is understood as a socially constructed system of meanings and relations, which provides social members with a way of identifying and interpreting the world. Thus, it creates the identities of subject as well as object. For individuals, discourse is an interpretive window through which one can see the world, engage in social activities, and construct one's identity. In a similar vein, a mainstream discourse in society plays a role as an interpretive framework enabling society to understand the world, engage in activities with others, and construct its identities.

As Foucault (1977, 1980, 2000) notes, on the other hand, knowledge is deeply associated with power – that is, knowledge reflects and exerts power. He states that "[t]he exercise of power perpetually creates knowledge and, conversely, knowledge constantly induces effects of power" (Foucault, 1980: 52). As for the relationship between knowledge and power relation, he notes that "there is no power relation without the correlative constitution of a field of knowledge, nor any knowledge that does not presuppose and constitute at the same time power relations" (Foucault, 1977: 27).

Discourse as a knowledge system reflects and constitutes certain power relations. Intertwined with power relations, discourse also becomes a site of social, political, economic, and cultural struggles, where various ways of interpreting and envisioning the world are confronting with one another. In relation to this, Howarth (2000: 9) maintains that "[t]he construction of discourses thus involves the exercise of power and a consequent structuring of the relations between different social agents."

The interpretive systems of some discourses can be shared by a broader range of social groups than are those of others. Widely accepted discourses may justify dominant social relations and the interests of dominant groups. As critical discourse analysts note, power of certain discourses can serve for the political purpose of domination at the expense of the marginalization of other discourses (Wodak, 1989; Fairclough, 2003).

Discourse and Hegemony

A discourse can be in a hegemonic status when its assumptions are consented by a broad range of social groups and social relations. In this case, hegemonic discourse reflects the hegemony of certain social groups that support dominant social relations. In the Gramscian notion, hegemony refers to dominant groups' intellectual and moral leadership over subordinate groups, which is based upon a broad range of consent from the latter.

For Gramsci, hegemony is distinguished from "direct domination" as it is preconditioned by the consent of subordinate groups. As Gramsci notes, social hegemony is based upon "[t]he 'spontaneous' consent given by the great masses of the population to the general direction imposed on social life by the dominant fundamental group [...]" (Forgacs, 1988: 306–307). While acknowledging that consent and coercion are closely interrelated with each other, Gramsci emphasizes the voluntary aspect of the former that is manifested, in principle, in the cultural, moral, and ideological leadership. In this respect, the leadership legitimated by the consent from a wide range of social groups is an important precondition for the dominant group's construction of a "historical bloc," which refers to the association at a certain historical point between the "complex, contradictory and discordant ensemble of the superstructures" and "the ensemble of the social relations of production" (Forgacs, 1988: 192). In relation to this, Gramsci (1971: 57–58) notes that "[a] social group can, and indeed must, already exercise 'leadership' before winning governmental power [...]; it subsequently becomes dominant when it exercises power, but even if it holds it firmly in its grasp, it must continue to 'lead' as well."

Insofar as hegemony needs a broad range of consent, it should take on a degree of universal bearing. This aspect of hegemony is closely related to Gramsci's emphasis on the need for a system of alliances among social groups as a precondition for it. In Gramscian terms, a social group cannot achieve hegemony if it remains sticking to its own economic-corporate interests. For a social group to be dominant, it needs to transcend its own economic interests to build political alliances with other groups. At the stage of the political alliance formation, as Gramsci notes, "one becomes aware that one's own corporate interests [...] can and must become the interests of other subordinate groups" (Forgacs, 1988: 205). As such, Gramsci suggests a need for constructing an awareness of homogeneity in political terms among diverse social groups that have different economic interests, for the purpose of constructing hegemony.

This insight of Gramsci is particularly worthwhile to note that hegemony implies a political phase in which both dominant and subordinate groups develop shared interests. As such, the rule of the dominant group can be regarded by subordinate groups not necessarily as oppressive but, rather, as beneficial to their own interests. In the hegemonic phase, the rule of a certain group is politically allied with the subordination of other groups, and thus is defended by both the dominant and subordinate groups. In cultural terms, this becomes a phase where the cultural activities of the dominant group take on universal bearing, which appear to transcend the particularism of any social group.

At the national level, a hegemonic group tends to be regarded as representing rather broader "national interests" than those of any particular group or class. In the concept of Gramsci's "national-popular" is implied that the intellectual activities of the dominant group are widely shared by the majority of the national population. In this way, hegemonic cultural and political activities are well associated with national energies. As for this, Simon (1991: 44) argues that "hegemonic class is one which succeeds in combining these patriotic struggles and ideas with its own class interests so as to achieve national leadership." Thus, an important way of securing hegemony for a social group at the national level is to successfully relate its own political economic interests to "national interests," leading to create "national-popular" collective energies.

The Gramscian notion of hegemony has influenced many cultural theorists in a variety of ways. Some discourse theorists, in particular, have tried to employ the concept of hegemony without prioritizing "fundamental" groups. A main criticism of the Gramscian notion of hegemony is about its assumption of centralized power based upon class identities. Supposing constructive decentralized nature of identities, Laclau and Mouffe (2001: 137–138), for instance, criticize Gramsci's thought in two ways: "(a) his insistence that hegemonic subjects are necessarily constituted on the plane of the fundamental classes; (b) his postulate that [...] every social formation structures itself around a single hegemonic centre." Presenting a somewhat different concept of hegemony from Gramsci's, Laclau and Mouffe argue that hegemony can appear in diverse sites of social relation.

Discourse, Orientalism, and Developmentalism

A number of studies have employed for their analyses the Foucauldian notion of discourse as a historically specific knowledge system. Among others, Said (1979) has used it for his analysis of the discourse of Orientalism. As noted above, Foucault maintains that discourse is a structural formation within which the objects and subjects of knowledge are constructed in a certain way. In this sense, the elements of knowledge are meaningful only within the system of knowledge itself. Employing this concept of discourse to his analysis of Orientalism, Said argues that any knowledge of the Orient is not free from the systematic web of meanings and relations of Orientalism. As he notes, "the Orient is not an inert fact of nature. It is not merely *there*, just as the Occident itself is not just *there* either" (Said, 1979: 4, emphasis in the original). In this respect, the Orient is the very construction of Orientalism.

As discourse requires a system of relations, the construction of the Orient is not possible without elements it is related to. In this regard, an important conceptual element is the Occident that is constructed in relation to the Orient within the systematic knowledge of Orientalism, reflecting the power relation between the two. In this way, both the Orient and the Occident are the historical constructions of Orientalism, which have affected the construction of reality for the interests of the latter. In this regard, Said (1979: 5) mentions that "as much as the West itself, the Orient is an idea that has a history and a tradition of thought, imagery, and vocabulary that have given it reality and presence in and for the West."

In development studies, post-development theorists provide insights into the understanding of the discourse of developmentalism. For them, developmentalism is no more than a discursive system reflecting the Western ways of looking at the world, entailing an epistemic hierarchy between the West and the non-West. Escobar (1995: 6), for instance, argues that "development" is "a historically produced discourse" or "a regime of representation." In this sense, the central concepts of developmentalism, such as the "developed," the "underdeveloped," or "poverty," are in no ways the faithful representations of reality out there, but are the very constructions of the discursive system and thus meaningful only within the system.

An important aspect of developmentalism is the construction of a hierarchy between the "underdeveloped" and the "developed," which serves for the latter's management and domination of the former. In this discursive system, the former is constructed as a negative image of the latter. In this respect, the hierarchical structure of developmentalism is somewhat similar to that of Orientalism, as is acknowledged by Escobar (1995: 6) that "[t]he study of development as discourse is akin to Said's study of the discourses on the Orient."

Developmentalism and Global Power Relations

"Development" is not a unitary concept, but is defined in plural ways. It can be a concept focusing on various social values, such as "fairness and equality," "quality of life and happiness," "level of humanity," and so forth. Nederveen Pieterse (2001: 3), for instance, defines it as "the organized intervention in collective affairs according to a standard of improvement." By adding that "[w]hat constitutes improvement and what is appropriate intervention obviously vary according to class, culture, historical context and relations of power," he opens up room for the plurality of the concept of development.

Insofar as "development" is the "improvement of society" in a broad sense, it has been always a question to any human society, and society has created various thoughts and ideas for development in any historical period and space.

When it comes to "developmentalism," however, the concept of development strongly takes on singularity, by prioritizing the value of economic development or economic growth over various important values of society, such as harmony, equity, solidarity, etc. The degree of development in developmentalism tends to be measured in simple quantitative indices such as GDP per capita.

The significance of developmentalism lies in its power to construct social reality. As for the discursive power of developmentalism, Escobar (1995: 41) mentions that it sets "the rules of the game: who can speak, from what points of view, with what authority, and according to what criteria of experience." In this way, it creates representations, institutionalizes social practices, designates identities, and transforms social reality according to its interpretations, imaginations, and classifications of the world.

Developmentalism in the global context can be understood mainly as a postwar construction, which reflects the transition of global power relations and of global political, economic and cultural circumstances. Post-development theorists trace the beginning of the global hegemony of developmentalism to the inaugural speech of U.S. President Harry S. Truman on 20 January 1949 (Esteva, 1992; Sachs, 1992). With regard to this, four circumstantial changes are notable after World War II.

First, in the cultural aspect, the discourse of civilization, which had supported a hierarchical relationship between the "civilized" and the "uncivilized" in the colonial era, lost its discursive appeal after the imperial world wars committed by the so-called "civilized" countries. In the wake of the wars, the distinction between the "civilized" and the "uncivilized" became far more blurred. This entailed a situation in which the power relations among different societies could no longer be defined by the discursive framework of the "civilized" and the "uncivilized."

Second, there was a hegemonic transition from Europe to the U.S. As discourse reflects power relations, this global hegemonic change accompanied discursive change. The U.S. had to formulate a new discursive framework supporting the new global power relation. In this respect, while the discourse of civilization had reflected European hegemony in the modern colonial era, the discourse of development echoed U.S. hegemony in the postwar era.

Third, former colonized countries retrieved independence and achieved sovereignty whose national statuses were formally equal to those of former colonial countries. As former colonized societies established modern state systems, neither were they to be defined as "barbarism," nor did they tolerate the attitude to designate them as such. In these new global power relations, a new discursive framework to define countries' identities was necessary.

Fourth, the onset of the Cold War increased the usefulness of developmentalism as an ideological tool for national or international mobilization of material and spiritual resources. In the Cold War context, developmentalism earned wholehearted support from capitalist elites, especially those in newly independent nations, by presenting the vision of capitalist national development vis-à-vis the vision of communist historical materialism.

In those respects, I generally define "developmentalism" as the "propensity to prioritize economic development of society through industrialization (or post-industrialization) and economic growth over other values, which arose as a hegemonic discourse around the globe in the mid-twentieth century." Under the global hegemony of developmentalism, humans' imagination about "development" has greatly shrunk.

The popularity of developmentalism after the mid-twentieth century reflected a hegemonic discursive change from the discourse of civilization centered on European power to that of development under American hegemony. With regard to this, Patterson (1997: 49) states that "[a]fter 1945, the United States, using arguments that echoed those of social Darwinists half a century earlier, began to project itself as the center and driving force of Western civilization." With this as momentum, "progress was measured in terms of economic growth [...]" (*ibid.*: 50).

The discursive change brought about a sea change in the global perceptual framework, entailing the appearance of new concepts, identities, and relations around the globe. The discursive transition was a historical point when former "savage" or "barbarian" worlds began to be termed as the "underdeveloped," while the "civilized" were the "developed." As an important concept characterizing the "underdeveloped" area was poverty, Escobar (1995: 22) pointed out that "[p]overty on a global scale was a discovery of the post-World War II period."

In terms of global power relations, the hegemonic discursive transition enabled former colonial countries, represented as the "developed," to maintain their cultural hegemony over the "developing" or "underdeveloped." Compared with colonial subjectivity, which was basically grounded upon antagonism between the colonizer and the colonized, the identities provided by the discourse of development did not necessarily assume the domination-subordination relationship. Rather, the relationship between the "developed" and the "developing" in the discourse of development was usually conceived of as a reciprocal one.

The "developing mission" was, in many cases, voluntarily executed by the national elites of the countries that were the very targets of development. This difference is observed in Foucauldian terms that development operates through "bio-power" rather than "sovereign" power – that is, "through the mobilization of interests and aspiration of Third World subjects and nation-states" (Brigg, 2002: 424).

Evolutionism, Developmentalism, and Eurocentrism

An important epistemic ground of developmentalism is its Eurocentric idea of progress. In the colonial era, European colonialists perceived as "savage" or "barbarian" other societies that supposedly had different societal forms from their own. Assuming a universal timeline for human progress, they supposed those different societies to be the past of Europe, somewhat equivalent to the medieval forms of European societies. By turning the "spatial difference" into the "temporal hierarchy," they justified their colonial projects as a "civilizing mission."

The modern idea of progress took on metaphoric bearing by illusively comparing social change to the development of living things (Nisbet, 1969). The discourse of development shares this episteme in assuming a universal linear path of progress from the "underdeveloped," "developing," to the "developed." As certain countries are termed as a temporarily advanced form, they are presented as the future societal form of the others, incurring a cultural hierarchy between them. In this framework, it is naturally assumed that "developing" societies should "catch up" with the "developed" through their internal transformation of socio-cultural systems (Rostow, 1960; Parsons, 1971; Inkeles and Smith, 1974). Here, "developed" societies are presented as a universal model of development.

A central idea deeply underlying various developmental thoughts of the West is evolutionism. As it posits the West at the top of the evolutionary hierarchy, i.e., the most evolved or developed, the remaining part of the world is identified as less developed or not developed. In evolutionism, the complexity of the world tends to be simplified into certain categories posited in different stages, such as: "Primitivism, savagery, barbarism, civilization" (Nederveen Pieterse, 2001: 19). This kind of stage theory transforms spatial differences into a temporal hierarchy. When the world is classified into some evolutionary stages, Nederveen Pieterse (2001: 19) notes, "global *space* appeared transformed into a *time* sequence, with Europeans as the only contemporaries, the sole inhabitants of modernity" (emphasis in the original).

Developmentalism is closely associated with Eurocentrism (Hettne, 1995; Cowen and Shenton, 1996; Leys, 1996; Rist, 1997; Mehmet, 1999). Eurocentrism is understood as an attitude to regard European experiences of history as the archetype of global history. Wallerstein (2004: 93) defines it as "any assumption that the patterns discerned by analyzing pan-European history and social structure are universal patterns, and therefore implicitly a model for persons in other parts of the world." It can be analytically divided into two interrelated epistemic propensities: European exceptionalism and Orientalism, of which the former is relevant to the construction of the superior self while the latter is to that of the inferior other (Kang J.-I., 2003a, 2004).

A notable characteristic of Eurocentrism is an imagined hierarchy between the West and the non-West. In Eurocentric discourses, virtually heterogeneous "others" tend to be constructed as a homogeneous entity with which negative attributes are associated, such as "irrational," "depraved," "childlike," and "abnormal," whereas similarly heterogeneous entities are homogenized into the "self" to which positive traits such as "rational," "virtuous," "mature," and "normal" are attributed (Said, 1979). As for the misleadingly simplistic distinction between the two worlds, Hobsbawm (1987: 16) once pointed out that "the (much larger) second world was united by nothing except its relations with [...] the first." In this regard, he appropriately questioned: "What else, except a common membership of the human race, had the Chinese Empire in common with Senegal, Brazil with the New Hebrides, Morocco with Nicaragua?" (Hobsbawm, 1987: 16)

To unilaterally designate certain societies as "underdeveloped" or "developing" deprives them of their own identities (Sachs, 1992; Brohman, 1995; Escobar, 1995; Rahnema and Bawtree, 1997; Nederveen Pieterse, 2001). In this representational framework, various forms of life and knowledge, which are not considered as belonging to the "developed," are marginalized (Apffel-Marglin and Marglin, 1990, 1996).[13] Nevertheless, this kind of episteme has historically provided a solid ground for colonialism and imperialism. As Hobsbawm (1975: 267) questions, "what was easier than to assume that those who represented the style of childhood or adolescence in the development of civilization [...] had to be treated like children by their mature 'parents'?"

As for the domination-subordination relationship between the "developed" and "developing," Tucker (1999: 1) points out that developmental discourse is "an essential part of the process whereby the 'developed' countries manage, control and even create the Third World [...]" Here development virtually becomes "the process whereby other peoples are dominated and their destinies are shaped according to an essentially Western way of conceiving and perceiving the world" (*ibid.*). Despite the relative decline of Western power, Eurocentric discourses are still consciously or unconsciously accepted around the globe (Alatas, 2006). In this respect, Eurocentrism is distinguished from other provincial ethnocentrisms and marginalized belief systems such as racism, which are criticized by mainstream discourses (Amin, 1989; Blaut, 1993; Shohat and Stam, 1994).

Organization of the Book

This book is organized in three parts. Chapters are arranged in a chronological order to easily grasp the historical emergence and change of Eurocentric developmental worldviews of Korean society.

Part I (Chapters 2–4) examines the discursive situation in the pre-developmental era of Korea. It investigates the characteristics and changes of *gaehwa* (enlightenment) and *munmyeong* (civilization) discourses, which provided representative Eurocentric worldviews from the late nineteenth century to the 1950s, concerning their relationship with the discourse of development. It also explains the background of the "discursive shift" from "*munmyeong*" to "*baljeon*" (development) in the Korean and global contexts. It shows that the discourse of "*baljeon*," which is a representative Eurocentric discourse in contemporary Korea, is genealogically linked to the discourse of "*munmyeong*" that was prevalent before the mid-twentieth century.

Chapter 2 traces the origins of Korea's Eurocentrism by analyzing the characteristics and changes of *gaehwa* and *munmyeong* discourses from the late nineteenth to early twentieth centuries. In the 1880s, Korea began to recognize the power of the West and the harsh reality of the emerging world order led by the West, employing the frameworks of modern *gaehwa* and *munmyeong* discourses. In the 1890s and 1900s, a hierarchy between the West and the East became manifest, as the West was typically represented as a world of *gaehwa* or *munmyeong*. The 1920s and the 1930s spanned a period when the universality of Western civilization was highly suspect.

Chapter 3 examines how the modern discourse of civilization disciplined Korea and justified the Japanese colonial rule in colonized Korea. For this, it analyzes articles from *Maeil Sinbo*, imperial Japan's official newspaper. The *Maeil Sinbo* problematized the level of Korea's civilization as not reaching that of the civilized, while raising its need for progress to civilization. The *Maeil Sinbo* designated Japan as the civilized to lead Korea to civilization, while justifying Japanese colonial rule as the rule of "civilization." Nevertheless, there were notable conflicts between the two peoples regarding the identities of civilization and barbarism.

Chapter 4 inspects the status of development discourse in the 1950s, which is reflected in President Rhee Syngman's addresses and the mass media texts. Above all, it demonstrates that the interpretive framework of *munmyeong* discourse was dominant in President Rhee's addresses. It also shows that the interpretive framework reflected in the 1950s magazines and newspapers was clearly distinguished from that of the developmental era.

Part II (Chapters 5–7) explores the characteristics and historical origins of, and changes to, Korea's development discourse from the 1960s to the present.

Chapter 5 discusses that it was the Park Chung-Hee era when developmentalism and *seonjinguk* discourse emerged as dominant discourses in Korea. Korea's developmentalism emerged in certain global and national historical environments, such as the emergence of U.S.-led developmentalism and the rise of a strong Korean developmental regime centered on the Park government. The discourse of *seonjinguk* was a representative development discourse, formed in the process of Korea's conceptualization of national status to be pursued through modernization as "*seonjinguk*."

Chapter 6 discusses the characteristics and changes of the discourse of *seonjinguk* in the historical circumstances of the 1980s and the 1990s. The 1980s was the period when the episteme of the discourse of *seonjinguk* came to be connected to internationalism amidst the global rise of neoliberalism. In the 1990s, the feature of Eurocentric universalism contained in *seonjinguk* discourse became more conspicuous amidst the Kim Young-Sam government's promotion of the "*segyehwa*" (globalization) project.

Chapter 7 investigates the structural characteristics of Korea's development discourse. It argues that developmentalism in Korea mainly consists of five elements: "Goal setting," "problematization," "crisis construction," "reminders of national potential," and "strategies." It shows how Korea's developmentalism has been reflected in the strategies of "*geundaehwa*" (modernization), "*segyehwa*" (globalization), and "*seonjinhwa*" (becoming advanced) in different historical circumstances.

Part III (Chapters 8–9) explores the characteristics of dominant discourses regarding national identities and worldviews at the regional level, e.g., Northeast Asia and Europe. It discusses the characteristics of development discourses in Korea, China, and Japan, and compares commonalities and differences between European and Northeast Asian discourses regarding regional identity.

Chapter 8 examines national identities and mutual perceptions reflected in the development discourses of Korea, China, and Japan. In Korean discourse of *seonjinguk*, Japan is generally represented as "*seonjinguk*," but having the feature of "*hujinguk*" in the matter of history and territory. China is perceived as a developing country in terms of the economic level, but as "*gang-guk*" (a strong country) or "*dae-guk*" (a great country) in terms of international influence. In Chinese discourse of development, the identity of a "developing country" connotes rather the potential and advantages of late-runners, rather than the deficiency and inferiority that are in the concept of "developing country" in Korean and Japanese discourses.

Chapter 9 compares the conditions and status of Northeast Asian regional identity with those of Europe, focusing on dominant discourses' construction of "self" and "others." This chapter demonstrates that both "primitive" and "practical" conditions for regional community are lacking in Northeast Asia because the awareness of similarities among intraregional countries is weak and confrontations are continuing among them in security matters.

Chapter 10, the conclusion of the book, critically reviews the influences and problems of Eurocentric developmentalism and *seonjinguk* discourse in Korean society in various aspects. It suggests ways to deconstruct and reconstruct them aiming for "true *seonjinguk*."

Notes

1 The romanization of Korean letters in this book follows the rule of the National Institute of Korean Language (www.korean.go.kr/front_eng/main.do), which better reflects Korean native pronunciation. As for the Korean name, this book follows the Korean practice, that is, family name first followed by given name. In the citation of Korean material, it writes the initials of the Korean given name along with the family name, as a Korean family name is shared by so many Koreans that they are hard to be distinguished merely by the family name.

2 See http://news.naver.com/main/read.nhn?mode=LSD&mid=sec&sid1=123&oid=156&aid=0000009015. All citations from Korean sources in this book are the author's own translation unless noted otherwise.

3 www.gasengi.com/main/board.php?bo_table=commu07&wr_id=753425.

4 The terms *seonjinguk* (先進國) and *hujinguk* (後進國) are made up with Chinese letters and are also used in China and Japan. They are differently read in Japan as *senshinkoku* and *koushinkoku*, and in China as *xian jin guo* and *hou jin guo*, respectively, with different connotations across countries.

5 National Institute of the Korean Language (www.korean.go.kr).

6 Sections 1–3 of this chapter are based on my analysis of three leading Korean newspapers, the *Chosun Ilbo*, the *Dong-a Ilbo*, and the *Hankyoreh*. The *Chosun Ilbo* and *Dong-a Ilbo*, which were founded in 1920, are the two oldest mainstream newspapers today, and the *Hankyoreh*, established in 1988, is considered one of the most influential progressive newspapers in Korea. Using the *Chosun Ilbo* archive and the Korean Integrated News Database System (KINDS) for the period 2000–2008, I have obtained 525 relevant editorials in the three newspapers that contain the terms *seonjinguk* or *hujinguk* in either headline or body.

7 Korea and Russia are not referred to as *seonjinguk* in the general sense but are regarded as *seonjinguk* in certain areas, such as information technology and soccer (Korea), and space technology (Russia), in specific contexts.

8 Japan tends to construct its identity as a member of the West (Ashizawa, 2008; Miyaoka, 2011).

9 In a similar vein, Quijano (2000: 216) argues that "[a]ll the forms of labor, production and exploitation were in ensemble around the axis of capital and the world market: slavery, serfdom, petty commodity production, reciprocity and salary."

10 As for auto-Orientalism, Befu (2001: 127) noted that "[i]t is a process of accepting the Orientalism of the West (Said 1978) by the very people who are being Orientalized." In a similar vein, Mora (2009: 418) referred to "internalized Orientalism" as an attitude that "[t]he East represents and expresses itself from the eyes of the West and with the image which the West fictionalized for it." Lee O.-S. (2002) used the concept of "*bokje* Orientalism" (copied Orientalism) in a similar context.

11 It is interesting to note that Korea is most frequently designated as *hujinguk*. This, however, shows a sarcastic attitude of self-criticism in certain aspects of Korean society. To designate Korea as *hujinguk* reflects an attitude to criticize that those negative aspects should not belong to Korea. In this respect, Korea is usually referred to as a certain type of *hujinguk* in a specific context, rather than "*hujinguk* in general."

12 In relation to this, Lee O.-S. (2002) points out that the Koreans have constructed their own "Orient" reflecting Western Orientalism and perceive other non-Western countries, such as India, through this Orientalist framework. This Orientalist image of India is, however, at odds with the Indians' own national identities based on three deep-seated identity sources: "Civilizational exceptionalism, post-colonial nationalism and secular democratic tradition" (Ollapally, 2011: 206). As noted above, even Korea is not free from the Korean version of Orientalist gaze.

13 These conditions facilitate the need for critical research that is "localized, grounded in the specific meanings, traditions, customs, and community relations" (Denzin, 2005: 935–936).

Part I

From "*Munmyeong*" (Civilization) to "*Baljeon*" (Development)

The 1880s to the 1950s

2 The Origins of Korea's Eurocentrism

Gaehwa and *Munmyeong* Discourses from the 1880s to the 1930s

The late nineteenth century witnessed a sea change in the Koreans' perception of the world. It was the time when the Koreans began to recognize the significance of European power and, accordingly, to adopt the Eurocentric interpretation of the world, for the first time in their history. The previous Confucian ethics-based perception of the West as "barbarism" was being replaced by a new awareness of the West as "civilization."

Recognizing the seriousness of the new world order in the "age of empire" (Hobsbawm, 1987), the Koreans came to be curious about the secret of the power of Western countries. For instance, *gaehwa* (enlightenment) theorists in the late nineteenth century endeavored to modernize Korea by modeling it after the West to achieve national wealth and strength. In terms of discursive relation, it was the process in which Korea was incorporated into a Eurocentric world order supported by Eurocentric discursive assumptions. In this process, Korean society began to set the West as the primary positive reference group in its modernization process.

The Korean discourses of *gaehwa* and *munmyeong* (civilization) reflected the rise of the Eurocentric world order and provided justification for the efforts to "modernize" Korea. Echoing the civilization discourse of the West, *gaehwa* and *munmyeong* discourses supposed a hierarchical distinction between *gaehwa* and *mi-gaehwa* (unenlightenment), and between *munmyeong* and *yaman* (barbarism), respectively. In these discursive frameworks, *gaehwa* theorist Yu Gil-Jun (1856–1914) (Yu, 2004 [1895]: 394–395), for instance, categorized countries into a three-tier classification system: *Gaehwa-guk* (enlightened country), *ban-gaehwa-guk* (half-enlightened country), and *mi-gaehwa-guk* (unenlightened country).

In those discourses, the non-West tended to be represented as the deficient counterpart to the sufficient West (Jeong Y.-H., 2004; Gil J.-S., 2004; Kim J.-H., 2005). Set as the deficient entity, *mi-gaehwa-guk* naturally comes to dream of achieving the status of *gaehwa* or *munmyeong*, while feeling shame at the self (Gil J.-S., 2004). In this regard, *gaehwa* and *munmyeong* frameworks contributed to the construction of Koreans' "auto-Orientalism," by assuming that what was desired by Korean society was something already existent in Western societies.

This chapter examines the long-term transition of the basic assumptions and implications of Korean *gaehwa* and *munmyeong* discourses from the 1880s to the 1930s, by concentrating on the varying images of the West in relation to Korea's self-identity. Special attention is paid to the temporal change of the discursive hierarchy between Korea (or the East) and the West concerning Eurocentric assumptions. For this, I have analyzed six historical newspapers representing Korea's early modern era: The *Hanseong Sunbo* (1883–1884), the *Hanseong Jubo* (1886–1888), the *Dongnip Shinmun* (1896–1899), the *Daehan Maeil Shinbo* (1904–1910), the *Chosun Ilbo* (1920–), and the *Dong-a Ilbo* (1920–).[1]

This chapter is organized in three main sections. The first section analyzes the historical context in which the new perceptions of the West emerged in the 1880s. The second section investigates the Eurocentric constructions of the West and Korea's self-identity, reflected in the concepts of *gaehwa* and *munmyeong* in the 1890s and 1900s. The last section explains the decline of Eurocentric *munmyeong* discourse and the reconstructive move of *munmyeong* discourse in the 1920s and the 1930s.

Appreciating the Power of the West: The *Hanseong Sunbo* (1883–1884) and the *Hanseong Jubo* (1886–1888)

During the nineteenth century, the military and economic gap between the West and the non-West widened rapidly. By the 1880s, there were "two sectors combined together into one global system: the developed and the lagging, the dominant and the dependent, and the rich and the poor" (Hobsbawm, 1987: 16). The dominant interpretive framework that justified this global gap was the Eurocentric discourse of civilization, which was based on the hierarchical distinction between the "civilized" and the "uncivilized."

For the Koreans, the late nineteenth century was the period when the significance of Western expansion began to be recognized. Their traditional view of the West as "barbarism" changed drastically during this period. Despite traditional Confucian scholars' indignant resistance to this change, as shown in their numerous petitions to King Gojong, *gaehwa* thought gradually spread among intellectuals.

Under the hostile global circumstances, the Koreans started to recognize the need to learn from the West to raise their national wealth and strength. Recognizing the West as a world of material wealth and physical power, *gaehwa* theorists became very interested in its remarkable achievements in the fields, in particular, of economy, machinery, technology, and military. They hoped to raise Korea's wealth and strength by learning the merits of Western systems.[2]

The early *gaehwa* theorists' aspiration for national strength was well reflected in the *Hanseong Sunbo* (hereafter the *Sunbo*) and the *Hanseong Jubo* (hereafter the *Jubo*). These newspapers' primary values regarding national transformation were concentrated in such concepts as "*bugang*" (wealth and strength), "*buguk gangbyeong*" (wealthy nation and strong military), and "*jagang*" (self-strengthening). In regard to this, an article in the *Sunbo* mentioned the following:

> These days, Western countries establish companies to attract merchants, which are actually the basis of wealth and strength (*bugang*) [...] In Western countries, steamships traverse the sea, freight cars run on the ground, and electric wires are laid and streetlights are turned on, the wonders of which are beyond description. They flaunt their wealth and strength all over the world and impress their neighbors by sending forces to every [corner of the] sea and conducting commerce with all countries, which is unprecedented. This has been possible only since they established companies.
>
> (20 November 1883; Jeong J.-S., 1983: 38)

This article recognized the importance of companies as the main source of national wealth and strength for Western countries and, furthermore, it appreciated the values of commerce and material development. This showed a degree of departure from traditional Confucian thought, which had rather pursued spiritual and ethical values than material interests.

The term *bugang* is a key word in this article. Things of modern engineering and technology, such as steamships, freight cars, and electric wires, were considered as the indicators of *bugang*. The West was seen as the possessor of *bugang*, and the main source of its power was considered to be the establishment of companies. In this sense, the wide gap between the West and Korea in wealth and strength was well recognized in the article.

Another important feature of the West that was perceived by the newspapers was its military power. The West was regarded as the world-dominating military power, which was based upon the development of machinery, technology, and industry. Thus, material wealth (*bu*) and military power (*gang*) were considered to be closely interrelated. The following is an excerpt from an article in the *Sunbo* describing the power of Britain:

> Mainland Britain is just an island country, but it developed navigation skills early and exerted its ambition around the world, broadening its territories, by taking advantage of machinery. [...] Britain gives top priority to military affairs. It subjugates its vassals by making many warships and completing military preparations, and it always keeps its military at the ready with the ambition of dominating its neighbors [...] The British people display respect for manufacturing industries and produce many machines that add convenience to life, and their *buguk gangbyeong* [national wealth and strong military] is the best in the world.
>
> (20 December 1883; Jeong J.-S., 1983: 93–95)

As in this article, the possessor of wealth was also recognized as the enforcer of military power, and the accumulation of wealth was considered to accompany military power. Thus, the West as the possessor of wealth was not necessarily an ideal world, as it was also the enforcer of military power around the world. In this respect, the Korean newspapers tended to perceive the West as the promoter of a new world order that was somewhat deplorable because of its militaristic, competitive, and conquering features.

In this regard, the *Sunbo* points out that "all countries in the world are now concerned with military affairs and compete with one another to become more powerful" (29 December 1883; Jeong J.-S., 1983: 115). As for the dominance of the West, the *Jubo* mentions that, among numerous countries in the six populated continents, "only the countries in Europe monopolize wealth and strength, and many countries in the other five continents are in the situation of being subjugated" (8 March 1886; Jeong J.-S., 1983: 748).

Furthermore, the West was perceived as behaving hypocritically and in its own self-interest. In regard to Western countries' aggressiveness towards others, the *Sunbo* stated, "the ancients who had said that '[Westerners] were not our race and their minds were always different [from ours]' did not deceive us" (22 July 1884; Jeong J.-S., 1983: 541). In a similar vein, the *Jubo* said, "one should be very careful when interacting with foreigners" (4 October 1886; Jeong J.-S., 1983: 842).

The attitude of criticizing the power-dominating world was strong in the Korean newspapers. The West was considered to be the main culprit in imposing the law of the jungle and the logic of power on the world. The *Jubo*, for instance, raised the mistrust of the world order in relation to international treaties, by writing the following:

> People who busily interact with one another only aim at profit, so how can we say that there is no law of the jungle? For example, France first subjugated Vietnam as its tributary, and England subjugated Burma. France and England always claimed treaties and international laws as the golden rule, but they have eventually subjugated others, while insisting on benevolence and righteousness.[3]
>
> (4 October 1886; Jeong J.-S., 1983: 842)

The Korean newspapers criticized the misuse of international laws and treaties by Western countries that were the very promoters of them.[4] The *Jubo*, for instance, denounced that "the countries are not afraid of ignoring international laws when it comes to self-interest, and do not feel ashamed when annulling treaties" (8 March 1886; Jeong J.-S., 1983: 748). This kind of recognition of the power-dominating world played a role in promoting the need for raising Korea's wealth and strength as an urgent strategy for its survival. In this respect, Korea had encountered a paradoxical situation in which it had to participate in a world that it did not necessarily welcome.

The colonial expansion of the West was justified by Western social ideas such as social Darwinism or social evolutionism. The main argument of Herbert Spencer, an English social theorist and representative social Darwinist, is that "the best forms of social organization emerge with unregulated competition among humans, which allows the most fit to survive, thereby elevating the level of society" (Turner, 2003: 77). Echoing the idea of natural selection suggested by Darwin, social Darwinism justifies competition and inequality among human societies as the driving force of social evolution. By this logic, the subjugation of weaker societies by the stronger is naturalized as a necessary process for social development. Social Darwinism is closely related to stage theories, as the processes of social evolution are often depicted as a succession of distinct stages, such as primitivism, savagery, barbarism, and civilization (Nederveen Pieterse, 2001).

Social Darwinism affected Korean intellectuals and those in other Asian countries in their understanding of the competitive world during their early modernization periods. Tikhonov (2010) argues that social Darwinism was a main ideological base upon which early Korean modern intellectuals justified their pursuit of national power and survival, and of "civilization," the "fittest status." However, the *Sunbo* and *Jubo* did not yet fully approve of social Darwinist ideas. Rather, they showed considerable reservations about those ideas, as shown in their critical attitudes towards the West-dominating competitive world.

While recognizing the wealth and strength of the West, the newspapers did not necessarily regard the West as the superior – the typical assumption of Eurocentric discourses. Rather, they showed a substantial degree of pride in Korea's history and its civilization, while expressing surprise at the "abrupt" rise of the West. As for the "rise" of Britain, the *Sunbo* stated, "England was destitute just a short time ago and has a short history, but it has achieved this development. We should research what made it possible" (20 December 1883; Jeong J.-S., 1983: 97). Citing a Chinese journal, another article from the *Sunbo* mentioned that "in ancient times, no country was more destitute than the West and no country was worse off than the West" (8 January 1884; Jeong J.-S., 1983: 137).

As such, the newspapers mainly considered the rise of the West as a recent and incidental phenomenon, reflecting Korea's traditional attitude of disregarding the West. On this, they tried to see much potential in Korea to become a country comparable to the West in its wealth and strength. While emphasizing Korea's great natural resources and historical heritage, for instance, the *Jubo* argued that "if we make efforts in developing policies to promote *bugang*, with these good resources, we should be able to reach most of the six continents, surpassing other nations" (23 August 1886; Jeong J.-S., 1983: 794).

In short, the 1880s was the period when Korean society began seriously to recognize the power of the West and a need to learn from it. While Korea began to depart from the traditional Confucian thought and to consider the West as "civilization," there was no clear Eurocentric hierarchy between Korea (or the East) and the West. While the West began to be recognized as "civilization," e.g. a *munmyeong-guk* (civilized country) strong in commerce and technology, the East was still regarded as a traditional kind of *munmyeong-guk* with rich cultural and natural resources.

The main reason why the *Sunbo* and the *Jubo* suggested the need to learn from the West in the 1880s was not that they perceived the West as an ideal world; rather, it was because they felt a sense of urgency for national survival under hostile international circumstances. In this respect, the articles of the *Sunbo* and the *Jubo* reflected Korea's paradoxical situation in which it had to accept the world order that it did not really welcome, and had to learn from the countries that it did not really want to learn from.

Eurocentrism in the Discourses of *Gaehwa* and *Munmyeong*: The *Dongnip Shinmun* (1896–1899) and the *Daehan Maeil Shinbo* (1904–1910)

The Dongnip Shinmun *(1896–1899)*

With regard to Korea's response to the expansion of the West in the nineteenth century, three temporal phases can generally be distinguished: Hostility, limited acceptance, and total acceptance (Kim J.-H., 2005). While traditional Confucian scholars' attitude towards the West was one of hostility, the *Hanseong Sunbo* and *Jubo* showed an attitude of limited acceptance, recognizing Western power albeit with great caution. However, when it came to the *Dongnip Shinmun* (hereafter the *Shinmun*), Korean modern thinkers tended to show a somewhat uncritical attitude of accepting Eurocentric ideas and the world order those ideas promoted.

With regard to national self, the *Shinmun* writers frequently demonstrated a manner of observing Korea from a "civilized man's" perspective by internalizing the values of the West (Jeong S.-T., 2004). As Gil J.-S. (2004: 73) noted, "it was the period of the *Dongnip Shinmun* when [the meaning of] *munmyeong* was totally transformed into Western civilization [...]" In this respect, the *Shinmun* can be considered as a harbinger of the period of total acceptance.

The ways for promoting *gaehwa* and *munmyeong* were actively discussed among Korean intellectuals after the *Gabo* Reform (1894–1896), and the *Shinmun* and the *Maeil Shinmun* were the main publications that spread those ideas in the general public (Noh D.-H., 2010a).[5] Among such terms as *gaehwa, munmyeong*, and *jinbo* (progress), which advocated the need for learning from the West in those times, the most popular one in the *Shinmun* was *gaehwa*. In fact, the concept of *gaehwa* at the time was so popular that people felt they had heard it to the point that "their ears were worn out" (*Dongnip Shinmun*, 2 November 1899).

In the *Shinmun*, a distinct hierarchy between the West and the East was implied, and "*gaehwa*" was the most dominant criterion to make this distinction.[6] One article in the *Shinmun* classified countries of the world into four hierarchical categories according to the degree of *gaehwa*, such as *gaehwa* (enlightened), *ban-gaehwa* (half-enlightened), *mi-gaehwa* (unenlightened), and *yaman* (barbarian)

(*Dongnip Shinmun*, 11 September 1899). Unlike the previous period when Korea was mainly perceived as another civilized country with a long history and valuable cultural heritage, the *Shinmun* generally viewed it as *ban-gaehwa* and suggested drastic self-strengthening reforms modeled after the West.

In the classificatory system of *gaehwa* discourse, only the West was categorized as *gaehwa*. As such, the idea of *gaehwa* adopted a Eurocentric civilizational view of history (*munmyeong sagwan*), which assumed that human history was one of civilizational progress led by the West (Lee W.-Y., 1996). The West was represented by various terms implying the highest stage of civilization, such as *gaehwa-guk* (enlightened country), *munmyeong-guk* (civilized country), *munmyeong-gaehwa-guk* (civilized enlightened country), *sangdeung-guk* (upper-class country), or *ildeung-guk* (first-class country).

Furthermore, Western knowledge and ideas were somewhat uncritically accepted. Colonial and racial ideas, which manifested the superiority of the West over others, spread in Korea under the name of "science."[7] One editorial introduced a study on Western dietary life in the following way:

> According to the analysis of various grains by Western chemists, wheat flour is the best for the human body, corn is the next, and rice has the fewest nutrients. We can easily perceive which one is superior and which one inferior by witnessing the robustness of Westerners, who eat wheat flour, and the weakness of Easterners, who eat rice.
>
> (*Dongnip Shinmun*, 25 August 1898)

Another editorial argued for the superiority of Western and Japanese customs over those of China:

> The Koreans always say that it is strange that Western women make their waist thin, that Japanese women paint their teeth, and that Chinese (Qing) women bind their feet. If we consider the merits and demerits of these in terms of people's lives, painted teeth and thin waistlines are not harmful for working, but the custom of binding feet not only obstructs work but also is harmful for health [...]
>
> (*Dongnip Shinmun*, 14 October 1899)

The content of this article reflects the decline of China in relation to the West and Japan. That is, various customs of Eastern civilization were considered old-fashioned and irrational when compared to those of the West. In this epistemic hierarchy, intervention by the supposedly rational being in the irrational being's affair was justified. In this regard, the article above added that "it is truly wonderful that Western women try to establish *jeonjokhoe* [foot-binding clubs] these days to change the bad custom of China's foot-binding" (*Dongnip Shinmun*, 14 October 1899).

Furthermore, another article explicitly reflected a colonial perspective regarding the British colonization of India:

> After England first conquered India, they lamented people's ignorance there and decided to educate them with new studies by spending 40,000 *ryang* of silver annually. [...] It is commendable that new studies are greatly promoted in India [...]
>
> (*Dongnip Shinmun*, 20 September 1899)[8]

This kind of perception, however, did not mean that the *Shinmun* was completely free from anxiety over Western expansion. Some editorials explicitly demonstrated their uneasiness about the aggressive behavior of the West. One editorial noted that "generally, the Westerners aim to get rid of different religions and dominate other races," adding, "they try to make themselves high alone by seeing high and walking broad in the world" (*Dongnip Shinmun*, 9 November 1899).

Nevertheless, the *Shinmun*'s mistrust and concern about the West were not strong enough to dispute the Eurocentric assumption of the West as the most advanced in the progress of civilization. Rather, the tendency came to be notable in the *Shinmun* to idealize the West and to consider its civilization as the archetype of modern civilization. As a way to learn from the West and to become a civilized country like the West, *gaehwa* and *munmyeong* were ardently promoted. In this respect, the 1890s can be considered a period when the Eurocentric thoughts of *gaehwa* and *munmyeong* widely spread in Korean society, to which the *Shinmun* greatly contributed.

The **Daehan Maeil Shinbo** *(1904–1910)*

In the first decade of the 1900s, the rivalry among Western countries intensified in their pursuit of new colonies. Amidst the expansion of the world economy, the gap between the colonial West and the colonized non-West remained significant (Hobsbawm, 1987). In intensifying colonial rivalries foreshadowing World War I, the term "imperialism" was on everybody's lips in the West (Hobsbawm, 1987: 60). In Asia, Japan was the only country that competed with the West in the colonial race. While the epistemic hierarchy between the West and the East was manifest, Japan came to be treated as somewhat equal to the "civilized" West with its victories over China (1894) and Russia (1904).[9]

In the Korean Peninsula, Japan's intention of colonizing Korea became manifest, which resulted in the Eulsa Treaty of 1905 that deprived Korea of diplomatic rights. In 1910, Japan "officially" occupied Korea under the legal discourse of international law created and enforced by "civilized" countries. Korea was declared illegal by the "civilized" world and fell prey to the discourse of "enlightened exploitation" (Dudden, 2005).

Korea's deplorable situation under the harsh international circumstances was recognized by the *Daehan Maeil Shinbo* (hereafter the *Shinbo*), and the need for learning from the West was urgently advocated as a way to overcome the national hardship.[10] A cause for Korea's endeavor to gain national strength was sought from its brilliant past. The *Shinbo* often contrasted Korea's past glories with its current miserable situation:

> Alas! O Korea, why have you alone met such bad luck? With such a miserable appearance, you are not like England that has broad territories around the world, not like Germany that sheds the bright light of studies, and not like the U.S. that boasts great wealth [...] You also produced heroes, were wealthy and strong, and were civilized in the past; thus, when China and India shone, you also rose with them. When such countries as Japan did not have the name of nation at the beginning, you already showed the development of culture. Alas, are you not considered a brother to China and India, and a senior to Japan? Then, how could you lose the past honor and meet this tragic bad luck today?
>
> (*Daehan Maeil Shinbo*, 27 March 1909)

In comparison with the West and Korea's own past, many aspects of contemporary Korea were easily subject to harsh self-criticism and auto-Orientalism, onto which the Koreans' severe feelings of frustration were projected in the colonized situation. One article wrote, "whether in the past or the present, whether in the East or the West, no public officials have been more negligent in doing their duties than those in Korea today, and no other ordinary people are as unenlightened as those in Korea today" (*Daehan Maeil Shinbo*, 6 October 1908). In addition to its own deplorable image, Korea had also to be faced with the ideal image of the West. In regard to this, an article argued that in the West "hope for humanity is unlimited and human progress is also unlimited [...]" (*Daehan Maeil Shinbo*, 13 August 1908).

Learning from the West was considered the only way out of this frustrating situation. Thus, the term *gaehwa* was still popular and influential in this context. According to one article, "the reason why our country today is in this pitiful situation is not because people do not have power but because we thought of *gaehwa* too late [...]" (*Daehan Maeil Shinbo*, 21 August 1907). However, the frequency of its use was greatly reduced with the increasing popularity of the term *munmyeong*.[11] The magazine *Gaebyeok*, which was published in the 1920s, mentioned that the term *gaehwa* had become popular with the public after 1894, and it was only after 1904 that the term *munmyeong* had popularized (Jeong Y.-H., 2006: 177). Thus, the first decade of the 1900s seemed to be the period when the concept advocating the need for reform shifted from *gaehwa* to *munmyeong*. With the increasing tendency to idealize the West, *munmyeong* was virtually coterminous with Western civilization and its universality was rarely doubted in this period.[12]

In regard to Japan's colonization of Korea, the secret to Japan's wealth and strength was sought from its "successful" accommodation of the West. Although the writers for the *Shinbo* recognized the *gaehwa* or *munmyeong* status of Japan, they did not lose their historical and cultural sense of superiority over Japan. Showing confidence in Korea's potential, the *Shinbo* argued that

Japan's advance over Korea was temporary and merely a matter of learning from the West. As such, *munmyeong* discourse in those times was used in more complicated contexts than was usually assumed in the simplistic binary distinction between superior *munmyeong* and inferior non-*munmyeong*.

An important social role of the sense of superiority over Japan was to promote resistance to Japanese colonialism. While Japan tried to justify its colonial rule with the discourse of *munmyeong* – for example, under the cause of "civilizing" Korea – Korea responded to it with a different focus on *gaehwa* or *munmyeong* – that of the past. In this regard, one article in the *Shinbo* argued the following:

> In the past, Japan was a country that had learned *gaehwa* from Korea. Its *Shintoism* was created on the basis of the things from the [Korean] *Silla* kingdom, its Confucianism and Buddhism were imported from the [Korean] *Baekje* kingdom, and other engineering and arts were all learned from Korea. So, no matter how powerful Japan is today, the Koreans will be willing to fight against it, but they do not have any intention to surrender, and thus will not tolerate colonization.
>
> (*Daehan Maeil Shinbo*, 7 January 1910)

The Koreans' sense of resistance to Japan in civilizational terms became clearer in the period of Japanese colonial occupation. As is shown below, there are many cases in which the Koreans discursively attack the Japanese rule and its civilization discourse with their own discourse of *munmyeong* in different contexts. This disputes Schmid's (2002: 15, 38) argument that Korean nationalists witnessed "how *munmyŏng kaehwa* was used [by the Japanese] to undermine their national sovereignty," and moved to contemplate alternative nationalist discourses such as "the national soul (*kukhon*) or the national essence (*kuksu*)." Schmid's argument largely derived from his assumption of the singular form of the discourse of *munmyeong gaehwa*, which ignored Koreans' active (re)constructions of the discourse reflecting their own understanding of national and global circumstances.

The Crisis and Reconstruction of *Munmyeong* Discourse: The *Chosun Ilbo* and the *Dong-a Ilbo* (1920s–1930s)

The Crisis of Eurocentric Munmyeong *Discourse*

As for the transformation of *munmyeong* discourse at the end of the first decade of the 1900s, Noh D.-H. (2010b) noted a tendency to distinguish between spiritual and material civilizations. The diversification of the concept of *munmyeong* implied that the Koreans recognized the possibility of the existence of other types of *munmyeong* that did not necessarily belong to the West. While appreciating the strength of the West as a material civilization, some intellectuals emphasized the importance of spiritual aspects. In this attitude, the Eurocentric perception of civilization was undermined and the authority of Western civilization shrank because it was designated as one type of civilization, that is, material civilization. This intellectual tendency later in the first decade of the 1900s became further manifest in the 1920s.

Just after World War I, the early 1920s witnessed a drastic decline in the authority of Western civilization in Korea. The belief in the linear progress of history pioneered by Western civilization came under serious suspicion in the wake of the unprecedented level of tragedies and atrocities committed by the so-called "*munmyeong-guk*" in their world war. This was a trend newly observed not only in Korea but also around the globe at the time. Thus, as Nederveen Pieterse (2001: 20) noted, "[c]yclical theories of history of a pessimistic cast prevailed, in the imagery of rise, decline and fall" after world wars.

Amidst the decline of the authority of Western civilization, the Koreans questioned its universality and desirability.[13] Departing from the previous attitude of idealizing the West, Korean newspapers often described the West as a world of uncertainty and confusion. Under the headline "The new tendency of Western civilization after the world war," the *Chosun Ilbo* (30 April 1921) mentioned that "recently, Europe is a world of transition and confusion," adding that "these transition and confusion are unique phenomena to Western countries after the big war."

Korean newspapers also developed relativist perspectives on *munmyeong* and began to recognize the values of diverse civilizations in different regions. In this regard, they raised basic questions about *munmyeong*, such as "what is *munmyeong*?" and "what is *yaman*?" An opinion column in the *Chosun* argued that "it is clear that a people who ignore humanity with a mere belief in power are *yaman*, and that a people who love peace and respect for justice are *munmyeong*" (*Chosun Ilbo*, 20 June 1921). According to this criterion, the West was not necessarily a world of *munmyeong*. In this regard, an article in the *Chosun* harshly criticized the pursuit of power by the West:

> If a Western scholar argues that psychology, politics, institutions, and economy are the elements of civilization, and exaggerates that they themselves are the civilized people, this is a bias of provincial pride and racial arrogance […] When we look into their psychology, what lofty ideals do they have, individually or nationally, except for invasion, plunder, misconduct, and pilferage? […] If we call them *munmyeong-in* [civilized people], this is not different from calling a thief a *gunja* [a man of virtue].
>
> (*Chosun Ilbo*, 20 June 1921)

Based on this critical perception of the West, the column concludes that a peace-loving civilization such as Korea is true *munmyeong*.

The West was repositioned as merely a region (e.g., that of confusion and transition), instead of the world. The *Dong-a Ilbo*, for instance, disputed the

British media's argument that the Imperial Conference of Britain was an institution for world peace:

> The first Imperial Conference of Britain after the world war was held in London [...] The British media designate it as "an institution of world peace" and compare it to the League of Nations. We are to comment on this interesting matter. As merely a meeting of Britain, the Conference discusses its national interests, that is, national defense, foreign policy, and the relationships between the mainland and its tributaries. Then, why do they call it an institution of world peace?
>
> (*Dong-a Ilbo*, 27 June 1921)

The Reconstruction of **Munmyeong** *Discourse*

Munmyeong in the 1920s came to connote a society's degree of artificial achievement, which was distinguishable from the state of nature (*Dong-a Ilbo*, 15 September 1925). As the concept of *munmyeong* took on diversity and specificity, various kinds of civilizations were recognized, such as "spiritual civilization," "material civilization," "civilization of science," "civilization of peace," "civilization of ethics," "civilization of invasion," "civilization of the East," "civilization of the West," and so forth. The concept of *munmyeong* was no longer monopolized by the West. Rather, Western *munmyeong*, as one of the various forms of *munmyeong*, was often regarded as materially developed but lacking spiritual and ethical aspects.

The Eurocentric hierarchy collapsed in Korea's *munmyeong* discourse after the world war. There was no ideal image of Western civilization at the expense of others. Rather, Western civilization (*seoyang munmyeong*) was regarded merely as a regional civilization with its distinguishable characteristics, and so was Eastern civilization (*dongyang munmyeong*). An article from the *Chosun* referred to Eastern civilization as *dodeok munmyeong* (civilization of ethics) and Western civilization as *gwahak munmyeong* (civilization of science), providing a relativist perspective on these civilizations (*Chosun Ilbo*, 26 July 1921). It wrote that:

> If we would like to discuss the values of human civilization by the situations of the East and the West, they [the West] may see us lacking in material development, but may not be able to say that our ethics has vanished too. Similarly, when seeing them, we may not be able to say that their scientific civilization is not developed just because they are weak in ethics.
>
> (*Chosun Ilbo*, 26 July 1921)

Based on this distinction between the Eastern and Western civilizations, this article went further to mention the need to combine the merits of the two civilizations, as follows:

> Therefore, as Eastern civilization has so long maintained the center thanks to its ethics, it would enjoy permanent peace by being combined with the Western civilization of science, and, at the same time, they [the West] may not be able to ignore the value of this kind of exchange either.
>
> (*Chosun Ilbo*, 26 July 1921)

As such, Korean newspapers showed a new tendency of considering *munmyeong* in terms of peace and humanity. The values of certain regional *munmyeong* were judged by the degree of their contribution to making universal *munmyeong* promoting humanity. As a product of human efforts, *munmyeong* was considered "advancing human behavior from bestiality to humanization" (*Dong-a Ilbo*, 15 September 1925). Judging by this concept of *munmyeong*, Western civilization was frequently regarded as lacking in spiritual virtue.

On the other hand, the Koreans discredited the West and challenged the Eurocentric notion of *munmyeong*, reflecting their feeling of victimization inflicted by a country self-claiming to be *munmyeong-guk*, i.e., Japan. In this sense, the re-conceptualizations of *munmyeong* and *yaman* were related to the resistance to the colonial occupation of Korea. The newspapers designated a civilization promoting the logic of power as pseudo-*munmyeong* or *yaman*, and peace-loving civilization as true *munmyeong*. This way of conceptualizing *munmyeong* and *yaman* provided justification to the Koreans' resistance to Japan's colonial rule. In this regard, the *Chosun* reported a speech from Yi Sang-Je, then president of the *Chosun Ilbo*, under the headline "Rise, youth of Korea, infringed by the civilization of invasion":

> The president of this newspaper, Yi Sang-Je, slowly approached the podium to speak on the topic of "the responsibility of the youth"; he urged the youth of Korea, infringed upon by the so-called modern violent science and the civilization of invasion, to stand up. He said that in order to save the world, Korea's youth should rise faster than those in any other country infiltrated by money and perverted science, to conquer the world of evil with the great power of true love.
>
> (*Chosun Ilbo*, 13 November 1925)

The new concept of *munmyeong* became the grounds upon which the Koreans criticized colonial rule and revealed its injustice. Under the criterion of this concept of *munmyeong*, Japan's oppressive colonial rule frequently fell into the category of *yaman*. The newspapers often pointed out that Japan's rule contradicted its own claim to be *munmyeong-guk*. As for the Japanese police's use of torture, the *Chosun* argued that "no torture exists under the judicial systems and police of a civilized (*munmyeong*) [nation]" (*Chosun Ilbo*, 9 March 1923). In another article, the newspaper raised a need for "civilizing the police" (*Chosun Ilbo*, 12 July 1924).

Despite the drastic change in the connotation of the discourse of *munmyeong* in this period, the authority of "science" did not wane significantly. The discourse's binary distinction between *munmyeong* and *yaman* was often supported by a variety of "scientific" forms of knowledge generated from the West. Citing the study of an American geneticist, the *Dong-a* reported that the more people are civilized, the higher their noses are (*Dong-a Ilbo*, 16 July 1926). Other articles introduced similar kinds of racial "scientific findings" in relation to *munmyeong*: For instance, civilized people have no wisdom teeth as a result of evolution (an English scholar's finding) (*Dong-a Ilbo*, 26 June 1929); civilized people have round-type faces (an American dental scholar's finding) (*Dong-a Ilbo*, 11 February 1939); and civilized people talk fast (an English stenographer's finding) (*Dong-a Ilbo*, 8 August 1936).

Conclusion

This chapter has examined the characteristics and changes of Korean *gaehwa* and *munmyeong* discourses in the late nineteenth and early twentieth centuries, showing that they did not simply imply binary hierarchical distinctions. The ways Koreans' perceptions of national self and the West were reflected in those discourses varied from period to period, reflecting different national and international circumstances.

In the 1880s, Korea began seriously to recognize the power of the West and the harsh reality of the world order. Departing from the traditional disregard of the West, the *Hanseong Sunbo* and the *Hanseong Jubo* advocated learning from the merits of Western social systems in order to raise national wealth and strength. However, their perceptions of the West were not necessarily Eurocentric. The West was frequently recognized as self-interested, belligerent, and untrustworthy. Furthermore, the "rise of the West" was considered a recent and incidental phenomenon; thus, it could be outrun by Korea and the East with appropriate effort. Korea and the East were still considered as the possessors of better ethics and cultural heritage, while the West was perceived mainly as the promoter of technology and industry.[14] Thus, in those newspapers in the 1880s, there was no apparent Eurocentric hierarchy between Korea and the West.

When it came to the *Dongnip Shinmun* and the *Daehan Maeil Shinbo*, a hierarchy between the West and the East became manifest. In this period, the West was typically represented as a world of *gaehwa* or *munmyeong*, while the East, including Korea and China, was *ban-gaehwa* or *ban-munmyeong*. The West was explicitly regarded as being at the highest stage of human progress and its civilization was considered as universal to be adopted by the non-West. In this respect, the 1890s and 1900s spanned a critical period when the Eurocentric hierarchy between Korea and the West was popularized in Korean society. Learning from the West was promoted as the way to make the nation strong enough to sustain and retrieve national sovereignty. The most popular concepts that reflected the need for learning from the West were *gaehwa* in the 1890s and *munmyeong* in the 1900s.

Despite its supposed second-tier status in the discourses of *gaehwa* and *munmyeong*, however, Korea was still regarded as a country that had brilliant historical and cultural heritage and exceptional natural conditions. Thus, the Eurocentric hierarchy was not yet considered as inherent and permanent; rather, it was incidental, temporary, and thus reversible, which was a notable difference between Koreans' Eurocentric attitude at the time and ordinary Eurocentric ideas.

The 1920s and 1930s spanned a period when the universality of Western civilization was highly suspect. In the wake of the unprecedented tragedies of World War I, which had been fought by the so-called *munmyeong-guk*, the authority of the West and Western civilization became greatly weakened. As reflected in the *Chosun Ilbo* and the *Dong-a Ilbo*, the concept of *munmyeong* was considered from a relativist perspective, and the values of diverse civilizations were well recognized. The West was repositioned merely as a region, instead of the world. Western civilization was perceived as a regional civilization strong in material aspects, while Eastern civilization was considered to be a spiritual and ethical civilization.

The newly emerged non-Eurocentric concept of *munmyeong* was utilized to criticize and resist against Japanese colonial rule. In this regard, peace-loving civilizations such as Korea were often considered as "true *munmyeong*" in contrast with "pseudo-*munmyeong*," promoting the logic of power. As such, the Koreans' *munmyeong* discourse in the early twentieth century contained a delicate feature that was not caught by the simplistic dichotomy between the "superior civilized" and the "inferior uncivilized."

In regard to the genealogy of Eurocentrism in Korea, the discourse of *munmyeong* in the late nineteenth century, which had spread Eurocentric thoughts and values in Korea for the first time in its history by designating the West as the pinnacle of civilization, gradually lost its discursive hegemony to the discourse of development after the mid-twentieth century with its authority seriously damaged after World War I. In this process, the "civilized" West began to be newly defined as the "developed" West, and Eurocentrism in Korea continued from the discourse of *munmyeong* to the discourse of *baljeon* (development), especially to that of *seonjinguk*.

Notes

1 For the articles from the *Hanseong Sunbo* and the *Hanseong Jubo*, I have referred to Jeong J.-S.'s (1983) translation. I have focused on "*gakguk-geunsa*" (international news) in the *Sunbo* and "*saui*" (editorial) in the *Jubo*, which are especially relevant to the perceptions of the West and international affairs. Using seven keywords such as "*seoyang*" (the West), "*oeguk*" (foreign country), "*seonjin*" (advanced), "*munmyeong*" (civilization), "*gaehwa*" (enlightenment), "*gurapa*" (Europe), and "*yaman*" (barbarianism) in the Korea Integrated News Database System, I have obtained a total of 326 editorials for the *Dongnip Shinmun* (81 cases) and the *Daehan Maeil Shinbo* (245 cases). Using "*munmyeong*" and "*yaman*" as keywords, I have obtained 353 articles for "*munmyeong*" and 62 for "*yaman*" from the *Chosun* archive, and 410

cases for "*munmyeong*" and 60 for "*yaman*" from the *Dong-a* database. There was no major newspaper published by the Koreans in the 1910s.

2 The understanding of *gaehwa* differed even within Korea. For instance, Yu Gil-Jun (2004: 393), reflecting the Japanese influence, noted that *gaehwa* is "the process through which various human things and affairs reach the status of ultimate good and beauty." In comparison, the *Dongnip Shinmun* (30 June 1896) mentioned that the term *gaehwa* originated from China, and defined it as a situation in which "one thinks about affairs with reason and does all things in realistic ways by enlightening his/her viewpoints." The terms "*gaehwa*" and "*munmyeong*" were often combined into "*munmyeong gaehwa*" in Korea.

3 The rapacious nature of the Western expansion was similarly recognized by modern intellectuals in other Asian countries at the time. A Japanese nationalist journalist Tokutomi Soho (1863–1957), for instance, argued the following in an article published in 1886: "The present-day world is one in which civilized people tyrannically destroy primitive people … The European countries stand at the very pinnacle of violence and base themselves on the doctrine of force … India, alas, has been destroyed, Annam has been destroyed, Burma will be next" (de Bary et al., 2006: 132).

4 One of the main objectives of the Japanese *Iwakura* mission in 1872–1873 was to investigate the possibility of renegotiating the unequal treaties made between Japan and Western powers at the time (Swale, 1998).

5 Noh D.-H. (2010a) noted that the most frequently used concept in the *Maeil Shinmun* was *munmyeong*, as in "*bugang munmyeong*" (strength and civilization) and "*munmyeong bugang*" (civilization and strength).

6 The term "*sugu*" was often used as the opposite to *gaehwa*. For instance, one editorial reported a person saying, "when talking about rural people's living, one may not know whether it is *gaehwa* or *sugu* […]" (*Dongnip Shinmun*, 2 November 1899).

7 With regard to racial studies, for instance, one editorial said, "in foreign countries, a study called ethnology is a great study and people studying ethnology are much respected" (*Dongnip Shinmun*, 6 April 1897).

8 Tikhonov (2010: 60) noted that the *Dongnip Shinmun* generally adopted social Darwinist ideas to think that "misfortunes were partly caused by the racial inferiority of the non-Western victims of 'civilization and progress.'"

9 Shortly after Japan's victory over China, Tokutomi Soho rejoiced at Japan's supposedly elevated status in the West-led world: "We are no longer ashamed to stand before the world as Japanese … The name 'Japanese' […] now signifies honor, glory, courage, triumph, and victory. Before we did not know ourselves, and the world did not yet know us. But now that we have tested our strength, we know ourselves and we are known by the world. Moreover, we know that we are known by the world!" (de Bary et al., 2006: 133). In regard to this, Tanaka (1993: 14–15) stated that "the Sino-Japanese War (1894–95) gained Japan respect as a power in Asia, while the Russo-Japanese War (1904–5) was seen to signal Japan's entry into the elite group of major world powers."

10 Another representative newspaper in this period was the *Hwangseong Shinmun*, which was published by pro-reform Confucian intellectuals. Despite the difference between this and the *Shinbo* in the general tone of argument, both agreed on the need for reform promoting *munmyeong* as a strategy for national survival. Noh D.-H. (2010b) noted that the *Hwangseong Shinmun* frequently used the term "*gaemyeong*" (enlightenment) for reform and the acceptance of Western knowledge. Baek D.-H. (2003: 172) also stated that the *Hwangseong Shinmun* "distinguished between '*munmyeong-guk*' and '*mimyeong-guk*' (uncivilized country) and agreed upon the need for *munmyeong-hwa* (civilization)."

11 The number of articles containing the term *gaehwa* was 16 for the *Dongnip Shinmun* and 13 for the *Daehan Maeil Shinbo*, while the number of cases for the term *munmyeong* was four in the former and 118 in the latter.

12 In this regard, Korean nationalists' efforts for *munmyeong gaehwa* are sometimes interpreted as mainly aiming at participating in the "global trend" (Schmid, 2002).

13 Many Asian intellectuals changed their perceptions of the West after World War I. The influential Chinese modernist Liang Qichao (1873–1929), who had been an ardent admirer of the West on the basis of social Darwinist ideas, dramatically altered his attitude after returning from Europe. He had observed the tragedies of the world war in Europe and saw the West as "sick and declining, the victim of its own obsession with science, materialism, and mechanization" (de Bary and Lufrano, 2000: 377–379).

14 During the *gaehwa* period, the concept of Korean ethics ("*yulli*") was influenced by the Western concept of ethics that was regarded as an element of civilization. However, Koreans' concept of "*yulli*" was rooted in traditional neo-Confucian values and, thus, its connotation and context of use were somewhat different from those of the West. Korean intellectuals frequently sought for their pride in Korea from "*yulli*" which they regarded as superior than those of other countries (Yi H.-G., 2011).

3 The Politics of Modern Discourse of Civilization in Colonized Korea

The 1910s and the 1920s

The colonial expansion of the West and Japan was deeply related to the diffusion of the discourse of civilization. The modern discourse of civilization justified modern Europe's colonial expansion by arguing that human history was to progress from "barbarism" to "civilization" and the Western civilization was to lead it in the forefront. On these grounds, European intellectuals claimed their "civilizational duty," such as the "white man's burden," to justify European expansion and colonialism around the globe (Patterson, 1997).[1] In this respect, modern discourse of civilization connoted the dominant-dominated relationship in itself.

The Japanese discourse of "*bunmei kaika*" (civilization and enlightenment) after the mid-nineteenth century employed the assumptions of modern discourse of civilization, and classified the world into three tiers: The "civilized," "half-civilized," and "barbarian." It designated the West as the "civilized," while identifying Turkey, China, and Japan as the "half-civilized," and Africa and Australia as "barbarian" (de Bary et al., 2006; Park Y.-S., 2008). In the 1880s when Japan gained confidence in its modern achievements through the Meiji Restoration, the idea that Japan was the half-civilized was replaced with the one that Japan was the "newly civilized of the East" or the "Britain of Asia," and its gaze of civilization discourse turned outward (Hahm D.-J., 2004: 376).

Japan justified the occupation of Korea under the cause of "civilization." The idea of "civilizational guidance" about Korea notably emerged in Japan in the 1880s. Fukuzawa Yukichi (1835–1901), a representative modern Japanese intellectual, supported the colonization of Korea with such logic that "Japan was strong and Korea was weak. And Japan had already forwarded to civilization but Korea had not" (Hahm D.-J., 2004: 382). Tokutomi Soho (1863–1957) argued in 1896 that "we have a duty to radiate the light of civilization beyond our shores and bring the benefits of civilization to our neighbors. We have the duty to guide backward countries to the point of being able to govern themselves" (de Bary et al., 2006: 133). Having won the Sino–Japanese War (1894–1895) and the Russo–Japanese War (1904–1905) consecutively, Japan attained confidence to think that it had reached the highest level of civilization comparable to the West.

Given the global influence of modern discourse of civilization in the colonial era, this chapter aims to show how the modern discourse of civilization in colonized Korea disciplined Korean society and justified Japanese colonial rule in the early twentieth century. For this, it analyzes the texts of the *Maeil Shinbo*, the official daily newspaper of the Japanese government-general in Korea, focusing on the concept of "*munmyeong*" (civilization) and its antonym "*yaman*" (barbarism). Through this, it attempts to reveal the basic premises, characteristics, and socio-political roles of the modern discourse of civilization reflected in the Japanese colonial newspaper, in regard to the colonizer-colonized relationship in Korea.[2]

The following sections will discuss: First, the way of problematizing the level of Korean civilization; second, the way of designating Japan as civilization and of justifying its rule as civilizational; and third, the occurrence of conflicts between the Japanese and the Koreans over the identities of civilization and barbarism.

The "Problematization" of Korea's Level of Civilization

One of the main sources of Korea's confidence in international relations in the *Joseon* (*Chosun*) period (1392–1897) was the civilizational pride that it was at the center of Confucian ethical civilization. When Western powers expanded to Asia, Korea's civilizational pride was a disturbing factor for its international exchange with the West. In the framework of Confucian discourse of civilization, Western civilization was close to "barbarism" as its expansion showed off its physical power. Having undergone the French invasion of Korea's Ganghwa Island (1866), followed by the American invasion (1871), Heungseon Daewongoon, the then actual ruler of Korea, established the Anti-foreign Steles across the country, which designated Western powers as "barbarians," and refused any interchanges and relationships with them. Korea's civilizational pride was a spiritual source for resisting against "Western barbarians" who were perceived as threatening its sovereignty.

In the framework of traditional civilization discourse, the Koreans tended to think of Japan's level of civilization as not reaching those of China and Korea. The frequent Japanese invasions of the Korean southern shores, especially after the mid-*Joseon* period, strengthened the Koreans' perception of the "Japanese barbarians." This perceptual tendency remained in Korea's modern discourses of *gaehwa* and *munmyeong* in the late nineteenth and early twentieth centuries. Then, what kind of discourse did Japan promote and utilize to respond to the Koreans' civilizational pride for its effective rule of Korea?

The Decline of Korea's Civilization and the Need for Improvement

For a stable dominance-subordination relationship, the intellectual and moral leadership of the dominant should be consensual (Gramsci, 1971). For this, the dominant should be perceived as being superior to the dominated and vice-versa, which means that the discourse naturalizing the hierarchy between the dominant and the dominated should be in a hegemonic status.

In regard to Japan's occupation of Korea, the urgent priority for Japan to stabilize its rule in Korea was to break down Korea's pride in civilization. Imperial Japan mobilized available resources to justify a hierarchy between Japan and Korea, and to make this be accepted by the Koreans. As an organ of imperial Japan, the *Maeil Shinbo* was the representative medium that made efforts to problematize the level of Korea's civilization through the discursive framework of modern civilization. It tended to criticize Korea's current status by emphasizing that Korea's civilizational level had been problematic and in need of improvement.

In this regard, an article in the *Maeil Shinbo* (19 March 1912) entitled "Civilization and filial piety and chastity" reported that:

> For thousands of years, Korea had maintained manners and honor, and its ethics had been clarified to produce devoted sons and virtuous women for generations [...] In this respect, Korea's civilization could be well said to have reached its zenith. However, for the past decades, its civilization has not avoided corruption and its custom has been getting weaker, with its humanity getting lowly, which have brought it close to the coarse and unenlightened situation [...] Thus, our Dear [Japanese] Emperor rules Korea to enhance our people's spiritual civilization, making people practice good manners and know honor. Under the royal grace of the Emperor, our people will hopefully observe spiritual civilization to recover civilization and humanity that have been handed down for thousands of years.

This article partly reflects Koreans' civilizational pride by admitting that their past civilization was somewhat splendid. However, it emphasizes that Korea's civilization has declined for decades to get close to the "coarse and unenlightened" situation currently. In this way, it problematizes Korea's current status to raise a need for Korea's change. As for the subject to lead Korea's change, this article presents the Japanese, i.e., the Japanese Emperor, instead of the Koreans. It is a characteristic of colonial discourse to make a perception that the colonized society is in a problematic situation with its people not having the capacity to solve it for themselves. In this respect, this article argues that the rule of the Dear Japanese Emperor is to advance Korea's spiritual civilization, and that Korean people will recover the past level of spiritual civilization under his "royal grace."

As Korea had constantly confronted foreign powers' threats since the late nineteenth century, Korean modern intellectuals shared a need to improve Korea's civilization to effectively face the modern world. Among various methods suggested by them for this, a criterion for distinguishing between nationalistic position and anti-nationalistic position would be to check their judgment of Korea's self-capacity and of the inevitability of depending on a foreign power. A representative Korean modern thinker, Yoon Chi-Ho

(1865–1945), for instance, advocated Korea's "enlightenment" under the rule of the civilized country, by criticizing Korea's supposed situation of barely maintaining "accidental independence," while choosing the benefit of "paradoxical positiveness" that would be brought about by the civilizational process even if it would be led by foreigners (Yu B.-L., 2013: 85). This kind of idea is somewhat relevant to the *Shinbo*'s article above as it supports imperial Japan's intent to rule Korea by disregarding Korea's own capacity, while interpreting Japan's intervention as a need for civilizational improvement.

In regard to the status of Korea's civilization, an article from the *Maeil Shinbo* (25 May 1918) introduces an American magazine article reporting that "by the time when Japan colonized Korea, the Koreans were definitely the most destitute race in the world, except for African black people." This article problematizes Korea at the time of Japanese colonization by designating it as having been in the most destitute situation. Then it mentions that change occurred in Korea after colonization, such as the increase in vehicles, and argues that "civilization stimulated Korea much." It further contends that it was imperial Japan which stimulated Korea in a destitute situation to move towards civilization. In this article's discursive framework, Korea, African people, and destitution are on the one side, and on its opposite side are Japan, vehicles, and civilization. Here the negative and positive values are contrasted on both sides respectively. It implies that the change from the former side to the latter side is possible, contingent upon the intervention of civilization like Japan.

While the problematization of "poverty" and the tendency of making hierarchy among countries according to the economic level became notable after the mid-twentieth century with the rise of development discourse, the article above problematizes "poverty" in the framework of civilization discourse and contrasts it with civilization. This shows that the level of wealth was an important criterion for judging civilization in the discourse of civilization. In fact, the civilized country was generally represented as the country of "*bugang*" (material wealth and physical strength) in the discourse of civilization.

Korea Inferior to "Civilization"

As for the status of Korea's civilization, an article in the *Maeil Shinbo* (8 January 1922) delivers the opinion of a Korean who has lived in the U.S. for more than 20 years. The writer of the article, Kim Yong-Ju, evaluates Korea from the "eyes of the civilized," having lived in the "civilized" U.S. He criticizes the level of Korea's civilization for being far less than he expected, and laments "how so far Korea has not escaped from the ancient emperor's time." He even designates Korea as a "barbaric country," and mentions that the gap between Korea and the U.S. in the level of civilization is as great as that between the sky and the earth. In this regard, he says that he has now realized the right reason for the Americans to ignore Asians, which he felt absurd when living in the U.S.

Another interesting point of this article is the writer's criticism of the Koreans' perception of reality. It says as follows:

> Our Koreans call Korea as a country of courtesy in the East and have an exaggerated delusive perception of Korea as the only precious one in the world. But what does the "country of courtesy" refer to on earth? How do they consider as if Western civilized countries have no manners and ethics? Furthermore, Korea in the past knew manners and practiced righteousness under the dominance of serious ethics, but according to what I saw and listened, the cases frequently appeared in which father and son sued and fought each other. Then, how could they be called as the people of the so-called "country of courtesy in the East?" [...] Civilized countries are feeling shameful to posit Korea in the rank of humanity, by calling Korea as the country of unenlightened or the people of barbarism. Then, no matter how we alone pretend to be respectful and elegant, how would the people in the world admit us?

From this article, we know that there was a notable tendency among the Koreans to think highly of their country as the "country of courtesy in the East" even under Japanese colonial rule. That is, there was a tendency in Korea to maintain the country's self-respect based on the identity of traditional civilization even amidst the influx of the so-called "new civilization." However, the article above argued that the level of Korea's manners and ethics was not higher than that of Western countries. The writer contended that it had no usefulness for the Koreans to pretend to be self-respectful alone in a situation where civilized countries designated Korea as the country of "unenlightened" or "barbarism" and felt shameful to posit it in their ranks.

As the article above indicates, the so-called "civilized countries" tried not to admit Korea as a main actor on the international stage, problematizing its level of civilization. In response to this, the Koreans tried not to lose their national pride, appreciating the level of Korea's traditional civilization. This can be understood as a way of Korea's discourse of traditional civilization responding to the expansion of the discourse of modern civilization promoted by the West and Japan. However, the discursive framework of the "civilized countries," which was backed up by physical power, tended to be perceived as more valid and universal than was Korea's. In fact, the discursive framework leading the imagination and arrangement of the world order was that of the "civilized countries," and the qualification for participating in the international order was only given to the so-called "civilized countries."

The attempt to make a hierarchy between Japan and Korea by emphasizing the inferior status of Korea's current civilization appeared widely in the *Maeil Shinbo*. In this regard, an article (2 July 1914) argues that Koreans' intellectual ability is not reaching that of the Japanese. It criticizes that there has appeared a tendency in Korean society to superficially imitate the civilized, bringing about harmful consequences such as extravagance. Another article (6 December 1919), in a similar vein, makes a clear hierarchy between Japan and Korea according to the level of civilization, by saying that "the level of Japanese civilization has progressed a step further than that of Korean civilization."

The Arbitrariness of Judging Korea's Civilization

Although the level of civilization was an important yardstick for defining countries' international status under the global hegemony of the modern discourse of civilization, the criteria for judging it were somewhat arbitrary. Reporting English journalists' visit to Korea, an article (12 November 1921) delivers a different perception of Korea's level of civilization from that of Kim's article above. This article, headlined "Sightseeing Korea … all facilities are those of civilized countries," reports the English journalists' impression of Korea as follows:

> Having entered and seen Korea, we came to have a different impression of it from what we had heard previously. The impression naturally appeared that its surprising potential and culture could be well comparable to those of other civilized countries. Before visiting Korea, we had not expected that there would be a railroad in Korea. What we had heard before was that the Korean people were feeling sorrow in bleak mountains and fields, being deprived of their property and getting intolerable mistreatment by Japanese officials. It was beyond our expectations that such a splendid railroad existed in Korea. And, according to what we heard from the representative of the railroad company, not only was Japan giving more than 20,000,000 in subsidies annually but the railroad company alone was contributing a great amount of more than 100,000 to devote to developing the Korean region.

In this article, the English journalists delivered their impression of Korea from the "eyes of the civilized." While comparing Korea to civilized countries, they implicitly showed their sense of superiority as civilized people. The main grounds for their judgment of Korea as being comparable to the civilized was the existence of a railroad. The adoption of new modern technologies was an important yardstick for judging a society's level of civilization. The English journalists perceived the Japanese as the subject "devoted to developing the Korean region." In this regard, they emphasized the benefits of the Japanese colonial rule, while mentioning that their previous thought was ungrounded that the "Korean people were feeling sorrow" under Japanese rule. This reflects that the legitimacy of colonialism, which was disguised as the project of civilization, tended to be commonly observed by both Western and Japanese intellectuals at the time.[3]

As such, there were various possible perspectives on the level of Korea's civilization. Among them, however, the notable one was an "in-between" identity, i.e., the identity between the civilized and the barbaric, in terms of the level of modern civilization. In regard to this, an article (26 October 1925) entitled "Civilization is our own property" reports a Korean intellectual Yoon Gab-Byeong's address as follows:

> Among 1,600 million humans in the world, there are three classes with the most civilized people followed by half-enlightened people and barbaric people. In these three classes, in which class are our Korean people located from an objective perspective? While admitting that it would never be a barbaric people, I would say it does not reach the civilized people either. Then, we are the half-enlightened people without question. Aren't we the people who will proceed to civilization, not remaining in a stalemate, while confirming that the path of civilization is our property?

This article follows the most general classification of then discourse of civilization, by categorizing the world into three tiers, e.g., the civilized, the half-enlightened, and the barbaric. Among these, it designates the Koreans as in the class of the half-enlightened, while emphasizing the need for progressing towards civilization without being stagnated. This reflects a representative view on Korea's "in-between" identity in terms of the level of modern civilization.

In a similar vein, an editorial (7 January 1928) entitled "Do not be comforted" argues that Korea's level of civilization is yet in "the crawling status in the cradle of modern civilization" although it has been contacting Western civilization for nearly one century. On these grounds, this article asks for "strenuous pioneering," rather than pursuing "being temporarily comforted," in order to progress in all fields such as education and industry.

Korea's Civilization as "Distorted" Modernity

Modernity or modern civilization, which imperial Japan attempted to implant, could not be duplicated in Korea in its original form. As Korea's own autonomous movement of modernization had been "stopped or distorted by the stronger modernity that had been implanted from outside" (Kim D.-N., 2004: 20), colonized Korea came to contain and display somewhat unnatural modernity in its historical context. In a way, colonized Korea showed a tendency to imitate the civilized by consuming hybrid modernity imported into it, displaying a type of colonized identity (Lee G.-H., 2004; Shin M.-J., 2004).

Some Korean writers for the *Maeil Shinbo* gave criticism to new trends in Korean society, which appeared with the inflow of foreign modern civilization. As for the trend of "new civilization" appearing among Korean women, a Korean female writer argued that it was as absurd as "putting a peacock's feather into the crow," and asked for progress towards substantial civilization without falling into the empty trend (*Maeil Shinbo*, 21 July 1920). Another article (7 November 1922), headlined "Modern life of civilization and people's misunderstanding," criticized the trend of pursuing the illusive "civilizational life," mentioning that "the new word of the so-called 'civilizational life' had become popular in recent years." Emphasizing the value of "substantial" life and civilization, it pointed out that the "unsubstantial" was the "uncivilizational."

In short, the level of Korea's civilization was generally represented in the *Maeil Shinbo* as not reaching the level of "sound civilization." The problematization of current status justifies social change. By problematizing Korea's current status, the *Maeil Shinbo* raised a need for Korea's change. After the problematization of current status comes a question: Who is and how to lead social change? As for this, imperial Japan utilized the *Maeil Shinbo* to make the Koreans have self-deprecating perception and identity by continuously highlighting the ignorance, misbehavior, and weaknesses of the Koreans (Cho S.-W., 2005: 16). The advocates of the Japanese colonial rule would have raised a need for borrowing the civilized foreign power, while its resisters tended to believe in Koreans' own capacity and potential. In this regard, the following section discusses in detail what interpretive framework and position the *Maeil Shinbo* employed to designate Japan as the subject to lead Korea's change.

The Superiority of Japanese Civilization and the Legitimacy of Colonial Rule

As noted above, the Koreans' evaluation of Japanese civilization has tended to be somewhat stingy through long historical times. Through the *Joseon* period, for instance, a notable perception was that Japan had been a kind of "barbarism" in the framework of Confucian ethics-based discourse of civilization. Around the late nineteenth and early twentieth centuries when Japan was emerging as a main actor on the international stage to colonize its neighboring countries including Korea, a notable perception of Japan among the Koreans was that although Japanese civilization was strong on material and scientific aspects, it was ultimately not reaching that of the West in those aspects, nor Korea's level of civilization in traditional and ethical aspects. In regard to the colonial relationship, the Koreans' attitude to deprecate Japanese civilization was closely related to the attitude to reject the Japanese "duty of civilization."

The *Maeil Shinbo* sometimes blamed the Koreans' tendency to underrate Japan. As for this, it is interesting to see that a Japanese writer of a *Maeil Shinbo* article (23 September 1921) criticized Koreans' resistance to the Japanese rule for deriving from "toadyism."

> As the idea of serving the great has been in people's mind for a long time, the improvement of the Korean people is impossible without removing it in any way. I really want to say to the Koreans that it is impossible without removing the spirit of serving the great [...] Comparing China and Japan, anyone would consider that Japan is small and China is big [...] I am suspecting if the Koreans' idea about Japan is not a kind of toadyism. That is, I am wondering if they do not have any idea that Japan is a small country but they have to serve it [...] If it is a big country like China, the Koreans never think it would hurt their honor even to be a half-tributary

> of it. If the Japanese is about to develop, the sense of aversion to it and the idea of independence emerge among the Koreans. That is, isn't the idea permeated among the Koreans that Japan is small? So, doesn't the idea exist even today to depend on a country that is considered bigger than Japan?

What the Japanese writer criticizes with complaint in this article is mainly the Koreans' willingness for independence without admitting Japanese rule. According to the writer's interpretation, it is because the Koreans are tinged with toadyism, the idea of serving big countries like China and Russia. While admitting that Japan is a small country compared with China, the writer expresses strong complaint about Koreans' attitude of disregarding Japan as a small country. He deprecates the Koreans' resistance as deriving from their "toadyism."

This article shows that the Koreans' so-called "toadyism" sometimes mentioned in the colonial historical view is a kind of idea raised by the Japanese as a way to interpret the Koreans' disapproval of the Japanese rule. Responding to that attitude of the Koreans towards Japan, the *Maeil Shinbo* had to make strenuous efforts to emphasize the superiority of Japanese civilization over Korea, while designating its rule as a necessity for Korea's improvement.

Japan as "Civilization" and the "Progress for Civilization"

The *Maeil Shinbo* affirmed, in general, that the Japanese civilizational level was a step above the Korean one. For this, it tended to equate Japan with civilization itself. One article (23 March 1914), for instance, designated the Korean observer team visiting Japan as "those at the forefront of civilization." It further reported that "in regard to the Tokyo Expo, Korean leaders and gentlemen visit Japan to directly observe the world's leading expo and various civilized situations there."

The most frequently appearing contents in the *Maeil Shinbo* regarding "civilization" are those about the distribution of the newspaper, as this is termed as the phenomenon of "civilization and progress," "the ray of civilization," "the sparkle of civilization," etc. The *Maeil Shinbo* justifies itself naturally by designating itself as an essential element of civilization, and its subscription as the phenomenon of civilization. In regard to this, one article (20 March 1913) argues that the newspaper is the source of civilization and that civilization and barbarism of society can be judged by the circulation of the newspaper. As the *Maeil Shinbo* was the only newspaper published in Korea in the 1910s, the early period of colonized Korea, it shows that imperial Japan designated the distribution of its propaganda instrument as the yardstick for "civilization and progress." On the other hand, the articles demonstrate that colonial Japan attempted to win over local Korean influentials through the medium of the *Maeil Shinbo*, as colonial Japan had difficulty in securing local officials' and intellectuals' support of its colonial rule (Shim J.-W., 2002).[4]

The *Maeil Shinbo* often carried articles introducing modern social changes, such as the increase of the division of labor, industrial development, and the expansion of social relations, by defining them as the phenomena of "civilization." An article (25 February 1921) entitled "Civilization and the division of labor," for instance, argues that "the division of labor is the expression of civilization." It contends interestingly as follows: "Women are advanced than men from the perspective of the division of labor [...] The urethral canal is separated from the deferent one with women, but these are combined for men. So, isn't it that men are undivisional of labor while women are divisional?" It is impressive to compare the division of labor, a characteristic of modern civilization, to the biological difference between the male and the female.

As such, "modern civilization" or "*munmyeong*" connoted positiveness, such as manners, order, non-violence, hygiene, and efficiency, while negativities were projected to the concept of "*yaman*," such as bad manners, disorder, violence, cruelty, dirtiness, inefficiency, etc.[5] As for the prison in Seoul, one article (14 May 1918) implies the humane aspect of civilization, mentioning that "even prisoners suffer less in the era of civilization."[6] Here "suffering less" is linked to "civilization."

When positiveness and negativeness, or the values of the good and the bad, are respectively projected into the concepts of "civilization" and "barbarism," the concept of "civilization" exerts an effect of disciplining social life and directing social change. In this regard, a series of articles in October 1917, which are entitled "Hygiene is the yardstick for civilization," emphasize the importance of hygienic life, insisting that the basis of the wealthy strong nation is hygiene. These articles intended to discipline social life in Korean society and to induce its change, by linking modern hygiene to the concept of civilization, which might have been quite unfamiliar to ordinary Koreans at the time. As for the Japanese, the *Maeil Shinbo* tended to highlight the dynamics of the Japanese in Korea by introducing their activities such as establishing schools, organizing groups, and leading economic activities, and infused into the Koreans that the Japanese were the first-rate people with diligence (Jeong H.-G., 2002: 127).

As such, the concept of "civilization," connoting the values of positiveness, played a role as a criterion of judging societies and their people. In this regard, an article (21 November 1919) entitled "Wedding expenses of the civilized country" made a comparison between Asian countries and the civilized, by pointing out that the wedding expenses of Japan and China were far higher than those of Western countries.

"Politics of Civilization," "Good Times," and "the Stubborn"

The *Maeil Shinbo* actively reported modern social changes and phenomena in colonized Korea, such as education, newspaper circulation, industrial development, custom change, and improvement of life, using the concept of "civilization." As for the Japanese rule, the newspaper designated it as the "politics of civilization," the "politics of royal virtues," or "strict and benign politics," emphasizing that this brought about good times in Korea. In this regard, one article (1 March 1914), for instance, argues that "since the annexation of Korea, Korean people have been enjoying the age of peace and happiness by virtue of strict and benign politics, and the bright and agile police." Another article (31 March 1914) distinguishes the period of pre-colonized Korea as the "old Korean times" from the "age of civilization" after that.

Imperial Japan's and its Korean collaborators' perceptions of colonial rule were well reflected in the so-called "song for congratulating civilization" (*munmyeong chukha-ga*), which was to welcome the Japanese governor coming to Korea. The lyrics of this song are introduced in an article as follows:

> Hey our Korean people, our lives are enjoyable in peace and affluence in the age of civilization [...] As the newly appointed governor-general of Korea, who has been closely tied with Korea, has come to Korea, isn't this a fortunate thing like reaching the sunny spring again? Hey our people, let's sincerely welcome him and wish for great blessings and the improvement of civilization.
>
> (*Maeil Shinbo*, 15 December 1916)

The *Maeil Shinbo* emphasized that the goal of the "civilizational" rule was to civilize Korea. In regard to this, an article (19 November 1920) reports a Japanese politician's mentioning of the ruling of Korea as follows:

> We wish for Korean people's well-being and, further, sincerely hope that we and our descendants altogether live in happiness as the Koreans and the Japanese get along very well with each other. So, we hope to make Korean industry run well and Korean lives improve, and to do better the education of the Koreans to make them civilized people. [...] How could it be useful for the Koreans if they are busy at political matters, while not paying attention to their economy and development at the present when they are teaching the Chinese letters at private schools, being unable to even make daily necessities? [...] For this Korea, we may have to guide it to a good place quickly.

The Japanese politician, the speaker in this article, argues that he hopes for Korea to be well. That is, he hopes that the Japanese rule makes Korean industry better, improves Korean lives, and advances Korean education to make Korean people civilized. He problematizes the traditional education and industrial status of Korea, and asks the Koreans to pay more attention to the economy rather than being "busy at political matters." In a sense of superiority, he implies that Japan already knows the "good place" for Korea, by mentioning that the Japanese will lead Korea to a good place quickly.

The *Maeil Shinbo* often called those not following the Japanese rule as the stubborn, and designated them as those sticking to old customs. In this regard, one article (27 March 1912) criticized that stubborn Koreans were not interested in the new education of young people, while keeping old customs and classifying political parties and people's status. The more the Korean elites are perceived as corrupt and incapable, the more the Japanese rule will have legitimacy. As for the Japanese role in educating Korea, this article further reported a case of the Japanese chief of the local military police who, allegedly, established a language night school and worked hard to educate, making a good case for the local government as the local Koreans responded positively and thoughts of civilization spread widely. The article compares the representation of Japan as civilization with that of those not following as the stubborn, naturally giving justification to the former.

As one of the main goals of elementary education in Korea in the early colonial period was to spread Japanese language, the term "language" in the article mentioned above seemed to refer to Japanese language. Imperial Japan utilized "new education" (or "modern education") for nurturing "loyal subjects" to destroy the traditional ruling structures of local societies.[7] The article above, on the other hand, implies that "the influence of traditional leaders and the traditional order, existent in local societies at the time, were not immediately destroyed, unlike the Japanese governor's expectation" (Shim J.-W., 2002: 226).

The *Maeil Shinbo* even directly advocated the legitimacy of colonialism. In this regard, a Japanese writer argued that the purpose of colonialism was "coexistence and co-prosperity" and to "enhance the happiness of the colonized" (*Maeil Shinbo*, 7 February 1927). In a similar vein, another article (14 February 1927) contended that "the ethical ground of the colonial movement" was to "expand civilization." This article further argued that it was the "sacred duty of civilization" to plan the welfare and development of the people unable to be self-reliant.

As examined above, civilization discourse reflected in the *Maeil Shinbo* was premised on the superiority of Japanese civilization to the Korean one. On these grounds, it argued that the Japanese rule was basically benign as it was to help the "civilization and progress" of Korea. Furthermore, the *Maeil Shinbo* emphasized that the civilization of Korea would be beneficial to both Japan and Korea. In this regard, the newspaper sometimes argued that the Korean and Japanese people were in the same race to demonstrate a unique civilization in collaboration in the future (*Maeil Shinbo*, 9 April 1923).

Identity Conflicts over "Civilization" and "Barbarism"

The concepts of "civilization" and "barbarism" in the early period of colonized Korea were main concepts incurring political domination and subordination, or obedience and resistance. The Korean writers for the *Maeil Shinbo* showed a tendency to accept the superiority of Japanese civilization and the legitimacy of its rule of Korea, arguing for the need for the Koreans to progress towards civilization under the Japanese rule.

Among the Koreans, however, the tendency to keep national pride was not weak, with confidence in their level of traditional civilization. It is notable that many conflicts between the Koreans and the Japanese were reported in the *Maeil Shinbo*, among which a great portion was about the emotional conflicts between the two peoples surrounding the identities of "civilization" and "barbarism."

Designating Korea as "Barbarism" and Its Resistance

In the 1920s, the *Maeil Shinbo* often reported the cases in which Korean students were resisting or on strike against Japanese teachers' designation of Korea as "barbarian." One article (7 June 1921), for instance, reported that Korean students were resisting against a Japanese professor's mentioning of Korea as barbarian.

> As Professor Gubo has studied the Korean people for many years, he is able to academically verify in detail that the Korean people have gradually degraded from civilization in the past to barbarism. Then, what could students say about it? And, it may be right to resist academically, but unfair to resist physically [...]

This article argues that the Japanese professor can verify academically Korea's gradual retreat to barbarism and asks Korean students to dispute it academically if they have a different opinion. As such, Japanese intellectuals attempted to give the inferior identity of "barbarism" to Korea, under the authority of modern academics. However, the "Japanese professor's admonition incurred students' fury on the contrary," as was reported in the article, demonstrating that Korean students did not shrink in front of Japanese professors' academic authority to resist more strongly against the attempt to designate Korea as barbarian.

Another article (16 July 1922) reports a case of Korean students' combined strike, as follows:

> Sojeonchon [a Japanese teacher who had been teased by Korean students due to her awkward English] tried to persuade students but only to fail to make them obedient. She wrote two letters, "virtue" and "force," on the blackboard, expressing uneasy emotion, and scolded students by saying humiliating words to Korean people that "you Korean people are the race still in the barbaric status and it is impossible to improve you without force." And, she ordered students to leave the classroom. Hearing such words from the teacher with whom they were already dissatisfied, the

> students got very angry and said to the teacher that "such an incapable teacher as you are not even in the Korean people," making the quarrel between the teacher and the students [...]

This article reports that the main cause of the students' combined strike was a Japanese teacher's designation of Korean people as a barbaric race. It shows well that the Japanese designation of barbarism was felt by the Koreans as an intolerable insult.

In a similar vein, an article (8 December 1927) reports the combined strikes of Korean students in Cheongju city:

> It is said that the cause of the combined strikes first derived from the school principal's improper speech and behavior, which created various problems to have finally exploded [...] The principal is, first of all, discriminating the peoples seriously. He not only argues for the discrimination of the Koreans, saying that the Koreans are born to be barbaric, but also is seriously egoistic and speaks nastily. To [Korean] students in class, he didn't hesitate to make a speech to recommend the policeman [for the students' future job], saying that "you will earn less than a third of my salary even if you become a doctor in the future" [...] It is also a cause that another teacher speaks and behaves similarly to the principal and, furthermore, has insulted Koreans by publishing a paper entitled "Koreans are barbarism" in a magazine.

These articles demonstrate that there was a kind of a sense of superiority among Japanese intellectuals, such as teachers and professors, over the Koreans by the criteria of modern civilization, which were implicitly or explicitly expressed in their everyday lives. They also show that there was a tendency among the Japanese to blame the Koreans for conflictive situations between the two peoples, by designating the conflict as mainly deriving from Koreans' "barbarism."

On the other hand, it is also observed that there were attempts by Korean intellectuals to academically dispute the Japanese attitude. An article (16 July 1921) entitled "Anatomy of barbarism," written by Korean Choi Young-Taek, emphasized that barbarism, such as cruel slaughter, appeared even in the so-called "civilized countries." On this ground, the article stated that any civilized people had barbarism, as if there were unethical and cruel persons in any society, and that it would be unfair to say that barbarism existed only in the Korean people.

Resistance against Western "Civilized" People

Promoting the modern discourse of civilization, the *Maeil Shinbo* well reflects the Eurocentric view of civilization. One article (5 June 1921), for instance, states that the West is in the status of strong civilized countries, among which England is the "head of Western countries." It further argues that the Europeans are always the pioneers of the economy, academia, the arts, etc., contributing to the progress of civilization, and being in the status of leading the trend of the world. Reflecting Japanese interests, it stresses that Japan has recently reached a status that can be called a "strong country of newest civilization," which is comparable to the status of Western countries.

As the hierarchy of peoples was made according to their civilizational level in the Eurocentric discourse of civilization, emotional conflict over the identities of "civilization" and "barbarism" was not a matter only between the Koreans and the Japanese. In the colonial situation, the so-called "civilized" people's expression of their sense of superiority over the "less civilized" was implicitly or explicitly rampant in everyday life.

In this regard, an article in the *Maeil Shinbo* (10 December 1924) with the headline "The civilized people who are gambling!" criticizes the Westerners' expression of their sense of superiority over the Easterners, as follows:

> I saw news in the newspaper that the members of English and American embassies had been caught by the cabin crew for gambling in the kitchen of a train from Tokyo to Kobe and had been handed over to the police [...] It seemed that the cabin crew had given warnings four times to them, catching their gambling, but they had not obeyed the crew with a bumptious attitude of being civilized people. I believe that they must have been stubborn to be finally arrested, disregarding the Easterners' warning, due to their sense of superiority in their minds. This is because Western races in the East are generally arrogant and unmannered, and supercilious and bumptious. The civilized people! The strong countries of the world! These are foul words to even hear! Would it be okay for you the civilized people to come to the East and disregard its rules?

This article reports a case about the gambling of an Englishman and an American on a Japanese train, who did not follow the crew's directions, with a bumptious attitude. The writer expresses an uneasy emotion to the "civilized people" and the "strong countries of the world," criticizing that the "Western races" in the East are usually "arrogant, bumptious, and supercilious." Thus, the writer asks the Westerners to reflect on themselves instead of boasting of being civilized.

As a capital city of the colonized, Seoul in the colonized period was a space containing the duality of "modernity" and "coloniality," which was reflected in people's perceptions and everyday lives. A duality appeared similarly in the attitude towards the "civilized countries" and "civilized people." This was somewhat reflected in people's critical attitude towards the civilized, as it also contained a sense of respect for them. In regard to the crime statistics of colonized Korean society, for instance, an article (12 May 1923) mentions that the "civilized people are different" as "there is no crime committed by foreigners except for the Chinese." It goes on to say that "this may be due to their small population, but deters us from saying that the crime increases according to the development of knowledge." Here the "development of knowledge" is considered as an attribute of the civilized.

As examined above, the concepts of "civilization" and "barbarism" under the hegemony of civilization discourse were the main causes of emotional conflict among peoples, as they were to designate the identities of countries and peoples, and make hierarchy among them. In everyday life, members of the so-called "civilized countries" expressed their sense of superiority implicitly or explicitly. While the Japanese claimed for the reciprocal relationship with the Koreans, beautifying its colonization under the cause of "civilization," the Japanese sense of discriminating against the Koreans was expressed in various ways. In response to this, the Koreans expressed their anger and resisted through such activities as combined strikes, academic disputes, individual fighting, etc.

Conclusion

This chapter has examined the characteristics of the discourse of civilization reflected in the *Maeil Shinbo* in the early period of colonized Korea, focusing on its feature of dominance. The *Maeil Shinbo* problematized the level of Korean civilization as not reaching that of the civilized in order to justify the colonization of Korea. Based on this, it raised a need for Korea to progress towards "civilization," while designating the Japanese, rather than the Koreans, as the subject to promote Korea's change.

As for the "progress" of society, a characteristic of colonial and imperial discourse is to underestimate the colonized society's own capabilities, raising a need for a foreign power's intervention. The *Maeil Shinbo* designated imperial Japan as "civilization" and emphasized its qualification for leading Korea to civilization, by claiming Japan's superiority of civilization over Korea. It sometimes argued that the Japanese and the Koreans should cooperate to make both countries better and ultimately create a unique civilization in the world.

Nevertheless, there were frequent conflicts between the Koreans and foreigners in colonized Korea, over the identities of "civilization" and "barbarism." The 1920s *Maeil Shinbo* reported many cases of Korean students' resistance and combined strikes, which were caused by the Japanese teachers' designation of the Korean people as "barbarians."

Conflicts over the identities of "civilization" and "barbarism" were not just a matter between the Koreans and the Japanese. In the hegemony of the hierarchical discourse of civilization led by the West, the expression of the sense of superiority by the so-called "civilized" over the "less civilized" was quite rampant in everyday life. Thus, the Westerners' seemingly bumptious attitude was sometimes the target of criticism by both the Japanese and the Koreans in the colonial era.

Notes

1 "The White Man's Burden" is the title of a poem composed by English Nobel Prize-winning author Rudyard Kipling. Published in the *New York Sun* on 10 February 1899, it clearly demonstrates Eurocentric racist prejudice in regard to American colonization of the Philippines.

2 The *Maeil Shinbo*, the official newspaper of the governor-general of Korea in colonized Korea, was published in the Korean language from August 1910 to just after Korea's Independence, November 1945. It was the only newspaper published in Korean in the 1910s and during the wartime period of the 1940s, making it important historical material for imperial Japan's rule of Korea. The *Maeil Shinbo* once designated itself as the "imperial organ" in Korea (*Maeil Shinbo*, 17 July 1912). As for the texts of the *Maeil Shinbo*, this chapter targeted those searched on the "Big Kinds" (www.kinds.or.kr) of the Korea Press Foundation for the period from 30 August 1910, the day of the first issue, to 31 December 1929. With 454 articles in total, searching for "*munmyeong*" (civilization, 332 cases) and "*yaman*" (barbarism, 122 cases), I have conducted an analysis of the texts, focusing on the basic assumptions and characteristics of the discourse of "*munmyeong*," particularly regarding the power dynamics between the dominant Japanese and the dominated Koreans.

3 Some American missionaries, journalists, and politicians, who had visited Korea in the colonized period, expressed a "sense of deep-rooted contempt for Korean people and strong repulsion towards Korea's independence" out of the sense of civilizational and racial superiority (Lee G.-S., 2007: 30). Their negative opinions about the Koreans affected American foreign policy regarding Korea. In regard to the Japanese colonization of Korea, U.S. President Theodore Roosevelt argued that Korea was clearly a Japanese possession, and that it was already shown that the Koreans could not self-govern in any way. George Kennan, who had traveled to Korea as an advisor to Roosevelt, even compared the Koreans to bugs and argued for a need for foreign powers' intervention in Korea (*ibid.*).

4 Korean Confucianists in the late nineteenth century felt an awareness of crisis from modern newspapers, regarding it as seditious media spreading the so-called "new thought" destroying human ethics (Kim G.-W., 2015).

5 As for the concept of "*yaman*," a Korean writer for the *Maeil Shinbo* (16 July 1921) explains as follows: "What would be called as having 'barbarism'? We can say that those with inhumane behaviors are to have barbarism and those with unethical manners have barbarism too. Looking at the barbaric town, we know that there is no humanity, justice, order, and discipline. Pointing to Germany's violent and cruel actions in the wartime, other countries called Germany the country of barbarism and inhumanity." Showing the negative connotation of the concept of "barbarism," the articles of the *Maeil Shinbo* reported: "The U.S. began corporal punishment [...] It is suspected that civilization has gone away and barbarism has returned" (21 March 1921); "The trial between brothers is barbarism" (25 June 1912); "Barbarism to setting fire to one's house" (18 June 1913); etc.

6 Unlike this propaganda, imperial Japan used corporal punishment on Korean prisoners before the so-called "cultural rule" of the 1920s (Lee J.-M., 2004), and even after that, it still inflicted torture on Koreans and was strongly criticized for this by Korean newspapers such as the *Chosun Ilbo* and the *Dong-a Ilbo*.

7 "*Seodang*," the traditional Korean school for elementary Confucian education, was widespread across Korea in 1905, with its numbers reaching more than 10,000, and imperial Japan attempted to destroy Korea's traditional education system and ruling system through the so-called "new education" (Kim G.-M., 2004).

4 Competition between Civilization and Development Discourses

The 1950s

At the global level, the 1950s was the period when the discourse of development rapidly emerged through the lead of the U.S. in the Cold War. While international power relations between the dominant and the dominated were mainly defined around the concepts of "civilization" and "barbarism" before the mid-twentieth century, as examined in previous chapters, the 1950s witnessed a notable tendency to justify them with the concepts of "development" and "underdevelopment." The judging criteria for societies gradually changed from "civilization" to "development," and the intervention in the "underdeveloped" by the "developed" took place under the cause of "development of the underdeveloped." The 1950s in Korea, the era of the Rhee Syngman government, was the period when the country was under the strong influence of those global discursive changes.

Bearing the limitation of national division and the wounds of war, Korea's industrialization level in the 1950s – most of the Rhee Syngman era (1948–1960) – was low, and its economy was quite reliant on external aid with weak infrastructure. In 1953, Korea's gross domestic product (GDP) was \$1.3 billion, and its gross national income (GNI) per capita was just \$67 (Table 4.1). In the 1950s, Korea's economic growth was slower than that in the developmental era after that.[1] The real growth rate of GDP was 5.8% on average from 1953 to 1959, and its size had grown 1.5 times to \$2 billion in 1959. GNI per capita had grown to \$82 in 1959, about 1.2 times.

In regard to the national economy, the Rhee Syngman government did not prioritize "economic growth" or "economic development" as an urgent national goal. The foci of the government's economic policy were, rather, put on "economic restoration" and "stability" in a situation where industrial infrastructure and everyday living facilities had been seriously damaged by the war and the increase of money circulation after the war threatened economic stability (Kim J.-G., 2012).

What, then, would have been Korean society's perception of "development" in the 1950s? Had there been the interpretive framework of developmentalism too, as in the development era? Had Korean society identified itself as "*hujinguk*" or an "underdeveloped country" in the framework of *seonjinguk* discourse at the time, and urgently pursued economic development as a way out of *hujinguk* status?

Table 4.1 Korea's Main Economic Indicators in the 1950s

Indicator by year	*1953*	*1954*	*1955*	*1956*	*1957*	*1958*	*1959*
GDP (nominal, $ billion)	1.3	1.5	1.4	1.4	1.7	1.9	2
GNI per capita (nominal, $)	67.0	70.0	65.0	66.0	74.0	81.0	82.0
GDP real growth rate (%)	–	7.2	5.8	0.7	9.2	6.5	5.4
Agriculture and fisheries (%)	–	8.7	2.1	–5.7	9.7	8.2	0.1
Mining (%)	–	11.0	17.1	14.9	10.7	9.5	10.9
Manufacturing (%)	–	13.9	17.7	16.2	8.5	10.5	10.0
Electricity, gas, and water (%)	–	26.6	–0.4	15.1	15.3	24.9	18.2
Construction (%)	–	22.7	–0.2	–7.1	25.0	2.4	21.3
Services (%)	–	3.8	6.0	4.0	6.7	3.5	7.2

Source: Bank of Korea, Statistics Korea

To answer those questions, this chapter examines how Korea responded to the global "discursive shift" from "civilization" to "development" after World War II, and how this affected Korea's perception of "development." For this, it reviews the status of development discourse in 1950s Korean society in relation to the status of the discourse of civilization. It also investigates in what discursive framework Korean society defined itself and perceived the West, in comparison with the Park Chung-Hee era. For this, it analyzes the texts of Rhee Syngman's presidential addresses, and those of popular magazines and the *Chosun Ilbo* articles published in the 1950s.[2]

This chapter is organized in four main sections. First, it demonstrates the dominant discursive framework appearing in President Rhee's addresses, focusing on Korea's self-identity and the representation of the West. Second, it analyzes the characteristics of the perceptions of development, which are reflected in the magazines and newspaper articles in the 1950s. Third, it looks into the perceptions of *seonjinguk* and *hujinguk*, contained in the magazines and newspaper articles in the 1950s. Fourth, it investigates the discursive framework of "*munmyeong*" (civilization) that is reflected in the magazines and newspaper articles in the 1950s, in comparison with the discursive framework of "*baljeon*" (development).

Korea and the West in the Discourse of *Munmyeong*: Rhee Syngman's Presidential Addresses

The 1950s was a period when the discourse of development was globally emerging under U.S. patronage and its influence was slowly expanding in Korea. Economic consciousness was rising across Korean society and the need for economic development began to be promoted by some Korean intellectuals. The use of concepts belonging to the discourse of development, such as "*seonjinguk*" and "*hujinguk*," was increasing in the mass media.

Yet, the influence of developmentalism was not strong enough in 1950s Korean society to define Korea's national identity and to provide a dominant interpretive framework of the world. For instance, a main discursive framework for President Rhee Syngman to define Korea's identity and interpret the world was not the discourse of development.

Rhee Syngman's Discourse of Munmyeong

A manifest difference is found between the presidential addresses of Rhee Syngman (the 1950s) and Park Chung Hee (the 1960s–1970s) in regard to Korea's economic development. While Park widely spread the assumptions of developmental discourse by setting the "modernization of fatherland" as the most urgent national duty (Chapter 5), Rhee tended to consider economic development merely as one condition for a wealthy and strong country, not as a national goal in itself.

Developmental concepts were rarely seen in Rhee's addresses. Rather, it was the discourse of *munmyeong* that President Rhee utilized for his main interpretative framework of national identity and the world. His important national values were expressed in terms of *munmyeong* discourse, such as "*munmyeong*," "*gaemyeong*" (enlightenment), and "*yaman*." In his addresses, positive national values were projected mainly into the concepts of "*munmyeong*" and "*gaemyeong*," while negative values into the concept of "*yaman*."

> People living in an organized society have progressed daily and have become very different from those in an unorganized society. Thus, certain societies are treated as "*migae*" (unenlightened), or "*yaman*" if they are worse than that. As such, there are distinctions among human societies.
>
> (3 June 1954)

> It is a duty of enlightened (*gaemyeong-han*) people to resolve private or public anxieties and complaints in legal ways. How could a people be treated as enlightened even when they did harm to the beneficial person?
>
> (28 June 1949)

National goals and vision tended to be expressed through the concept of "*munmyeong-guk*" (civilized country) or "*gaemyeong-guk*" (enlightened country), and the future direction of Korea was suggested also in such terms as "*munmyeong*" or "*gaemyeong*." In addresses, such as one entitled "We will establish a nation well comparable to any civilized country in the world" (3 July 1957), President Rhee frequently appealed to people to intensify the national level of "*munmyeong*" and "*gaemyeong*." He emphasized that the Koreans should glorify their country and hand down a country to the future generations, in which they could enjoy enough wealth. He hoped that Korea would be a country well treated and respected by others in the world.

In regard to national goal and vision, the concept of "*bugang*" (wealth and strength) was also used frequently. In an address entitled "Cooperate, the South and North Koreans" (1950), for instance, President Rhee mentioned that "we will enjoy freedom and pleasure as a country of *bugang* by improving agriculture and developing industry and commerce in the world." As in the notion of "*munmyeong bugang*," the two concepts were often used together. There were differences, however, in connotation between the two. While *munmyeong* tended to be a concept focusing on cultural, historical aspects, the concept of *bugang* highlighted economic and military aspects.

As the concept of *bugang* connoted economic and military aspects, it appeared more frequently in addresses about industry and economy. In this case, it generally referred to the increase of material power. Given the stress of *munmyeong* discourse on spiritual aspects, the concept of *bugang* tended to be emphasized as a need in practical terms, rather than as an ultimate vision for the country. For instance, it was regarded as a need for the country to survive in the international order that was putatively dominated by the rule of the jungle. In this regard, an address insists as follows:

> In the world today, there are two ways of making people one's slaves. One is through military forces, having others as slaves and taking the position of the rich while playing as rulers, and the other is through economic power, producing many products and making ignorant people buy them. Those ignorant people are prevented from producing their own and are forced to ask the rich for food. This is called an economic slave. Although one can be an independent country in political terms, it will lose the political independence if it does not avoid the status of economic slave [...] one can be an independent country and free people only when it develops its economy [...] Now that we should make the nation wealthy and military strong, we are fighting for independence, cooperating with our allies, and searching for the way for *bugang* (wealth and strength) with our resolution to strengthen economic independence for our welfare [...] Although we are full of glory and hope, we have to collect wealth in order to upgrade our living [standards] and to compete with the so-called enlightened people. With wealth, we are able to strengthen our military, the forefront of anti-communism. Those things are not possible without economic power, so we need to make a country of *bugang munmyeong* by expanding the rights of commerce to the world, collectively or individually. With that, we can retrieve our glory inherited from our ancestors and can be a developing people. We should not lose this opportunity, recognizing it as a good fortune, and should use it.
>
> (15 July 1957)

Rhee Syngman's Perception of Korea

While *bugang* was emphasized in regard to national survival, *munmyeong* was the main concept used to designate Korea's identity. Within the discursive framework of *munmyeong*, Korea was generally identified as a country of *munmyeong* and *gaemyeong*, having long tradition and history, and manners and morality. It was notable that the "civilized status" of Korea was emphasized in Rhee's address, despite its unstable and insufficient political, social, and economic conditions in the 1950s. In this respect, Rhee's *munmyeong* discourse was somewhat close to the non-Eurocentric *munmyeong* discourse that had appeared after World War I. In Rhee's addresses, it was emphasized that Korean civilization had been respected by others and should be further admired in the future. The following addresses show this point well.

> Our country has been enlightened people from the past, keeping the duty of the Three Principles and Five Disciplines and, thus, has been admired as a country of manners. What we have learned from childhood is that only the human is the noblest among all creatures in the universe because we humans know ethics and manners, unlike all other animals.
>
> (18 November 1957)

> Through the last election, we have seen that our people are developed and enlightened. With this, we have known the level of our people's enlightenment, and this is what we can boast to others [...] I believe in you and also ask you to become further respected by all people in the world by doing well.
>
> (25 March 1958)

In Rhee's addresses, it is interesting to note that the tendency of negatively constructing Korea's identity was rarely seen, although a need for achieving national wealth and strength was constantly raised. In Rhee's era, the discursive power of developmentalism was weak, and the tendency of problematizing Korea's "underdevelopment" was not strong enough to negatively identify Korea. In fact, Korea was self-identified basically as a "*munmyeong-guk*" in the dominant framework of *munmyeong* discourse at the time. While raising a need for constant reforms in recognition of the law of jungle in the international order, President Rhee endeavored to maintain national pride. In a way, this might have reflected his political interests to stabilize his rule.

A dominant perception in regard to Korea's identity was that Korea had a boastful level of civilization while it was lacking in terms of *bugang*, e.g., material power. President Rhee considered that Korea could be a country of "*munmyeong bugang*" when it was strong economically and militarily. Thus, he raised a need for people's efforts for national reforms in such a phrase as "*sin saenghwal*" (new life) (1950).

Rhee Syngman's Perception of the West

Korea's national identity, as a "*munmyeong-guk*" of spirit, was formed in relation to the perception of the West, which had been a "significant other" for Korea's identity since the late nineteenth century. In general, Korea was considered as comparable to – or even better than – the West in terms of *munmyeong*, while not reaching its level of *bugang*. Thus, the discursive focus tended to be put on the aspects of *bugang*, rather than *munmyeong*, in regard to the West. In terms of *bugang*, the West was considered as an entity from which Korea should learn to survive in the harsh international order. The following addresses show this point well.

> A wealthy and strong country like the U.S. makes close relationships with the countries in the East and the West, having decided that it cannot live alone [...] Since Japan made a commercial treaty with the Americans, it had been seven times in 30 years that countries such as Britain, the U.S., and France sent warships to our country trying to force us to open our door [...] If our government officials had been bright politicians and had expanded diplomacy and commerce, we might have avoided the disasters that we experienced after then, while having achieved *bugang*. In darkness and corruption, all things had become in such a way, and we should search for a correct way for the future, taking lessons from the past.
>
> (10 August 1949)

> Countries like Britain and Japan had a difficulty in feeding their populations in the islands, so Britain first developed industry and produced various commodities with machines, saving human power and time. This made it easy to produce cheap and solid products through mass production, which were exported to countries overseas. Through this, the British earned money to use and, with the money left, they established cities and buildings, moving around the world and waging war for the right of commerce. Having achieved unprecedented developments of modern industry and commerce, the Westerners came to the East, destroying all economies, and had achieved the countries of *bugang* in the world.
>
> (9 September 1952)

As is seen in those addresses, the *bugang* of the West was basically envied but was also criticized in the sense that it had been achieved by damaging others. By the criteria of *munmyeong*, this was to be regarded as lacking "ethics and manners" and fell under the category of "non-*munmyeong*" or "*yaman*." While "*bugang*" was considered to indicate the status of *munmyeong* in material aspects, its limitations were also well recognized in terms of the means used to achieve it. In this sense, while the West was perceived as a positive reference group in Korea's reforms for *bugang*, it was far from an ideal image.

President Rhee did not lose a critical attitude towards a tendency of evaluating the degree of *munmyeong* or *gaemyeong* by material criteria. While pursuing *bugang* for Korea, he did not feel much shame in its lack of *bugang* in relation to the West. In an address, he delivered a biting criticism of the influences of materialism and the Western criteria of *munmyeong*.

> The so-called *munmyeong* in the world is different from what our country boasted in the past. Instead of referring to the pursuit of the welfare and benefits of humanity by guaranteeing peace and security with ethics and manners, it usually refers to improving human living [standards] by developing materials and making cities big and new. No matter how one respects the old wisdoms of ethics and manners and sacred life, he cannot be treated as a person of *munmyeong* if living in a mud house or in a stone house. No matter how one's thought is mean and has no progress in ethics, he is treated as a man of *gaemyeong* if living in a good house and making concrete streets. In this sense, *munmyeong* and *bugang* have become the same noun, and people of *bugang* build good houses and make cities, while poor people are treated as unenlightened no matter how they have ethics and manners. If one is poor, it is difficult for him to stand in front of the world. So, unless we reach the status of *munmyeong*, we are not to be treated as *munmyeong*, and in this situation without *bugang*, we will not be treated well. This is why every country sets the achievement of the status of *bugang* as its biggest goal. In this respect, all of the competitions and wars in today's world are mostly aiming for widening the rights of commerce.
>
> (2 July 1954)

He reproved the world order dominated by the West and the logic of power as follows.

> In retrospect on Western history, European civilization has continued through wars, with previous things being replaced by new ones. Thus, only Europe is continuing wars until today and is coming to the East with the intention of conquering it. It has not escaped from the low level of animals in the law of the jungle, determining rise and fall through war. The disaster has come to the East, and the logic of the survival of the fittest will continue for a long time. Only those who are able to wield power to oppress the weaker will take a superior position, but this runs counter to the correct way of *munmyeong* in the Confucianism of the East.
>
> (1 October 1954)

In those respects, Western civilization of *bugang* was perceived as having limitations rather than being ideal. In this regard, there was a tendency to consider it as having both the feature of *munmyeong* in terms of *bugang* and the feature of *yaman* in terms of its violence and aggressiveness.

The perception of Japan was somewhat similar to that of the West. In the discursive framework of *munmyeong*, Japan was basically considered a country of *bugang* while having limitations in terms of *munmyeong*. Reflecting the Koreans' anti-Japanese sentiment deriving from Japanese colonial history, Rhee expressed strong anti-Japanese sentiment in his addresses. In an address entitled "Make sure that there are no pro-Japanese and pro-communist people" (13 May 1954), he categorized five pro-Japanese types including "those who have a belief that Korea can't compete with Japan with its weak power as Japan is a wealthy and strong country in the East." He argued that pro-Japanese people, along with pro-communist people, were those whom should be watched most strictly.

As for Japan, an address insists that:

> When Japan was living alone as an island in the East Sea, it earned the *gaehwa* of the East by learning our civilization and manners. Now the Japanese are boasting that they have been a civilized people since the past, while admitting that they received the civilization of the East from Korea. In the recent past, Japan got a chance to adopt the so-called Western civilization and learned Western military materials and war strategies, and eventually conquered Korea. They even said in the past that their king had been a brother of our king, but now the situation is that we have something to learn from them and also have something to teach them. By the way, what we are trying to teach them is that they can be treated as the best country of *gaemyeong* only when they learn and practice Eastern people's teachings for co-prosperity in the peaceful world, rather than learning Western people's ways of destroying with one another in the law of the jungle.
>
> (30 December 1957)

In those respects, the need for *bugang* was mostly presented in terms of practical purpose for national survival. As for the individual, *munmyeong* was a kind of duty for a person to be a human, but *bugang* presented a practical need in order not to be a slave of others. In this context, there was a high degree of caution about accommodating the West. While the need for learning from the West was raised, the need for selective acceptance of it was also emphasized.

The West was regarded as having various social and cultural problems, of which Korea should be cautious.

> Today people having children in the West have many concerns. The education of children has recently become a big issue in the schools of the U.S., and there are debates about it. Many of them envy and praise us to see that the Koreans serve and respect their parents and elder people. This has resulted from Americans' recent policies of removing all disciplinary and punishing measures, and of letting their children free. We have to be very careful about that.
>
> (1 October 1954)

On the other hand, an address worried about the movies imported from the West.

> Among the movies imported from foreign countries, some are difficult to bear to watch, and others are committing barbaric customs, such as either trickery and burglary or shooting guns at people and seeing them bleeding. As a result, children learn homicide, dispossession, and illegal behaviors, and we have to be cautious of this.
>
> (2 January 1959)

In those respects, the hierarchy between Korea and the West did not clearly appear in Rhee's addresses. Rather, Korea and the West were perceived as the possessors of different kinds of civilization, each having strength in different aspects. In this respect, the discourse of *munmyeong* in the Rhee era reflected the Koreans' own unique interpretative framework in which they maintained national pride while taking a critical attitude towards the West.

Munmyeong *and Anti-Communism*

Given that anti-communist discourse was prevalent in the Rhee era (Cho H.-Y., 1998, 2003; Kim J.-H. and Cho H.-Y., 2003), the discourse of *munmyeong* was often combined with anti-communist ideology. In the anti-communist discourse, the distinction was made between democracy and communism, and Korea and the West were defined as the countries of democracy or freedom. In Rhee's addresses, it is interesting to note that the countries of freedom and democracy were often equated to the countries of *munmyeong*. In relation to this, communism was designated as the idea ignoring valuable tradition and culture, such as the Three Principles and Five Disciplines.

> There are some things that we should not throw away. For instance, we cannot amend the Three Principles and Five Disciplines that we have been learning from the past. If we throw this away and make all the same rank without discerning adults and children or seniors and juniors, we will be back to the status of *yaman* 4,000 years ago. So we have to necessarily teach, learn, and abide by it [...] The communist way is to pull down those who are in the upper position to make them equal to those who are in lower positions. The idea of making all equal is to destroy the world through revolutionism. This is what they argue for, but we do not admit it as a way of making equality in a democratic society.
>
> (30 December 1957)

This address emphasizes the importance of the Three Principles and Five Disciplines, while criticizing communists' equality for the way of destroying the world order. Ignoring this kind of human ethics, communism was treated as being close to *yaman*, which the *munmyeong* of Korea should fight against.

As such, a cause for fighting against communism was sometimes sought from the framework of *munmyeong* discourse. In this respect, President Rhee's anti-communism can be more appropriately understood in relation to *munmyeong* discourse, as both were the notable dominant discourses in his era.

The Mass Media Perceptions of Development in the 1950s

Developmentalism problematizes the "underdevelopment" and "poverty" of society to prioritize the transition to the status of "development" through industrialization and economic growth (Sachs, 1992; Escobar, 1995).[3] In Korea, developmentalism has problematized Korea's underdeveloped condition relative to *seonjinguk*, and pursued the developmental goal of "*seonjinguk*" with diverse strategic discourses at different historical times, such as "*geun-daehwa*" (modernization) in the 1960s–1970s, "*segyehwa*" (globalization) in the 1990s, and "*seonjinhwa*" in the 2000s (Chapter 7). In the distinction between *hujinguk* and *seonjinguk*, Korea's developmentalism has set a transition from the former to the latter as an urgent national goal, and Korea's economic growth and modernization have tended to be actively promoted for national needs rather than people's direct needs.

This section mainly questions whether those developmental perceptions notably appeared in the 1950s, the pre-developmental era, as well. If not, what were the perceptions of the economy and development at the time? To answer this, the analysis of this section focuses on the concepts mainly used in economic perceptions, the problems and goals recognized in economic terms, and whether arguments are made for escaping from the status of *hujinguk* or for economic growth and modernization aimed at the rank of *seonjinguk*.

For this, it analyzes the articles of popular magazines and the *Chosun Ilbo* in the 1950s. With ten search words on the online archive of the Korea Magazine Museum, which are related to economic and development perceptions, it has obtained 57 articles from 38 volumes of 21 magazines.[4] It has identified 1,662 articles from the *Chosun Ilbo* archive, with the same search words used for the magazines.[5] To compare development discourse with *munmyeong* discourse in the 1950s, it has used "*munmyeong*" as an additional search word to obtain 16 articles from 13 volumes of ten magazines and 31 articles from the *Chosun Ilbo*.

Frequency of Developmental Terms

An easy way to observe a discursive transition of society is to check the change in the use of concepts belonging to concerned discourses. In a discursive transition, it would be notable that the frequency of concepts belonging to the declining discourse decreases while that for the emerging discourse gradually increases. In this respect, this section investigates the difference between the 1950s and the 1960s in the number of searched cases for each search word to check the uniqueness of the use of economic concepts in the 1950s compared with Park Chung-Hee's developmental era (Table 4.2).[6]

Table 4.2 Comparison of the 1950s and the 1960s in the Number of Searched Cases Concerning Economic Perceptions

	Magazines		*The Chosun Ilbo*	
	The 1950s (1950–1959) (unit: volume)	*The 1960s (1962–1971)*	*The 1950s (case)*	*The 1960s*
Gyeongje seongjang (economic growth)	1 (4.0%)	8 (12.7%)	7 (0.4%)	101 (11.9%)
Gyeongje baljeon (economic development)	2 (8.0%)	6 (9.5%)	26 (1.7%)	32 (3.8%)
Gyeongje gaebal (economic development)	1 (4.0%)	18 (28.6%)	24 (1.5%)	164 (19.3%)
Geundaehwa (modernization)	1 (4.0%)	25 (39.7%)	6 (0.4%)	171 (20.1%)
Gongeophwa (industrialization)	1 (4.0%)	1 (1.6%)	10 (0.6%)	15 (1.8%)
Gyeongje jaegeon (economic reconstruction)	3 (12.0%)	1 (1.6%)	10 (0.6%)	6 (0.7%)
Buheung (rehabilitation)	16 (64.0%)	4 (6.3%)	1,489 (94.7%)	360 (42.4%)
Total	25 (100.0%)	63 (100.0%)	1,572 (100.0%)	849 (100.0%)

In terms of the number of searched articles, the analysis shows that "*gyeongje jaegeon*" (economic reconstruction) and "*buheung*" (rehabilitation) are higher in the 1950s than in the 1960s. The frequency of "*buheung*" is especially higher in the 1950s in newspaper articles, indicating that it was notably popular in the 1950s before rapidly losing its popularity in the 1960s. The result also shows that the frequencies for "*gyeongje seongjang*" (economic growth), "*gyeongje baljeon*" (economic development), "*gyeongje gaebal*" (economic development), and "*geundaehwa*" (modernization) are higher in the 1960s than in the 1950s, indicating that they were more frequently used in the Park era. Among them, especially notable terms are "*gyeongje seongjang*" and "*geundaehwa,*" whose frequencies become rapidly higher in the 1960s.

The analysis demonstrates that the perceptions of the economy were made in different conceptual, discursive frameworks between the Rhee Syngman and Park Chung-Hee periods. Compared with the Park era, the feature of developmental discourse is relatively weaker in the 1950s as is reflected in the lower frequencies of such concepts as "*gyeongje seongjang,*" "*gyeongje baljeon,*" and "*geundaehwa.*"

The Perceptions of Economic Goals and Problems

In the 1950s, Korea keenly felt a need to recover the industrial infrastructure, on the assumption that it had been historically distorted and destroyed through such unfortunate incidents as Japanese colonial occupation, national division, and war. As the frequency analysis in Table 4.2 indicates, the interpretation of Korea's economic situation was made with different concepts from those in the development era.

In that regard, this sub-section analyzes the texts of the magazines and newspaper to investigate in detail the characteristics of the perceptions of economic goals and problems in the 1950s. The analysis of the magazines shows, first, that the concept appearing with the highest frequency in regard to national economic goals was "*gyeongje buheung*" (economic rehabilitation) (seven cases), followed by "*gyeongje jalib*" (self-supporting economy – five cases), and "*gyeongje jaegeon*" (economic reconstruction – four cases). Other manifest goals reflected in the magazine texts are: "independent reconstruction," "rehabilitation of agriculture," "overcoming backwardness," "overcoming underdeveloped economy," "escaping from the vicious circle of poverty," and "increase of national income" (one case for each). These results demonstrate that public awareness of the national economic goals was mainly expressed in such concepts as "*buheung*" (rehabilitation), "*jalib*" (self-supporting), and "*jaegeon*" (reconstruction) in the 1950s.

Then the analytical foci are put on the contents of the texts. In regard to the recognition of economic goals and visions, an article in *Saebyeok* (1 November 1956) mentions that the "ideal goal of the reconstruction (*jaegeon*) project is to balance between financial stability and economic reconstruction (*jaegeon*) [...] and whether the Korean nation could build the ground of industrial economy will be decided in three or five years."[7] Another article argues that "in the middle of the nation's total efforts for the great mission of constructing a self-supporting economy (*jalib gyeongje geonseol*), our country has become an unprecedented aid-recipient country due to the severe destruction by the war" (*Jayugongron*, 1 December 1958).[8]

The tendency to focus on the national economic goals of "reconstruction," "self-supporting," and "rehabilitation" appears notably in the newspaper articles as well. As for the popularity of the concepts of "economic reconstruction" and "economic self-supporting," an opinion column in the *Chosun Ilbo* (19 June 1957) entitled "Methods for facilitating economic reconstruction" mentions that "everyone talks about economic reconstruction and, sometimes, cries out for economic self-supporting."

As for the primary causes of Korea's current economic problems, the articles in the magazines and newspaper tended to attribute them to the historical circumstances, such as Japanese colonial occupation, the national division, and the Korean War. As for the Japanese occupation, a dominant idea was that the Korean economy was not able to develop a sound economic system for itself, because it had been incorporated into the Japanese economic system, as a supplier of raw materials and foods and as a logistics base. The Japanese occupation was considered a main historical incident that had interrupted the accumulation of national capital and technology and distorted the productive system of Korea. As for the national division and the war, there was a tendency to perceive that the fragmented and distorted features of the Korean economy had become aggravated by the national division after Independence and, further, that the Korean economy severely lost its vitality undergoing the destruction of industrial facilities during the Korean War.[9]

This kind of historical interpretation of the Korean economy was notable in the magazine texts, especially in those published before the mid-1950s. For instance, an article in *Jayusegye* (25 January 1952), entitled "Method for rehabilitating the Korean economy," argues:

> Our Korean economy had suffered severe oppression in developing national capital by Japanese colonial policies. It had been constructed in a distorted dependent structure, playing a role as a supplier of raw materials and foods, and as a market for products for colonial Japan [...] The evil 38th parallel line had dichotomized Korea, while the political confusion after Independence and the U.S. military government's policy for maintaining the status quo had created a vacuum situation in the economy [...] A ray of light of stability had begun to shine on the Korean economy just before the Korean War. [However, the] invasion of North Korean communist troops totally trampled on the efforts of reconstructing the Korean economy.

Here the positive evaluation of the Korean economy just before the Korean War is notable, when "a ray of light of stability had begun to shine." This kind of "past-oriented" perception was common in the early and mid-1950s. As was implied in the concepts of "rehabilitation" and "reconstruction," the first goal of the Korean economy tended to be set to recover the level of productive power and industrial facilities in the heyday of the colonial period and in the pre-war conditions.

The main concepts of "rehabilitation," "reconstruction," and "self-supporting" were considered mutually interdependent: That is, reconstruction was possible through rehabilitation and vice versa, or the self-supporting economy was possible through both of them. Given that developmental discourse tends to show a future-oriented tendency to present a "rosy" future based on the problematization of the present and the past, that kind of past-oriented economic awareness in 1950s Korea is somewhat noteworthy.[10]

Perception of Agriculture

Another tendency notably appearing in the mass media in regard to the Korean economy was to emphasize the importance of agriculture. Articles in the magazines and newspaper considered the rehabilitation of agriculture as a key to the rehabilitation of the Korean economy, on the grounds that Korea had traditionally been an agricultural country and most of its population was engaged in agriculture. In this regard, there were such arguments that the export of grains would enable the rebalance of Korea's international trade and building of a self-supporting economy, and that the prosperity of the rural area would make possible the escape from the "vicious circle of poverty" towards national economic development.

Some articles asked for the implementation of strong governmental measures against the situation in which Korea as an agricultural country imported agricultural products, while agricultural people suffered a great economic burden due to agricultural products imported at low prices. Articles also emphasized that the rehabilitation of the agricultural area and agricultural people was a required condition for improving people's material life in the country.

For instance, an editorial in the *Chosun Ilbo* (11 November 1958), entitled "Discrepancy between grain price policy and economic development," points out that the policies disregarding the plummeting grain price impoverish agricultural people and areas. Thus, it mentions that the appropriate grain policies are "needless to emphasize as agriculture is regarded in Korea as the ground of the world, which would be the case even for advanced industrial countries whose agricultural population is just 10% of the whole." The editorial recognizes the prosperity of the agricultural area and the increase in agricultural productive power as the vital elements of Korea's economic development. In this regard, it argues that "the destitution of agricultural people and low agricultural productive power would make the so-called vicious circle, unique to *hujinguk*, continue and, if so, the goal of economic development would become just pie in the sky."

In a similar vein, an article in *Shincheonji* (5 October 1953) argues that "key elements for rehabilitating our Korean economy are, anyway, the market for industrial products, together with the good harvest of agricultural products." As for the goal of the national economy, it further insists that "generally, national finance and people's lives will not be that destitute in Korea if agriculture is doing well and ordinary production factories are running well every year." Here a "plain," non-theoretical perception of economic goal, e.g., the reduction of people's destitution, is notable, rather than an "abstract" and "sophisticated" one, e.g., national remodeling for an urgent developmental goal. As for a satisfactory condition for the Korean economy, it suggests a situation in which "agriculture is doing well and ordinary production factories are running well every year."

However, the discursive focus on agriculture gradually came to compete with the inflowing Western theories of development that were oriented towards industry-based economic growth. For instance, *Shintaeyang* (1 March 1959) introduces Spengler's argument that "it cannot avoid backwardness if the economy is not differentiated, employing unskilled labor and farmers using simple skills," and "this is why the spokesperson of underdeveloped countries emphasizes industrialization and believes the economies of underdeveloped countries can be modernized through industrialization."

With the rise of developmentalism around the globe, the Western theories of development earned power, and agriculture became treated as a "traditional element" that should be discarded through modernization. In a situation in

In another article entitled "Backwardness of our economy (1): A comparison in per capita income – $50 for Korea and $1,500 for the U.S.," the writer of the article above argues as follows in regard to *hujinguk* and *seonjinguk*:

> The term "*hujinguk*" (underdeveloped countries) refers to countries lagging behind in economic development, in comparison with countries advanced, that is, "*seonjinguk*" (developed countries). Thus, it would be appropriate for us to comparatively designate developed and underdeveloped countries, using certain criteria for comparing economic status in the international perspective.
>
> (*Chosun Ilbo*, 8 September 1955)

The discursive process of defining Korea as "*hujinguk*" accompanies a degree of self-contempt. Being defined as the "alienated other" to *seonjinguk*, it is imagined as an embodiment of the attributes of backwardness. In regard to Korea's backwardness, an article in the *Chosun Ilbo* (9 September 1955) argues that "the Koreans are people generally stuck in undernourishment or malnutrition," and goes further to argue as follows:

> As nutrition is not sufficient, they [the Koreans] are always inert, and being inert, they can't work efficiently. They can't avoid a fool's condition of going to work in the morning, reading newspapers, chatting, going to a coffee shop, and repeating yawning and drowsiness. As work is not efficient, productivity does not go up, and as productivity is low, foodstuffs are lacking eventually. The causal operation of this vicious circle of production and consumption is our reality. The way of operating the economy is fundamentally different from that of *seonjinguk*, in which people's lives are becoming prosperous as they eat well and work hard, resulting in the increase of production.

Assuming a fundamental difference between Korea and "*seonjinguk*" in economic and everyday activities, this article emphasizes that "economic development is a process of transforming our fatalistic framework to the developmental framework of *seonjinguk*."

As the concept of *hujinguk* was being newly introduced to Korean society, the social debate about the definition of *hujinguk* was, on the other hand, a social process of constructing *hujinguk*. This process proceeded under the influence of global developmentalism. Given this, it was also a process in which Korea's discursive space concerning national development was incorporated into that of the hegemonic West.

Debates about Korea's Identity

The rise of the discourse of *seonjinguk* accompanied a change in national identity. While Korea was generally identified as a *munmyeong-guk* of spirit and ethics in *munmyeong* discourse, it degraded to the status of *hujinguk* with the rise of a developmental discourse. In the global developmental regime, Korea was merely categorized into a group of *hujinguk* with other countries in Asia, Africa, and Latin America.[15] Here was reflected a Eurocentric epistemic tendency to see the non-West as the object of Orientalism, disregarding its diversity and uniqueness.[16]

As the terms "*seonjin*" and "*hujin*" reflected developmentalist ideas, the magazine articles containing those terms tended to highlight Korea's backwardness. One article, for instance, says that "Korea belongs to underdeveloped societies," or "we are definitely the people of *hujinguk*," while suggesting ways to overcome it (*Hyeondae*, 1 December 1957).[17] The "backwardness" of Korea became strong in the Eurocentric discursive framework and, in this process, a discursive hierarchy between Korea and the West became manifest.[18]

Meanwhile, some intellectuals expressed a feeling of humiliation about the labeling of Korea as *hujinguk*. An article in *Hyeondae* (1 December 1957), entitled "General features of Korea's backwardness: Deformed modernization and a backward new class," deplores that backwardness has deprived the nation of its pride by bringing about the trend of blindly pursuing the West. It further argues:

> Backwardness always causes the loss of tradition. Losing immunity to the virus of a foreign trend is due to the loss of the health of tradition that should be possessed in nature. No matter how it possesses such things, the grief of backwardness accompanies a self-abusive tendency. So, they don't have a room in mind to think that noble authority is hidden in themselves, being busy looking outside and prying about neighbors. Here imitation becomes everything [...] When existentialist literature appeared in France after the war, there appeared numerous imitations of Sartre's work "Le Mur" in our country. There is no chance that existentialism, a product of over-consciousness having appeared at the peak of mechanization in Western civilization, would be exactly fitting to us who are eating *kimchi* with *doenjang* [soybean paste] soup. Shamelessly, cultural people in *hujinguk* are engaged in the megalomania of worrying about *seonjinguk*, while they are not in a situation of being able to be concerned about their country's own affairs [...] As such, backwardness makes us unconscious of an important fact that creativity is losing, as the loss of self is promoted while awkward imitation is done habitually [...] Like a saying that "even precious ritual utensils are sold in three-year poverty," we have been deprived of national pride while we are suffering from the vicious circle of poverty.
>
> (*Hyeondae*, 1 December 1957)

While being keenly critical of the Koreans' tendency to blindly imitate *seonjinguk*, this article shows a degree of "assimilative" attitude towards Eurocentrism, as it adopts Eurocentric concepts and discursive framework in recognizing Korea's "backwardness" (Kang J.-I., 2003b). Thus, the writer of this article emphasizes a need to overcome backwardness through reform and innovation, out of the feeling of shame over Korea's reality. In relation to this, he finishes the article with a statement cited from college students' conversation: "Hey, until when should we hear such words as 'underdeveloped country' or '*hujinguk*,' instead of building factories and making products?"

Nevertheless, the prepositions of development discourse were not soundly accepted by Korean intellectuals. Critical attitudes were also notable towards the tendency of defining a country's identity by economic and material criteria. Especially, there was resistance to the tendency to identify Korea as *hujinguk*. An article in the *Chosun Ilbo* (12 June 1959), entitled "What is *hujinguk*," shows some Korean scholars' criticisms of the concept of *hujinguk*:

> *Hujinguk* is a term indicating a situation that economic development does not reach the normal level from the viewpoint of the Westerners. How to decide its level concretely is not clear so it is unacceptable for us that we are *hujinguk*.
>
> Eastern societies are considered as *hujinguk* (backward) today by Westerners' criteria because they developed capitalism later than Western societies and the transitions from the feudal agricultural social system to the capitalist system were not smooth. However, it is not that all *hujin* areas show the characteristics of *hujinguk*. Although "Africa" can be designated as an uncivilized area, it is undeniable that "Asia" has been affecting Western cultures, while maintaining its unique spiritual civilizations, traditions, and values. Therefore, even though we may accept our economic backwardness (*hujinseong*), we cannot say that in terms of cultural aspects.

Those arguments emphasize that the concept of "*hujinguk*" is not only a category created by Western criteria but is also quite ambiguous. In regard to the tendency to define Eastern societies' "backwardness" in economic aspects, they dispute the validity of the concept of "*hujinguk*" by assuming the superiority of the East in terms of "spirit," "tradition," and "culture." In this regard, another article shows a stance of distinguishing Korea from "other *hujinguk*," arguing that "we have to look around the footsteps of countries in Latin America and the political phenomena in countries of *hujinguk* in Asia and Africa, which are howling in the confusion of revolutions and dictatorships, and we should be careful not to follow those paths, as boasting ourselves with the long history of 5,000 years" (*Saebyeok*, 15 October 1959).

As Korea was treated as *hujinguk* regardless of its "level of civilization," the perception of the elements causing its "backwardness" became de-contextualized. In the economic aspect, for instance, the cognitive tendency of attributing Korea's distorted economy to Japanese colonialism, national division, and the war gradually weakened, while the trend of emphasizing the elements suggested in

Western development theories, such as a "vicious circle of poverty," became gradually notable.

In this respect, the expansion of a development discourse in Korea contributed to abstracting the understanding of Korea's socio-economic situation, according to Western theoretical frameworks. The development discourse gradually overpowered various local historical narratives that had appeared in diverse local historical contexts. In this sense, the development discourse arose as a global discourse integrating the histories of the East and the West into one temporal-spatial dimension.

Difference in the Perception of the West

The majority of the *Chosun Ilbo* articles that contained the terms *seonjinguk* and *hujinguk* in the title were international news articles. In general, the newspaper articles tried to catch up with foreign news about the development of underdevelopment that had been promoted under the leadership of the U.S. and the Union of Soviet Socialist Republics (USSR) in the Cold War circumstances. Thus, the international news reported in the newspaper was mainly about international aid, such as the plans and status of aid from the U.S. and the USSR, aid plans of international institutions, aid recipients' economic development status, and so forth.

The newspaper's international news on international development contributed to popularizing development discourse in Korea, which distinguished the West and the non-West according to the "degree of development." Here the international relationship was mainly framed in the "aid provider-receiver relationship" between the developed West and the underdeveloped non-West, making a hierarchy between the two.

International news articles also contributed to popularizing the concepts of "*seonjinguk*" and "*hujinguk*," as the former was used as a translation for "developed countries" and the latter for "underdeveloped countries." For "underdeveloped countries," such terms as "*migaebal-guk*," "*mibaljeon-guk*," and "*hujinguk*" were used interchangeably at the beginning, but the tendency of convergence to the term "*hujinguk*" became gradually notable. For "developed countries," some terms were also used other than "*seonjinguk*," such as "*gongeop-guk*" (industrialized country) and "*baljeon-guk*" (developed country), before the convergence tendency to the term "*seonjinguk*" became conspicuous.

Some international news from American sources covered the U.S. evaluation of Korea's economic development status. An international news article in the *Chosun Ilbo* (6 April 1958), entitled "Korea's economic development is notable – the U.S. Department of Commerce points out," reports that "the U.S. Department of Commerce announced that Korea's economy showed growth and stability during the first half of this year." Another article reports that "the New York Times commented that South Korea had achieved 'notable rehabilitation and development' since it was invaded by puppet North Korea" (*Chosun Ilbo*, 27 June 1958). In this regard, Korean society was somewhat sensitive to the external assessment of it. The recognition and evaluation of Korea's economy by the U.S. and international institutions were considered an "objective indicator" of Korea's development status and exerted influence on Korean society.

On the other hand, there were also many articles that did not use such developmental categories as "*seonjinguk*" and "*hujinguk*" when referring to countries. This shows that the use of those developmental terms and categories had not settled down yet in the 1950s. In this regard, an article in *Beobryulgwa Gyeongje* (1 February 1954) reported that "in the same democratic camp, other countries' price trends showed a decline by 20–30 percent, whereas Korea's one showed a 60 percent increase." Here it is notable that it categorizes non-communist capitalist countries including Korea into the "same democratic camp," instead of distinguishing *seonjinguk* and *hujinguk* among them, even when referring to them in economic aspects. Some articles in the magazines referred to Asian countries as "countries in the East" and Western countries as "countries in Europe," instead of using the concepts of *seonjinguk/hujinguk*. Others mentioned countries just by their names without categorizing them.

When the articles did not use development terms, their interpretation of economic phenomena tended to be different from development theories. As for Asian countries' low productive power, the article above mentions that "countries in the East including Korea have been stagnant in the development of productive methods because their geographical conditions, such as soil fertility, are so advantageous" (*Beobryulgwa Gyeongje*, 1 February 1954). Here is rarely shown the idea of development discourse that tends to focus on such internal factors as traditionalism for a country's backwardness. In relation to "countries in the East," the article calls the West "countries in Europe," and the U.S. as "the number one industrial country in the world" or a "giant-like industrial country." It is also notable that the article compares Korea, countries in the East, countries in Europe, and the U.S. with one another, as historical and regional cases for productivity development, without hierarchically classifying them into "backward" (underdeveloped) or "advanced" (developed) countries.

The discussion above shows that the perceptions of countries can widely differ according to discursive frameworks. In a development framework, there appears a hierarchy among countries, but without it, the perception becomes different. In relation to this, an article in the *Chosun Ilbo* (15 May 1950), entitled "First seeing Thailand," introduces Thailand as "the country of elephant and temple – underdeveloped but Utopia." This article's perception of the "underdeveloped" country as "Utopia" is somewhat distinguished from development discourse that tends to treat it as the object of problematization and of "professional prescription."

Worldviews in *Munmyeong* Discourse in the 1950s

The cognitive trend of the non-Eurocentric discourse of civilization, which had manifestly appeared after World War I, came to be more notable after

World War II. As formidable violence was recognized in material and scientific civilization, the West was considered dangerous to be able to cause the collapse of humanity, rather than to lead the progress of humanity. In contrast, the values of Eastern civilization were appreciated as alternative ones to help overcome the limitations of the West.

In this context, the critical attitudes towards modern civilization and the modern world, led by the West, notably appeared in the mass media texts as well in the 1950s, somewhat similar to those observed in Rhee Syngman's presidential addresses. The majority of writing in the magazines and newspaper that contained the term "*munmyeong*" pointed out the limitations of the material, scientific civilization of the West, and expressed concern about it. Articles in the magazines tended to designate material, scientific, and modern civilization as the fundamental causes of people's anxiety, nervousness, and confusion. Introducing Spengler's idea of the "decline of the West," an article in *Shintaeyang* (1 March 1959), for instance, argues that "new machine civilization is dominating people, determining humanity, controlling society, and mechanizing the masses more than any other time in the past," and "as a result, there are trends of taking pride in Eastern spiritual civilization as if it would soon dominate the world while Western material civilization would soon collapse."

The degree of distrust of modern civilization was generally proportional to the degree of trust of the East. In this regard, a pervasive idea was that the East was the very civilization with potential to solve the problems of the West. A column article published in the *Chosun Ilbo* (1 January 1959), for instance, argues as follows:

> Now humanity is in a crisis of being degenerated into the non-human animal even though it is said to stand at the peak of material civilization. Human beings are now devaluing humanity. It is the sin of Western modern civilization, rather than that of the East, which has driven human beings into this inhumane world. It is because the scientific civilization of the very recent modern era has run only to mechanical civilization, totally deviating from spiritual civilization. It is because ancient people's, that is Eastern people's, pursuit of spiritual aspects has changed into pleasure-seeking and imitation that pursue the benefits and wealth of Western material civilization […] It would be, after all, Eastern thoughts that will save human beings. Humankind can get eternal life only when we drive ourselves into the civilization in which people love and respect one another, can live being content amidst poverty, and can find pleasure from humble food and drink.

Insofar as Western civilization was assumed to blindly pursue scientific technology and material wealth in the non-Eurocentric discourse of civilization, it was likely to be framed as a kind of foolish civilization. Pessimism about the modern world prevailed in *munmyeong* discourse as it recognized that the world led by the foolish civilization would be dangerous. As for the lagging of the East in material, scientific aspects, the *munmyeong* discourse tended to attribute it to the East's brilliant past and advantageous natural conditions and, thus, the lagging was temporary. As the East was considered as materially lagging but spiritually advanced in relation to the West and vice versa, a need for mutual harmony or mutual complementation was emphasized.

However, the cognitive trend of the non-Eurocentric discourse of civilization drastically changed with the rise of the discourse of development. In development discourse, material and scientific elements became primary criteria for judging the world and were pursued ceaselessly. In this respect, the discourse of development was a kind of praise for material, scientific civilization. It disregarded the varying "degrees of civilization" among non-Western countries, and grouped them together under the blanket term of "*hujinguk*" according to material, scientific, and economic criteria.

The rise of a development discourse accompanied the spread of blind belief in science and technology and, thus, effectively dampened skepticism about the civilization of material and science, and about the progress of modern civilization. In terms of global power dynamics, the newly emerged development discourse effectively replaced the stranded Eurocentric discourse of civilization, saving the global hegemony of the West (Brohman, 1995; Escobar, 1995; Patterson, 1997; Latham, 2000; Nederveen Pieterse, 2001).

The degree of accepting the assumptions of development discourse was inversely proportional to the degree of pride in Korea's civilization and culture. The stronger the acceptance of development discourse was, so were the positive perception of the developed West and the feeling of emptiness in Korea's civilization.[19]

In those respects, the 1950s in Korean society was a period of discursive shift when the dominant status of *munmyeong* discourse was gradually challenged by the rise of the discourse of development. As the discourses of civilization and development crossed into the public discursive space, the concepts belonging to each discourse were sometimes used interchangeably. An article in *Chojeom* (25 January 1956), for instance, mentions that "the country that produces and consumes the large amount of fine fuel is the country of *bugang* (wealthy and strong) and of *munmyeong*." Here is shown developmental cognition to judge countries by the amount of fuel production and consumption, while the term "*munmyeong-guk*" is still used. In a similar vein, an article in the *Chosun Ilbo* (5 April 1959) uses "*munmyeong-guk*," instead of "*seonjinguk*," as a contrasting concept to "*hujinguk*": "[The population of] *hujinguk* expanded more than [that of] *munmyeong-guk*." As such, a sign of a discursive shift was reflected in the mixed use of those concepts and cognitive tendencies by the mass media.

Conclusion

This chapter has examined the state of development discourse in the 1950s, reflected in President Rhee Syngman's addresses and the articles of popular magazines and a newspaper, in comparison with that in the developmental era. Above all, it has demonstrated that the interpretive framework of *munmyeong* discourse, rather than a development discourse, was prevalent in Rhee's presidential addresses. In this regard, it is interesting to note that the central concepts of a development discourse, such as "*seonjinguk*" and "*hujinguk*," were barely found in his addresses. National goals and vision were presented in such concepts as "*munmyeong-guk*" (civilized country) or "*gaemyeong*-guk" (enlightened country), rather than "*seonjinguk*."

Economic development tended to be perceived as a practical condition for national wealth and strength (*bugang*), instead of being set as an urgent national goal in itself. In regard to national identity, Korea was generally defined as "*munmyeong-guk*," albeit with a low level of "*bugang*." The tendency to idealize the West, in relation to Korea, was not notable as Korea's civilization of ethics was considered as ultimately more valuable than the material civilization of the West.

This chapter has also examined the status of developmental discourse and *seonjinguk* discourse reflected in the magazines and newspaper in the 1950s. It has argued that the awareness of economic problems and goals appearing in such concepts as "*buheung*" (rehabilitation), "*jaegeon*" (reconstruction), and "*jalib*" (self-supporting) were distinguished from the developmental use of "*seongjang*" (growth), "*baljeon*" (development), and "*geundaehwa*" (modernization) in the Park Chung-Hee era. A notable tendency also appeared to recognize Japanese colonialism, national division, and the Korean War as the main causes of the distortion and destruction of Korea's economic structure, while setting the pre-war conditions as the primary objective of "*buheung*" and "*jaegeon*." This was contrasted with the development discourse's future-oriented tendency of setting the goal of entering into the ranks of *seonjinguk*. It has also shown a notable perception that Korea's economic fundamentals should be established through the rehabilitation of agriculture, based on Korea's national identity as an agricultural (or agriculture-based) country. This is also distinguished from the attitude of development discourse to consider "agriculture" as a "traditional element" to be reduced for national industrialization.

In regard to the perception of *seonjinguk*/*hujinguk*, this chapter has demonstrated that Western theories of the development of underdevelopment and the international politics concerning aid to underdeveloped countries were well introduced to Korean society through the mass media. The concepts of *seonjinguk* and *hujinguk* began to popularize in the inflow of Western development discourse, as "developed countries" and "underdeveloped countries" were translated into those Korean terms, respectively. Korean intellectuals suggested a need for economic development, out of the feeling of shame of Korea being designated as "*hujinguk*." On the other hand, there was also notable resistance to Western development discourse by disputing the validity of identifying countries by Eurocentric material criteria. In terms of global discursive hegemony, the diffusion of a development discourse in Korean society was a process in which the discursive framework of interpreting and prescribing Korea's economy came to be under the influence of Western discourse.

This chapter has noted that the material, scientific, and modern civilization of the West was negatively framed in the non-Eurocentric discourse of *munmyeong* in the 1950s. In *munmyeong* discourse, the Eastern civilization of spirit and ethics was basically regarded as an alternative to overcome the limitations of Western civilization. In this respect, there was no clear hierarchy between the East (or Korea) and the West in *munmyeong* discourse.

In those respects, the 1950s in Korean society was a period when development discourse and *seonjinguk* discourse began to be constructed in Korea's public discursive space under the influence of Western discursive hegemony. However, as *munmyeong* discourse was still dominant, the discourses of development and *seonjinguk* did not yet secure a dominant position enough to present a prevailing national goal, vision, and identity.

Notes

1 The developmental era of Korea can be defined in various ways. In a narrow sense, it can be defined as a period when the Korean developmental state led by the Park Chung-Hee regime aggressively pursued Korea's economic development, i.e., the 1960s–1970s. However, it can also be understood as a period that has been going on since the 1960s in the sense that developmentalism and developmental discourse (e.g., *seonjinguk* discourse) are still in a dominant position despite the replacement of the developmental state by the post-developmental state with neoliberal character in the 1990s.

2 It has obtained 453 cases of President Rhee's addresses in the fields of politics/society, industry/economy, and culture/sports/tourism from the online contents of the National Archives of Korea (www.pa.go.kr). The mass media materials have been obtained through a search of the Korea Magazine Museum database and the *Chosun Ilbo* archive for the period from 1 January 1950 to 31 December 1959.

3 An article published in *Shinsegye* (1 January 1962a) well shows a critical attitude towards the Western discursive tendency of problematizing "poverty": "The bear is not poor. I am not poor either. The bear and I merely have the sorrow of Genesis. Working for a half year and hibernating for another half year, I would really be frustrated if suddenly told to live like rich Westerners. While most of us are living like this, it is said that most of them [Westerners] are toiling and moiling in factory or farm all through the year except for holidays. If we envy them, we would be poor, poorer than a bear being brought by a circus troupe."

4 It has, first, used eight terms for the search, which belong to developmental and *seonjinguk* discourses: "*gyeongje seongjang*" (economic growth), "*gyeongje baljeon*" (economic development), "*gyeongje gaebal*" (economic development), "*hujin*" (backward), "*seonjin*" (advanced, developed), "*gaebal dosang*" (developing), "*geundaehwa*" (modernization), and "*gongeophwa*" (industrialization). It has also used two more terms for the search, which are known as main economic concepts during the 1950s: "*gyeongje jaegeon*" (economic reconstruction) and "*buheung*" (rehabilitation). The most searched magazine was *Saebyeok* with seven volumes, followed by *Shintaeyang* and *Shincheonji* (five volumes each), and *Hyeondae* (four volumes).

5 Among these, the number of articles for "*buheung*" takes the overwhelming majority with 1,489 cases. The number of cases except for "*buheung*" is 173.

6 It has checked the number of searched articles for a ten-year period in the Park Chung-Hee era (1 January 1962–31 December 1971), with the same search words and methods that have been used for the period of the 1950s, to compare the use of developmental concepts between the 1950s and the 1960s.

7 The congratulatory messages of politicians and high government officials appeared on the cover of the first issue of *Gyeongje Gongron* (10 May 1957), demonstrating economic awareness at the time: "Be the model of economic rehabilitation," "be the guide for industry promotion," "for the establishment of self-supporting economy," "be the guide for the improvement of agricultural economy," "perform the mission of rehabilitating industry," etc.

8 The main principles of the economic development plan for 1959–1960 (the "long-term plan for economic rehabilitation"), which were announced by the Department of Rehabilitation in June 1958, were as follows: 1 supporting the economy to maintain appropriate defense power and consumption levels; 2 preparing for investment to advance towards a self-supporting economy on stable financial ground; 3 promoting people's awareness of production (*Chosun Ilbo*, 22 June 1958).

9 It is estimated that about half of industrial facilities were lost due to the Korean War, and industrial productive power fell down to a third of the pre-war level as of August 1951 (Choi S.-O., 2003).

10 An article in *Shintaeyang* (1 April 1958) entitled "It is possible to reach the self-supporting economy: Could backwardness be overcome?" was published as one of the special articles on "the prospect of Korean society in ten years." It recognized the economic level of ten years ago or the highest economic level in Japanese colonial rule as sufficient conditions for a self-supporting economy, suggesting the five-year plan in the Nathan Report as a strategy for it.

11 Among 12 volumes searched by "*hujin*," ten volumes were published after 1955, indicating that the terminological use of "*hujin*" rapidly increased after the mid-1950s.

12 An advertisement on the cover of *Jaejeong* (1 September 1955) introduces Nurkse's book *Problems of Capital Formation in Underdeveloped Countries* (1953), as follows: "Sixty seven percent of world population are now living in poverty with less than \$50 per capita income annually. How could underdeveloped countries escape from the 'vicious circle of poverty' inherent in their national economies? This is the dizzy wheel of: The narrowness of market scale – sluggish attraction of investment – lack of capital – low level of productive capacity – low income level – narrowness of market scale. What would be the diagnosis and prescription for this task of the century? An ambitious good book, forthcoming!" According to Park T.-G. (2005), foreign economists, who were frequently cited in Korea in the 1950s, include Arthur Lewis, Raul Prebisch, Paul Baran, Ragnar Nurkse and Gunnar Myrdal. He also notes that Korean universities began to teach courses on economic development in the late 1950s.

13 An article in *Jeonggye jaegye* (10 December 1959) introduces *hujinguk* like this: "When we interpret *hujinguk* as referring to the country that we commonly call *hujinguk* – that is, the country whose industry and economy are underdeveloped and national income level is low, being newly independent and having short experience of democracy, and not getting much benefit of the modern machine civilization of the twentieth century, we can generally call the U.S. and countries in Europe *seonjinguk*, and countries in Asia, Africa, the Middle East, and Latin America *hujinguk*."

14 An article in *Gyoyukgwa Hunryeon* (20 July 1963) mentions that "*hujinguk* in the economic aspect refers to a country whose real income per capita is less than \$100, by the criterion of national income level, and the country having between \$100 and \$300 is *jungjinguk*, and one having above this is *seonjinguk*."

15 An article in the *Chosun Ilbo* (9 September 1955), entitled "Backwardness of our economy (2)," argues: "Whether it is fateful sorrow or not, all of the countries in

Southeast Asia lie in this situation. Not only Korea but all countries, such as communist China, Taiwan, Cambodia, Laos, Vietnam, Thailand, Malaysia, India, Pakistan, the Philippines, Indonesia, have below $100 per capita income, mostly at $50~60 level. Among the countries thinking of themselves as cultural ones having a long history, it is difficult to find a country poorer than Korea in terms of per capita income, and our people have to recognize this special reality."

16 Since the modern age, mainstream Western elites have had a cognitive obsession: which society or region is superior and more advanced (Nederveen Pieterse, 2001)? After World War II, the linear progressive view of history unfolded in the circumstances of the Cold War. For instance, *Digest* (1 January 1950) introduces a British politician's statement under the headline of "Has the Soviet economy really been rehabilitated?": "We can know how the companies of the Soviet Union are lagging behind those in the West and the U.S. by the fact that the Soviet exultantly announces their new use of things that have already been used in European countries."

17 An article in the *Chosun Ilbo* (9 September 1955) argues: "Watching a documentary movie about the war in Ethiopia, we thought that Ethiopia was a barbaric country never comparable with us. However, every person in this country should realize that Korea known to the world through the recent war is represented in the foreigners' view exactly as a country like Ethiopia that we thought before. There may be indignant patriots calling it nonsense but, above all, we have to exert strenuous effort on our undeniable reality."

18 Articles without the discursive framework of *seonjinguk* did not clearly show a cognitive hierarchy between Korea and the West. Countries frequently appearing as an exemplary case of economic reconstruction in the magazines were West Germany and the Netherlands, but most of the articles did not show an attitude of hierarchically comparing these countries and Korea. For instance, an article in *Gyeongje Gongron* (10 May 1957), entitled "Learn from the rehabilitation of the Western German economy," perceives the post-war economic level of West Germany as lower than that of Korea, saying that "the West German economy, which fell into the lower economic level than our country's in a few years after the war, demonstrated a surprising status of rehabilitation."

19 An article in *Shinsegye* (1 January 1962), entitled "We are about [the rank of] staff sergeant," shows well the hierarchical perception of Korea and the West based on the prepositions of *seonjinguk* discourse: "The rich country is certainly the U.S. Let's consider the U.S. as a general [...] If we make a hierarchy, the countries of *seonjinguk* are general officers. While belonging to Western Europe ranked as general officer, countries like Italy cannot be called as such. Let's count it as a field-grade officer [...] We can see countries in Latin America as company-grade officers [...] Wouldn't Japan be about a captain or a lieutenant? [...] Countries of the so-called '*hujinguk*' are enlisted men. Most countries in Africa and Asia are at the rank of enlisted men [...] Maybe we are at the rank of a staff sergeant." In addition, this article asks: "While we are said to boast the history of five millennia, what did we do during that time as we are this poor?"

Part II

The Rise of Developmentalism and its Current State

The 1960s to the Present

5 The Rise of Developmentalism and *Seonjinguk* Discourse

The 1960s and the 1970s

The global rise of the discourse of development was reflected in the rise of developmentalism in Korea in the 1960s. With the advent of the Park Chung-Hee era (1961–1979), a national priority was put on economic growth and industrialization under the cause of the "modernization of fatherland" (*joguk geundaehwa*). Korea's interpretative framework of national identity and worldview rapidly changed from the discourse of "civilization" to that of "development."

While the tendency to identify countries by the criterion of "civilization" weakened, the attitude of interpreting the world by economic indices, such as economic growth and national income, gained currency. The country with an advanced level of industrialization and high level of income was called "*seonjinguk*," while the opposite was designated as "*hujinguk*" (backward country). Accordingly, the rise of developmentalism and development discourse accompanied the rise of the discourse of *seonjinguk*, one of the most popular development discourses in Korea.

The discourse of *seonjinguk* is a system of knowledge based on the distinction between idealized "*seonjinguk*" and its marginalized other, "*hujinguk*." In this framework, social change is interpreted in regard to the transformation from *hujinguk* to *seonjinguk*. That is, a process of certain social change accompanying industrialization and economic development is typically understood as a process moving from the status of *hujinguk* to that of *seonjinguk* on a linear universal path of progress.

It has historically provided the Koreans with a dominant interpretative framework of the world in their modernization process, justifying national change prioritizing rapid economic development. The ideal image of *seonjinguk*, in particular, has played important roles as a "positive significant other" in Korea's modernization process, being a national goal and vision, desirable model, reference point, and so forth.

This chapter examines the forming and unfolding processes of developmentalism and *seonjinguk* discourse, along with their discursive characteristics, during the Park Chung-Hee era in the context of global discursive change. For this, it analyzes Park's presidential addresses, which are the documents best reflecting dominant values in the period, and *Chosun Ilbo* articles, which represent a slice of dominant public discourse, focusing on the formation and transformation of Korea's national identity and worldview within the framework of the developmental discourses.[1]

This chapter is organized in five main sections. First, it examines the state of developmentalism and modernization discourse in the Park Chung-Hee era through the analysis of Park's presidential addresses. Second, it investigates the change in the way of looking at Korea's tradition and history, which was incurred by the rise of development discourse. Third, it explains the main characteristics of *seonjinguk* discourse reflected in Park's presidential addresses. Fourth, it discusses the change in Korea's national identity, incurred by the rise of *seonjinguk* discourse. Fifth, it introduces the characteristics of *seonjinguk* discourse, reflected in newspaper articles.

The Formation of a Developmental Regime and the Rise of a Development Discourse

Historical Background

It was not until the Park Chung-Hee era when the development alliance was manifestly formed for the cause of rapid economic development of Korea. Having held power through a military coup in 1961, the Park regime sought to compensate for its lacking legal legitimacy with aggressive economic development of the nation. For this, it willingly became developmental nationalists prioritizing Korea's economic development to join the global developmental regime.

The Park government launched a full-out development project to "create infrastructure for the self-reliant economy and to break off the vicious circle of poverty through high growth" (Kim J.-G., 2012: 28). For this, it established the Economic Planning Board and set out the Five-Year Economic Development Plan in 1962, the first effective national project for economic development in Korea. From 1964, it promoted strong export-oriented industrialization as a main development strategy by providing exporting companies with various incentives and advantages in taxes, loans, subsidies, etc. (Ryu S.-Y., 1996; Lee D.-J., 2009).[2] The Park government mobilized all available sectors of the nation "from above" for the cause of "*joguk geundaehwa*" (Kim Y.-T., 1999a).

The Park Chung-Hee era was the time when the accumulation of capital was made through productive activities, instead of aid, grants, or distribution, and industrial capitalist class such as "*jaebeol*" (*chaebol*, conglomerate) notably emerged (Seo J.-J., 1991). The state and big corporates became close partners connected through "institutional networks," endeavoring to succeed in the common goal of national economic development (Kim Y.-T., 1999a: 160). In this situation, *jaebeol* grew notably under the auspices of the government. The political-economic alliance of the state and the big corporates (or *jaebeol*) became a main ground for the formation of Korea's developmental regime.[3] Korea's developmental regime could take advantage of propitious external conditions, such as "the benefits of U.S. hegemony and the Cold War system," "the formation of the international division of labor with Japan," and "the unprecedented expansion and prosperity of the world economy" (Yoon S.-W., 2006: 70).

In the global context, the emergence of the Korean developmental regime occurred "when U.S. hegemony was at the peak temporally and where powers of the Cold War crossed spatially" (Kim C.-G., 2003: 73). Upon Independence from Japanese colonial rule, Korea became rapidly incorporated into the U.S.-led world order through U.S. military rule and the Korean War (Lee S.-H., 2004). Being a front line against the North Korean and Chinese communists, South Korea's geopolitical importance was well recognized by Washington. At the same time, the importance of U.S. hegemony was also well recognized by the Korean ruling elites.

The U.S. saw poverty and underdevelopment as a fertile ground for communism in the Cold War context (Wiegersma and Medley, 2000). Thus, economic development took on a strategic bearing as a vital tool for containing communism. In this respect, the appearance of the Park Chung-Hee regime, which discursively combined developmentalism and anti-communism, was generally welcomed and supported by the U.S. (Ryu S.-Y., 1996; Ma S.-Y., 2002; Jeong I.-J., 2009).

Given the knowledge-power relationship, the rise of the developmental regime accompanied the rise of a developmental discourse that supported and justified it. The Park era was the time when the discourse of development emerged to a dominant status for the first time in Korea. The Park regime was the first ruling group in Korea that actively accommodated and utilized the global discourse of development for its national goal-setting and for its political legitimacy.

Developmentalism and development discourse in the Park era effectively contained the oppositional political groups' resistant discourses centered on such values as democracy, socio-economic justice, and equality, by justifying the developmental dictatorship and the so-called "Korean-style democracy" (Cho H.-Y., 2003). Furthermore, developmentalism in this period became associated with anti-communism inherited from the previous period. It provided a discursive ground for the formation of an anti-communist developmental state under such a cause that development was a way to win communism and to ultimately achieve the unification of the two Koreas.

The combination of developmentalism and anti-communism became greatly manifest in the late 1960s, due to such incidents as the dispatch of Korean troops to Vietnam, a North Korean raid on the Blue House in 1968, and the Pueblo incident. This brought about a new type of dominant discourse promoting defense and economy at the same time, e.g., "defense on one side and (economic) construction on the other side" (Kim J.-H. and Cho H.-Y., 2003).

Park Chung-Hee's Development Discourse

With the rise of developmentalism, the discursive focus moved to "development" in regard to a national identity and goal. The terms related to economic development, such as "*jeungsan*" (production increase), "*geonseol*" (construction), "*suchul*" (export), and "*baljeon*" (development), appeared as central concepts in Park's addresses. Economic issues, such as rapid economic growth and the increase of income, came to be considered as the most important national goals and the nation's ultimate historical mission to achieve. For this, the importance of economic activities was emphasized, such as efforts for production, construction, and frugal life.

Accordingly, an (economically) developed country, rather than a civilized country, was set as the nation's future vision and people were compared to workers and warriors for the sacred goal of national reconstruction. Industrial nationalism was actively utilized for the mobilization of the nation (Kim H.-G., 1998: 105).

Above all, it is notable that the interpretative framework of the *munmyeong* discourse was rarely seen in Park's addresses. Dominant views on national identity, national vision, and the world were mainly expressed around the values of economic development. Park's development discourse was based on the thorough problematization of poverty, especially that of Korea.

> It is needless to say that the instability and confusion Korea is facing today derive mostly from "poverty." The escape from poverty and the improvement of people's life [...], the progress of democracy, the construction of a welfare state, the increase of national power for the unification of the Koreas through winning communism are eventually dependent upon success in the construction of the economy [...] We are truly on a tense forked road whether we are to endlessly wander suffering poverty and sorrows under the label of backwardness or to create a new history of freedom and prosperity bravely escaping from this stagnant reality.
>
> (15 August 1964)

Park's developmentalist worldview in regard to national identity and vision was particularly notable, as the dominant interpretative framework in the preceding Rhee era had been the *munmyeong* discourse and this was still prevalent in the public space in the early Park era. In this respect, Park Chung-Hee can be considered to be the most notable historical figure who led the rise of developmentalism in Korea.[4]

Park's developmentalism was often expressed in the concept of "modernization" (*geundaehwa*), which referred to a process of escaping from poverty and weakness towards a wealthy industrial country. The primary goal of the modernization project was set first as a kind of war against poverty, and economic development through industrialization was regarded as the most effective way to accomplish it. President Park considered industrialization as the decisive driving force of modernization, and tended to equate the power of industry with national power (29 September 1967). He asked the people to become a working people, while designating those who were actively working for the modernization of fatherland as true patriots (15 September 1965).

Park understood the project of the modernization of the fatherland as "the process of conquering the dark sides and replacing them with the bright sides" (3 October 1965). In this regard, he also mentioned it as "the process of change for rapidly modernizing, reforming, and renewing various traditional, reactionary, and old things" (18 August 1969). The contrast between "modern" and "tradition," "reform" and "reaction," and "renewal" and "old things" are manifest here. While the primary goal of the modernization of the fatherland in the Park era was to achieve economic development, it actually aimed for the overall transformation of the whole nation in all aspects (Heo E., 2010).

Park's devotion to the modernization project, centered on the values of production and construction, was so strong that he made "production increase" an important criterion for evaluating various affairs in the country. In one address, for instance, he raised a need for "reducing the criteria of judging all issues to the increase of production, while removing unproductive ideas and customs," and mentioned "how rapid our country's development would be if, at least, lawmakers and governmental officials come to have economic development and the direction of production as the criteria of judgment" (11 June 1965). Using such phrases as "productive politics" and "productive journalism," he further emphasized that all fields and functions of the country including politics and journalism should contribute to the increase of production (11 June 1965; 15 August 1967).

Truly, Park Chung-Hee attempted to mobilize the entire nation for the increase of production under the cause of modernization. His national goal and vision of this kind directly induced the emergence of developmentalism and development discourse in Korea, whose discursive power, in turn, supported his ambitious project to be successful.

Change in the Perception of Korea's Tradition and History

A need for social change arises from the problematization of the current situation, and the need for change increases in proportion to the seriousness of the current problem. A problem as well as the solution to it is recognized within the interpretative framework of discourse and, accordingly, the goal and direction of social change vary according to discourses. The discourse of civilization, for instance, raised a need for a civilizing process by problematizing the situation of barbarism, while the development discourse justified economic development based on the problematization of poverty and underdevelopment.

The tendency to interpret Korea's identity in the framework of *munmyeong* greatly weakened in the Park Chung-Hee period. Park's view on Korea in the 1960s tended to be expressed in such negative terms as "poverty," "backwardness," and "weakness." He considered Korea's past and present basically as in the situation of struggling with poverty being used to idleness and complacency. In this regard, Park recognized Korea's history as a history of regression. For him, "boastful national culture was merely an exceptional part of national history" and, thus, he believed that "the only way to reconstruct the nation was to thoroughly reflect on the [regrettable] past of the nation" (Choi Y.-S., 2007: 47).

Park's notable perception of national self was, above all, that Korea had always been poor throughout its history. This interpretation of history made a ground for the efforts for "revolutionary" national change to be justified. Park's nationalism considered it as a national historical mission to escape from poverty and backwardness for the goal of national restoration.[5] He assumed economic development and modernization as the most effective strategies for it.

For Park, the Koreans' traditional thatched house was a symbol of poverty and weakness. He argued that "the thatched house, which we have inherited from our ancestors for 5,000 years, will be rarely seen at the end of the third Five-Year Economic Plan" (15 April 1971). Later, reflecting on the achievements of economic development, he stated that "the dirt of 5,000-year-old poverty is now disappearing slowly around our living environments" (10 December 1976).

In this respect, the problematization of poverty was the most fundamental element justifying his aggressive developmental modernization project.[6] As Korea was perceived as having been constantly in an economically poor and incompetent condition, his problematization of poverty was closely related to his denial of Korea's past and history. As Choi Y.-S. (2007: 47) mentions, "Park's aspiration for and devotion to modernization derived from a deep-rooted hatred towards our history."

As for Korea's identity, Park Chung-Hee attempted a thorough perceptual departure from the previous period. While Rhee Syngman emphasized Korea's civilizational identity as a *munmyeong-guk* in the preceding period, Park criticized this as a groundless narcissistic worldview ignorant of reality.

> It would not matter to be narcissistic, calling ourselves a nation of calm morning or the country of courtesy in the East, as long as we are to close our doors as in the past, maintain the policy of seclusion, build walls against neighbors, and live like a frog in a small pond.
>
> (17 April 1967)

For him, the stark historical reality of Korea was, rather, of a country having been trapped in poverty and backwardness than a country of civilization, or a weak country accustomed to poverty and complacency. He related this to Korea's history of colony and emphasized a need to raise national power.

The aspiration for power was manifest in Park's historical viewpoint. Above all, he showed an attitude to admit the "order maintained by power," rather than criticizing it. While President Rhee often expressed critical views on the evolutionary international order led by the West in such terms as the law of the jungle and the survival of the fittest, President Park tended to take the world as it was. He regretted Korea's past as it had been too weak to survive the international competition. He often expressed remorse and shame of Korea's lagging behind in the power-dominating competitive international order. In this regard, he mentions in an address as follows:

> Looking back on the past century's Korean history, I am wondering why the Koreans left those many traces of humiliation [...] We always fell behind in competition. Our society in the past fell behind by one, two, or sometimes ten steps, when the international society was developing and progressing day by day in every field in such ways as modernization, production and industrial revolution, and the diffusion of education [...] We will fall behind by a year if we are lingering for a day.
>
> (30 November 1967)

Park Chung-Hee sought for the values of Korean tradition from "power" rather than from civilizational features. He launched a project for the "creation of new culture" under the cause of the restoration of the nation, through which he discovered Korean war heroes in history, such as Yi Sun-Shin, Gang Gam-Chan, Kim Yu-Shin, Sambyolcho, Euljimundeok, while emphasizing the "history of having overcome national disasters" (Park N.-J., 2005; Choi Y.-S., 2007). The Park regime selectively developed spiritual culture and national culture only useful for the national goal of modernization and economic development (Lim H.-S., 2012).

In this regard, Choi Y.-S. (2007: 65) notes that "Park Chung-Hee saved no efforts for supporting national tradition useful for national security and modernization, such as Admiral Yi Sun-Shin and King Sejong, but streamlined everyday cultures and heritage for the reason that they were inconvenient and ineffective." In those respects, it was the worldview admitting the law of the jungle, along with the self-denial of tradition and history, which made a discursive background for justifying Park's modernization mission.

As is well known, Park Chung-Hee considered his term in office as a "period of revolution" for escaping from the misfortune of the past. He argued that the direction of impotent national history dramatically changed with the appearance of the revolutionary government.[7] He interpreted it as a period when the transition occurred for the first time in national history from the unproductive, pre-modern, dependent situation to the productive, modern, and independent one. He considered it a period of national rebirth for a strong nation. In this regard, one address argues as follows:

> We are now at the turning point in 5,000-year national history. That is, we are on the threshold of the overflowing new era, in which we endeavor for ambitious progress escaping from regression and stagnation, and aim for independence and prosperity by getting out of the fetters of backwardness and poverty.
>
> (3 October 1965)

As modernization theorists sought for the cause of underdevelopment from society's internal pre-modern, feudal thoughts and lifestyles (Rostow, 1960), Park Chung-Hee assumed modernization in the cultural sphere as a pre-condition for successful economic growth. He suggested a need for change in ideas and thoughts by such drastic ways as "thoroughly clearing" the past and throwing away all "pre-modern," "non-scientific" elements as soon as possible.

> We have to boldly eliminate all of the wrong elements that made sick our nation's culture, ideas, education, and everyday life [...] Thus, we have to repel all of the pathological elements that are feudal, pre-modern, unscientific, non-independent, and non-democratic in all fields such as ideas, education, self-governance, everyday life, etc.
>
> (9 October 1965)

Furthermore, Park Chung-Hee asked people for change to the extent of "human remodeling." He assumed that deep-rooted conventions in people's behaviors and thoughts became internal hindering factors for modernization. He argued: "Without the human remodeling of ourselves, our nation cannot successfully create new history, that is, the accomplishment of the mission of the modernization of fatherland and national restoration" (28 September 1968).

At the New Year press conference in 1968, Park Chung-Hee asked people to be reborn as "modern-type humans." He designated the economy in its original term, such as the increase of production and income, as the "first economy," while defining the elimination of non-economic elements interrupting economic development as the "second economy," such as the project of spiritual reformulation. A need for change to the level of "human reformulation" was reflected well in the *Samaeul* (New Village) Movement in the 1970s, which took on a feature of political ideology for mobilizing peasants (Kim D.-Y., 2004).

In those respects, Park's nationalism contained a paradox of denying the national past. Nevertheless, his presentation of national vision in the framework of development discourse greatly appealed to people. As Kim H.-G. (1998) notes, his "industrial nationalism" or developmental nationalism, which aimed for modernization and economic growth for the nation's escape from the poor past, seemed to have succeeded in earning widespread consensus from people to create discursive hegemony in the 1960s.

The Rise of the Discourse of *Seonjinguk*

In the Park Chung-Hee era, developmentalism took concrete shape in its subordinate discourse of *seonjinguk*. The rise of *seonjinguk* discourse at the time was manifest in the rapid increase of the use of related terms and concepts. Compared with the previous Rhee Syngman era when developmental concepts, such as "*seonjinguk*" and "*hujinguk*," were rarely found in presidential addresses, Park Chung-Hee's presidential address demonstrated the significant increase in these concepts.

Characteristics of **Seonjinguk** *Discourse*

The discourse of *seonjinguk* took on some characteristics in Park's addresses. First of all, it contained linear evolutionism, supposing the transition from *hujinguk* to *seonjinguk* as a universal developmental path of human society. In this respect, *hujinguk* was described as a "catching-up" country tracing the path of *seonjinguk* that achieved development ahead, and *seonjinguk* was understood as a country more suitable to survival in the competitive international circumstances. The countries on the way to *seonjinguk* from *hujinguk* were termed "*jungjin-guk*" or "*gaebal-dosang-guk*" (developing country) (1964; 1 November 1968).

Park considered the "catch up"-style modernization process through industrialization as the best way to *seonjinguk*. In this regard, there appeared a tendency to understand Korea's development as a linear journey towards the goal. In an address made in 1967, he compared Korea's economic development to a train journey towards the destination of top industrialized country or *seonjinguk*, in which everyone could live wealthy.

> If I may exemplify this economic plan we are promoting now, you may consider it as a train journey to Seoul. When you arrive in Seoul, then you will be rich. Then, where are we now? […] In my view, we are nearby I-ri [in North Cheonla Province] […] When we do another Five-Year Economic Plan, that is, the third one, we arrive in Seoul over the Han-River Bridge. Then, we will be living wealthy. We all will be rich. Our country will become a top industrialized country in Asia. We will be at the level of competing with Japan for the top place […] We have also to develop heavy industry […] We have to quickly develop this strategic area in order to catch up with modern advanced industrial countries in the future […] If we finish the second Five-Year Economic Plan, our housekeeping will be far better than now […] We need only do another Five-Year Economic Plan that is the third. Then, we will be able to catch up with the rank of *seonjinguk* as a sound modern industrial country. This is what we are now referring to as the modernization of fatherland.
>
> (18 April 1967)

This address clearly showed an assumption that *hujinguk* was behind and *seonjinguk* was ahead on a temporal scale. It perceived that Korea could escape from the status of *hujinguk* through the Five-Year Economic Plans to become industrial *seonjinguk*. President Park intended for the people's consensus on his development project by suggesting a vision that everyone would be rich if the national plans were successfully completed.

As catching up with *seonjinguk* was set as an urgent national goal, the concept of *seonjinguk* played an important role as a "significant other" in Korea's modernization process. Korea's change and achievement occurring in the process of modernization tended to be compared with the level of *seonjinguk* as a positive reference point. For instance, while the visible achievements of economic development in such fields as construction and export began to be appreciated from the mid-1960s, a dominant perception was that they were not yet matching those of *seonjinguk* (6 July 1966).

Second, the discourse of *seonjinguk* took on economism, prioritizing economic values as the most important criterion for judging national affairs over other (social and cultural) values. With the rise of the discourse of development, the "progress of humanity" began to be measured in economic aspects by such indices as national income per capita (Patterson, 1997: 49). In Park's addresses, the main feature of *seonjinguk* was appreciated mainly in terms of the degree of economic development, and the countries having a high income and advanced level of industrialization were regarded as *seonjinguk*. The so-called "Third World" countries in Southeast Asia, Africa, and Latin America, whose income levels were low, were designated as *hujinguk*. In regard to the national income level, President Park mentioned in an address that "although our economy is praised for its rapid growth, it is just over $200 in per capita income. There are many *seonjinguk* whose per capita incomes are over $1,000, $2,000, $3,000, or $4,000" (1971).

The level of per capita income for *seonjinguk* changed in different historical circumstances. As for this, $1,000 was generally suggested in the early 1970s, but it is interesting to note that $3,000 or $5,000 was presented in the late 1970s when Korea had already achieved the level of $1,000 in per capita income.

> Envisaging the status of our fatherland tomorrow, which will be grandly joining the rank of *seonjinguk* after having achieved the high industrial society, I deeply appreciate you, the people's efforts and cooperation up to today [...] Now our economy has just gone over the level of $1,000 in per capita income. In order to rise to the level of *seonjinguk*, it should go up at least to $3,000 or $5,000.
>
> (27 March 1979)

Third, it showed a degree of Eurocentrism by assuming the historical experiences and social phenomena of Western countries as the reference points for Korea's change. The discourse of *seonjinguk* was basically a knowledge system that was constructed by the Koreans in their specific historical circumstances, in which *seonjinguk* existed as a representation of the ideal country. The Koreans attributed their own positive values to countries that were called *seonjinguk*, e.g., those in the West, and created a Eurocentric hierarchy between Korea and the West. In developmental terms, Western countries were mainly referred to as *seonjinguk* whose industry and economy were advanced and income levels were high (9 June 1966; 23 March 1972).

Before the Park era, the West had been mainly perceived in the framework of the discourse of *munmyeong*. For instance, the West was called "*munmyeong-guk*" in the Rhee Syngman period but was perceived basically as material civilization containing violence. Thus, the West was far from an idealized image. In a sense, it was treated as a lower level of civilization compared with Korea and the East which were based on the civilization of spirit and ethics (Chapter 4).

The status of the West dramatically changed, however, in the discourse of development in the Park era. As the West was described as an entity for Korea to catch up to on the path of economic development, it retrieved the feature of temporal advancement over Korea. In the hierarchical framework of the *seonjinguk* discourse, the West came again to enjoy a superior status over Korea, being represented as countries for Korea to catch up to as soon as possible.

Fourth, it contained internalized Orientalism. The negative values in developmentalism, such as poverty, weakness, and idleness, were projected onto the concept of *hujinguk* that was at the opposite point to *seonjinguk*. As Korea was designated as *hujinguk* in the early 1960s, the self-criticism of Korean society widely appeared. In an inverse proportion to the degree of idealization of *seonjinguk, hujinguk* became marginalized. Internalized Orientalism formed a negative or deficient self-identity against the representation of *seonjinguk* but, on the other hand, it provided a strong motivation for escaping from the status of *hujinguk*. In this regard, President Park mentions as follows:

> What I want to especially emphasize today to people is that we are poor and backward people for sure, the people of *hujinguk*. But we should have the dream, confidence, and courage to become wealthy like others, the people in *seonjinguk*, in the near future, by standing independently on our own efforts.
>
> (2 May 1965)

Fifth, nationalism was deeply reflected in the discourse of *seonjinguk*, especially in relation to Park's aspiration for power. The escape from *hujinguk* and entry into the ranks of *seonjinguk* were set as a national destiny determining the survival of the nation. In this regard, the national goal of *seonjinguk* was pursued, in a way, on the assumption that *seonjinguk* was the ultimately desirable evolutionary form most suitable for surviving the competition of the world. The aspiration for *seonjinguk* was well expressed in the nationalistic term "*joguk geundaehwa*." In this respect, the discourse of *seonjinguk* at the time can be understood as a sort of nationalistic developmental discourse combining developmentalism with Korean nationalism.

Historical Background of the Rise of **Seonjinguk** *Discourse*

The Park Chung-Hee era can be defined as a period when the discourse of *seonjinguk* arose as one of the notable dominant discourses in Korea. Specific national and global circumstances promoted the rapid spread of the discourse of *seonjinguk* in Korean society.

First of all, there was the influence of modernization theory promoted by American social scientists. Modernization theory spread around the world under U.S. hegemony.[8] It framed the relationship between the non-West and the West into that of traditional society and modern society, and suggested the transition from the former to the latter as the ideal social change.

In this respect, the theory shared much in common with Korea's developmentalism and the discourse of *seonjinguk*. Rostow's modernization theory, for instance, was well introduced by the Korean mass media, such as *Sasanggye*, a renowned popular magazine in the 1960s, and other major newspapers. His ideas were somewhat popular at the time, to the extent that they frequently appeared in public writings about economic development, and were even introduced in textbooks for middle and high school students (Park T.-G., 1997). Besides, as Rostow advised on U.S. policy on Asia, his ideas exerted great influence on American development advisors involved in Korea's economic development plan.

The discourse of *seonjinguk*, reflected in President Park's addresses, resembled Rostow's modernization theory in terms of its structure and contents. The common elements between the two include the binary distinction between *hujinguk* (traditional society) and *seonjinguk* (modern society), the assumption of a linear developmental path, the suggestion of the modernization of catching-up with the West, and so forth. In this regard, a perception began to appear from the mid-1960s that the Korean economy had reached the level of "take-off," which was reminiscent of Rostow's five stages of economic growth. For instance, Park Chung-Hee argued that "we have recently succeeded in establishing the ground for independent economy, and it is approaching the take-off stage at which it can reach the 'plains of independence'" (25 September 1966). When Rostow visited Korea in 1965, he argued that the country was at the stage of "take-off," which gave confidence to Korean intellectuals that Korea could take off according to his theory. His theory became a criterion for the Park government to evaluate its economic development project (Park T.-G., 2004: 156).

Second, the Cold War situation inducing competition between the U.S. and the Soviet Union for international aid was a good condition for the spread of the discourse of *seonjinguk*. As military and economic aid from the U.S. and the Soviet Union to the "underdeveloped" countries drew attention nationally and internationally, developmental terms appearing in the foreign media were also used in the Korean media. For instance, developmental terms in international news, such as "developed country," "underdeveloped country," and "development," were translated into "*seonjinguk*," "*hujinguk*," and "*baljeon*," respectively. In the *Chosun Ilbo* published in the 1960s, articles using those developmental terms mostly appeared in regard to international news.

In those respects, it can be said that the term "*seonjinguk*" was conceptualized in Korean society, reflecting the term "developed country" in global development discourse and the term "modern society" in modernization theory. In a similar vein, we can understand that the term "*hujinguk*" echoed the concepts of "underdeveloped country" and "traditional society" in those discourses.

Third, the historically visible achievements of the economic development project led by the Korean developmental regime contributed to the spread of *seonjinguk* discourse. The discourse of *seonjinguk* provided a concrete or easily recognizable interpretative framework for abstract developmental questions, such as "why we need to develop" or "why the modernization of fatherland is needed." In this regard, it defined Korea as *hujinguk*, setting *seonjinguk* as the concrete goal of development.

The notions and interpretative frameworks of the discourse of *seonjinguk* dovetailed nicely with the Park regime's political need, which sought to compensate its weak political legitimacy with the achievements of economic growth and modernization. It is important to note that the Koreans historically felt "as if" they were experiencing the "transition towards *seonjinguk*" as the Korean economy rapidly grew in the Park era. Korea's historical experience of rapid modernization and economic development gave them confidence in modernization or in the mission of the "entry into the rank of *seonjinguk*." This became historical grounds for reinforcing their belief in the main assumptions of the discourse of *seonjinguk*.

While facing resistance from students and opposition political powers, the Park regime succeeded in drawing wide consensus on its "developmental dictatorship" at least before the "October Restoration" in 1972. With the development discourse, it could effectively control opposition discourses centered on the value of democracy (Cho H.-Y., 2003). In a situation where discourse for "bread" was more powerful than that for "liberty," the discourse of *seonjinguk* played an important role as a hegemonic discourse in serving the political interests of Korea's ruling class at the time.

Change of Korea's National Identity in the Discourse of *Seonjinguk*

With the rise of the discourse of *seonjinguk*, there occurred a big change in Korea's national identity. Whereas Korea was mainly defined as a *munmyeong-guk* (civilized country) in *munmyeong* discourse in the Rhee Syngman era, it was degraded to "*hujinguk*," struggling with poverty and weakness in the discourse of *seonjinguk*. While Korea as a civilized country of spirit had enjoyed an equal position with the West as a material civilization, Korea as *hujinguk* retrieved its inferior position to the *seonjinguk* of the West in the discourse of *seonjinguk*. In the temporal aspect, Korea was no longer considered contemporaneous with the West, but came to be posited in the past of the contemporary West. After all, the hierarchical relationship between Korea and the West reappeared on the assumption of the lacking status of the former in relation to the sufficient condition of the latter in the discourse of *seonjinguk*.

The attitude of perceiving Korea as a *munmyeong-guk* was rarely seen in Park Chung-Hee's address. Not only did he hesitate to use the term "*munmyeong-guk*" for Korea, but he also criticized the attempt to enhance national self-identity as showing a narcissistic attitude of ignoring the stark reality of the nation (17 April 1967).

Korea's Identity in the 1960s

Park Chung-Hee did not hesitate to define Korea as *hujinguk* in the early 1960s, highlighting its state of poverty and backwardness. In an address, he decisively mentioned that "we are clearly poor people, backward people, and the people of *hujinguk*" (2 May 1965). In regard to students' protests against the Korea-Japan meetings for historical reconciliation and the establishment of a diplomatic relationship, he laid blame like this: "The students in a poor country are not preparing for a great leap into the future, but [participating in demonstrations]" (3 June 1964). As such, Park intended to infuse the identity of a poor country or *hujinguk* into the Koreans as a motivation for drastic national change.

Hujinguk in Park's addresses appeared as a country pre-modern in terms of modernization, less industrialized in terms of industry, and incapable of being self-reliant in terms of the economy. It was also a country with low productivity, low motivation for production, and dependent on "unscientific" production methods. It was often referred to as a newly established country, having earned independence after World War II. In Park's addresses in the early 1960s, Korea's identity tended to be defined as *hujinguk*, as a newly established country with a pre-modern status.[9] Accordingly, it was set as an urgent national historical mission to escape from the status of *hujinguk* and, in this respect, Korea was designated as a country aspiring for *seonjinguk* by means of modernization.

From the mid-1960s, around the end of the first Five-Year Economic Development Plan, President Park evaluated his modernization project as having produced visible achievements. He emphasized that the country had entered into the level of industrialization and a new fatherland was being constructed. Showing confidence in achieving planned economic development, he mentioned that the construction boom was rising in every corner of the country. An address in this period stated that "today, a flash shines in regard to the modernization of fatherland and new ethos sprouts in our constitutional politics" (17 July 1965).

Park publicized that his economic development project was proceeding well as planned and the nation was surely moving towards a hopeful future, escaping from the unfortunate past. In this regard, an address in 1969 interpreted the 1950s, the 1960s, and the 1970s as follows.

> In retrospect, the 1950s was a period of uncontrollable confusion and insecurity, and the 1960s was a period of having retrieved stability by

> arranging and clearing out the confusion, and I expect that the approaching 1970s will be a period of mission for eternalizing the hard-retrieved stability.
>
> (10 October 1969)

As the achievements of modernization were recognized, a move of change in national identity also appeared. Reflecting Park's confidence in economic growth, Korea's identity was frequently defined as a kind of developing country (or *jungjinguk, gaebal-dosang-guk*), rather than *hujinguk*, in the mid- and late 1960s. There even appeared a perception that Korea was one of the most successful developing countries.

> We are facing an "adult Korea" today as of 15 August [...] "Adult Korea" today has become a dashing developmental and adventurous country that is never shameful in front of the world. The fact that our country Korea is counted as the most desirable and successful country among numerous developing countries in the world signifies a good sign for our ultimate mission for achieving the unification of the Koreas, and makes a strong ground for it.
>
> (15 August 1968)

President Park perceived his ambitious project of the Five-Year Economic Plan as a main strategy for moving towards *seonjinguk*. In this regard, he considered that Korea had taken a leap to *jungjinguk* through the second Five-Year Economic Plan. Based on this, he presented a national blueprint that Korea would leap to upper-class *jungjinguk* through the third Five-Year Economic Plan.

> Our economy in the 1960s has achieved a rapid growth through the first and second Five-Year Economic Development Plans. This is representative in the world, and our economy has constructed the ground for a leaping industrial country and for an exporting country. From this year on, we are newly enforcing the first year project of the third Five-Year Economic Development Plan, aiming for upper-class *jungjinguk*.
>
> (2 August 1972)

Park's perception in this kind seemed to have broad support from the people. Experiencing a somewhat unstable beginning, the Park regime became greatly stabilized after the mid-1960s by virtue of its achievements in economic development, and this was reflected in its victories in the presidential and general elections in 1967 (Hong S.-R., 2005). There appeared a wide range of support of the Park regime around the nation in the mid-1960s, as the material grounds for national mobilization expanded due, in part, to the effects of national economic growth (Cho H.-Y., 2004).

Korea's Identity in the 1970s

The ground for the legitimacy of the Park government, however, weakened in the 1970s. As contradictions inherent in rapid economic development erupted, the material ground for the people's consensus notably shrank (Cho H.-Y., 2004). Notable political and social incidents consecutively occurred around 1970, such as protests against the constitutional amendment for Park's third term in 1969, Jeon Tae-Il's self-immolation by fire for labor rights in 1970, and student protests and the Gwangju Daedanji Uprising in 1971.

In response to resistance, the Park regime invoked the garrison act and declared a state of national emergency in 1971, and eventually declared the *Yusin* (Restoration) system in October 1972. It took the strategy of prioritizing oppressive measures, while strengthening its authoritarian features and sowing the seeds of its collapse (Cho H.-Y., 2004; Park T.-G., 2009; Lee D.-J., 2009). In discursive terms, it was the period when the resistant discourses centered on the values of economic distribution, human rights, and political freedom began to rise against the hegemony of development discourse succinctly phrased as "Let's Live Wealthy!" (Kim D.-J., 2001; Cho H.-Y., 2003).

However, those socio-political situations were not reflected well in Park Chung-Hee's discourse of *seonjinguk*. Rather, it is interesting to note that Korea's national identity in the 1970s was suggested in more hopeful ways than before. The confidence in economic growth increased in this period, and a notable national identity was that Korea had not only escaped from the status of *hujinguk* but also had experienced some of the most exemplary economic growth among *jungjinguk* or developing countries in the world. In this regard, one address mentions:

> According to the UN [United Nations] statistics about the 120 countries' economic growth rates during the past ten years in the 1960s, our country Korea is ranked third from the top. In the statistics of export increase among the 120 countries, our country Korea is ranked top, that is, we are the top in the world. Our country achieved the highest economic growth among developing countries in the past ten years, having become a top student and an exemplary country [...] Our economy will become totally self-reliant after the third Five-Year Economic Development Plan [...] Besides, our income will be more than double that of today, as our country will go up to the high level in the world or among *jungjinguk*.
>
> (17 April 1971)

In the political aspect, the discourse of *seonjinguk* played a role as a hegemonic discourse in the 1960s, as its suggestion of the national mission of escaping from *hujinguk* drew widespread consensus among the people. However, the discourse of *seonjinguk*, reflected in Park's addresses in the 1970s, showed a stronger tone as a dominant political discourse to appease the discourses of opposition powers, as the resistance to the regime strengthened. In terms of industrial structure, the Park government intended to bring about strategic change to heavy and chemical industrialization in the early 1970s. The nurturing of heavy and chemical industry was emphasized, and the level of heavy and chemical industrialization was recognized as an important condition for *seonjinguk* (3 July 1973).[10]

President Park more actively mentioned the goal of *seonjinguk* in the 1970s, showing confidence in entering into the ranks of *seonjinguk* by the late 1970s or the 1980s. As the addresses showed above, he mentioned that Korea would become "a totally self-reliant country" or "a top-class country among *jungjinguk* in the world" after the third Five-Year Economic Development Plan. In this regard, an address in the early 1970s expected a national income of $1,000 and national exports of $10 billion in the late 1970s, and recognized those numbers in the economy as the level of *seonjinguk* (10 April 1971).

Entering into the mid-1970s, there began to appear evaluations that Korea as a top-class developing country had grown up enough to compete with *seonjinguk*. This reflected a perception that Korea had become a country of top-class *jungjinguk* as was aimed by the government economic project in the early 1970s. In this regard, Park mentions in an address as follows:

> It is not much to say that it is an unprecedented record in the world that a developing country like ours, whose resources are lacking and modernization has been late, has become able to expect $10 billion in exports in such a short time as ten years [...] Our country has been an exemplary developing country so far, being in a position of getting praise and encouragement from *seonjinguk*, but now its position is changing to a serious competitor to *seonjinguk*, getting challenges from outside.
>
> (30 November 1976)

The designation of Korea's identity as an "upper-level *jungjinguk*" became prevalent in the late 1970s. A notable perception was that Korea would enter into the ranks of *seonjinguk* in the near future, and its achievement of self-reliant economy as a highly industrial country was impending. In this regard, a presidential address in the late 1970s emphasized that "we will achieve a high industrial society and rise to the rank of *seonjinguk* in the early 1980s, the near future" (13 January 1978).

In an address made in 1979, Park interpreted the 1960s, the 1970s, and the 1980s: "Today is the most rewarding period in our long national history when we envision the great flight in the 1980s, having experienced development in the 1960s and leap in the 1970s" (15 March 1979). Accordingly, the entry into the ranks of *seonjinguk* was set as an important historical mission that should be achieved by the contemporary generation (26 February 1979).

The change in Korea's self-identity, which appeared in *seonjinguk* discourse in the 1960s and the 1970s, well reflected the rapid expansion of Korea's economy at the time (Table 5.1 and 5.2, and Figure 5.1). Korea's GDP growth rate from 1961 to 1979 was about 10% average, the highest rate in the

Table 5.1 Korea's Main Economic Indicators in the 1960s

Indicator by year	*1961*	*1962*	*1963*	*1964*	*1965*	*1966*	*1967*	*1968*	*1969*
GDP (nominal, $ billion)	2.2	2.4	2.8	3.0	3.1	3.8	4.4	5.4	6.8
GNI per capita (nominal, $)	85.0	91.0	104.0	107.0	110.0	131.0	150.0	178.0	221.0
GDP real growth rate (%)	6.9	3.8	9.2	9.5	7.2	12.0	9.1	13.2	14.5
Agriculture and fisheries (%)	15.0	–6.4	9.9	16.1	1.1	8.8	-5.1	0.1	9.1
Mining (%)	5.6	16.5	14.8	10.0	20.5	17.2	22.6	20.4	16.0
Manufacturing (%)	5.5	15.3	16.3	9.5	22.1	18.8	23.9	23.1	17.6
Electricity, gas, and water (%)	6.8	25.5	12.6	22.7	21.9	23.9	28.0	25.4	33.1
Construction (%)	9.6	14.5	17.3	5.6	24.3	21.4	18.9	38.5	38.2
Services (%)	0.9	7.4	5.8	1.4	6.7	11.0	12.8	15.8	14.2

Source: Bank of Korea, Statistics Korea

world. In particular, the growth rate of manufacturing reached as high as 17.5% average during that period. The size of GDP had grown as much as 30 times, from $2.2 billion in 1961 to $64.3 billion in 1979, and GNI per capita had increased 20 times from $85 to $1,709. A hopeless, "underdeveloped" country, Korea's surprising economic growth at the time was sometimes termed as the "Miracle of the Han River."

In this respect, the Koreans historically experienced the "realization of rapid modernization" through their full-out national development project, which was not shared by other countries that had failed in effective economic development to consider it as a hollow dream suggested by the West (Rivero, 2001). This historical experience of the Koreans strengthened their belief in the validity of the evolutionary development scheme featured in the discourse of *seonjinguk*.

The Rise of *Seonjinguk* Discourse in the *Chosun Ilbo*

The emergence of the discourse of *seonjinguk* was notable in the mass media during the Park era. Compared with the preceding Rhee Syngman period, the use of terms belonging to *seonjinguk* discourse, such as "*seonjinguk*" and "*hujinguk*," greatly increased in the newspaper. The relations between the terms became more stabilized as well.

The use of the term "*seonjinguk*," in particular, was rapidly on the increase from the 1960s to the 1970s, while that of the term "*hujinguk*" was in decline. In the data of *Chosun Ilbo* articles, published in the Park Chung-Hee era (1961–1979), the number containing the term "*seonjinguk*" was 125 in total. Among these, 18 cases were published in the 1960s (1961–1969) and 107 cases

Table 5.2 Korea's Main Economic Indicators in the 1970s

Indicator by year	*1970*	*1971*	*1972*	*1973*	*1974*	*1975*	*1976*	*1977*	*1978*	*1979*
GDP (nominal, $ billion)	8.2	9.5	10.8	13.8	19.5	21.7	29.8	38.3	53.7	64.3
GNI per capita (nominal, $)	257.0	292.0	324.0	406.0	563.0	610.0	826.0	1,047.0	1,454.0	1,709.0
GDP real growth rate (%)	10.0	10.5	7.2	14.8	9.5	7.9	13.1	12.3	10.8	8.6
Agriculture and fisheries (%)	-0.7	5.4	2.9	6.6	6.3	5.3	8.9	3.0	–10.0	11.5
Mining (%)	16.1	16.2	13.9	29.5	15.9	12.9	19.6	16.2	23.6	9.4
Manufacturing (%)	15.8	17.4	15.0	30.2	16.5	13.0	20.9	16.3	24.7	10.2
Electricity, gas, and water (%)	17.7	22.8	12.2	17.9	13.3	12.9	21.7	7.6	33.3	7.0
Construction (%)	4.2	–2.2	–2.0	23.1	11.2	5.8	9.3	28.3	28.0	4.6
Services (%)	13.6	11.8	8.0	11.2	6.9	7.6	9.6	10.4	10.2	7.9

Source: Bank of Korea, Statistics Korea

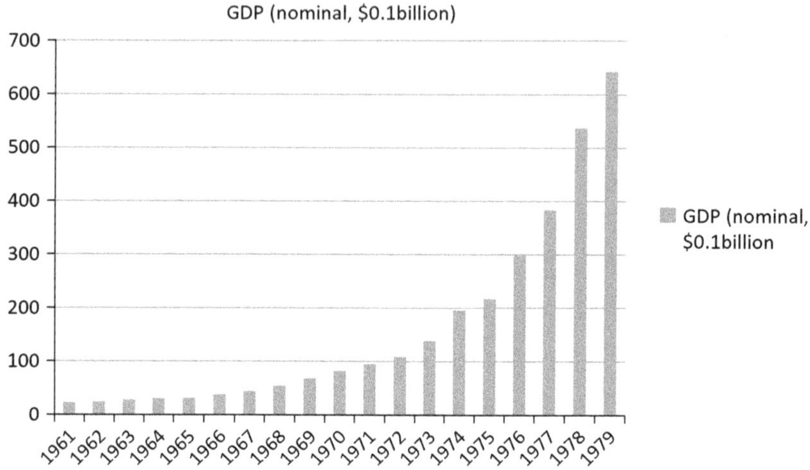

Figure 5.1 Change in Korea's GDP from the 1960s to the 1970s
Source: Bank of Korea, Statistics Korea

were in the 1970s (1970–1979). The stark increase of the term "*seonjinguk*" in the 1970s is notable. In comparison, the number of articles containing the term "*hujinguk*" was 77 total. Its use decreased from 53 cases in the 1960s to 24 cases in the 1970s. The change of trend in the use of both terms may reflect the transition of discursive focus from "escaping *hujinguk*" in the 1960s, based on the self-identity of *hujinguk*, to the "entry to the rank of *seonjinguk*" in the 1970s with the identity of *jungjinguk*.

Perception of **Seonjinguk** *in the* **Chosun Ilbo**

In the 1960s *Chosun Ilbo*, the concept of *seonjinguk* generally referred to a country advanced in industrialization, development, and capitalism. Its variants included "*seonjin gongeop-guk*" (advanced industrial country), "*seonjin gaebal-guk*" (advanced developed country), and "*seonjin jabonjuui-guk*" (advanced capitalist country). The advanced features of *seonjinguk* were somewhat limited to material aspects, such as economy, industry, technology, and capitalism.

In regard to culture and the environment, *seonjinguk* was much criticized. While President Park portrayed *seonjinguk* in very positive ways, focusing on its economic power, there were many cases in the *Chosun Ilbo* that pointed out the dark sides of industrialization, such as environmental destruction, the devastation of humanity, and the increase in crime. For instance, an opinion column entitled "The wrongdoings of *seonjinguk*" pointed out:

> There is an advantage of going behind others in industrialization and economic development. That is, we do not need to repeat the

> wrongdoings committed by *seonjinguk* when they developed ahead [...] In *seonjinguk*, we cannot wash our hands in the water of rivers, not to mention drinking it, due to industrial sewage, and the fish in it are all dying and the seaweed in the sea close to land are also being annihilated. We do not need to make our land and river like that, do we? If we use pesticides thoughtlessly as bugs eat trees in the mountains, it would kill not only bugs but also kill birds that eat those bugs or cause their extinction by making them lay eggs without shells. We should not become a country repeating the wrongdoings of *seonjinguk*, which are regretting sacrificing natural environments for the development of material civilization.
>
> (*Chosun Ilbo*, 4 November 1969)

This column emphasized that Korea should not resemble the negative aspects of *seonjinguk* in its pursuit of economic development. The dilemma of development aiming for *seonjinguk* was well expressed in one article's mention of "polluted *seonjinguk*, hungry developing countries" (*Chosun Ilbo*, 7 June 1972). As such, *seonjinguk* in the newspaper at the time was far from an ideal representation. Compared with President Park's addresses, the mass discourse showed a more careful attitude toward *seonjinguk*.

The increase in the use of the term *seonjinguk* in the 1970s reflected the increase of public attention to it. As *seonjinguk* was a newly emerging buzzword, people wondered what *seonjinguk* was and what it meant to Korea. In this regard, a featured article entitled "The Korean meaning of *seonjinguk*" noted that "in the Korean meaning of *seonjinguk* are well reflected what values the Koreans emphasize, that is, what national future they pursue" (*Chosun Ilbo*, 9 March 1972). As such, the concept of *seonjinguk* became a popular notion people widely used in regard to their social transformation and national future. Based on a survey, this article reported Koreans' perceptions of *seonjinguk* as follows:

> In Koreans' perceptions, *seonjinguk* can be summarized as countries such as the U.S. or Western countries, which are wealthy in economic aspects and advanced in art and culture, science and technology, and thinking and behaviors.
>
> (*Chosun Ilbo*, 9 March 1972)

According to this article, *seonjinguk* was perceived as a country advanced not only in the economy but also in culture and thinking. In general, however, the concept of *seonjinguk* mainly focused on the country's material aspects at the time, and there was a considerable level of resistance to the tendency of perceiving *seonjinguk* as advanced in cultural aspects. The article reported that those most frequently referred to as *seonjinguk* were the U.S., Japan, Britain, West Germany, and France. It pointed out that the Koreans hardly came up with Scandinavian countries when they thought of *seonjinguk*, and argued that these countries had many things to learn in Korea's modernization.

On the other hand, the article raised a need for a careful approach to *seonjinguk*, by mentioning that the Koreans tended to think about *seonjinguk* too optimistically. In this regard, it argues:

> Too positive perception of *seonjinguk* implies that we are ignorant of its negative aspects [...] In Koreans' view on *seonjinguk*, there is a possibility that we cannot carefully prevent such problems as the deterioration of living environments, which can be caused by wrong *seonjinhwa* [becoming advanced] or modernization (which have already been appearing in *seonjinguk*), and conflicts between classes, which are caused by ignoring distributional justice. This is the time when the national future, goal, and value for Korea should be re-established.
>
> (*Chosun Ilbo*, 9 March 1972)

This article also reported that some Koreans had included such countries as the Soviet Union and China in the category of *seonjinguk*. As such, some Koreans tended to think of *seonjinguk* as big countries. The inclusion of those countries that are not generally considered as *seonjinguk* today, shows a somewhat unstable aspect of the notion of *seonjinguk* at the time. This also implies that there was no consensus among the public on the concept of *seonjinguk*, although it was popularizing generally referring to Western countries.

National Identity and Goal in the Chosun Ilbo

The newspaper well reflected Koreans' confidence in economic development during the 1970s in regard to their national identity. Similar to presidential addresses, it tended to construct Korea's identity as *jungjinguk* (or developing country) in the 1970s.[11] This accompanied a transition of discursive focus from *hujinguk*, as in the context of escaping from "*hujinguk*," to *seonjinguk* as an achievable goal in the near future.

National opinion leaders actively promoted the need for catching up with *seonjinguk*, and the national desire was high for entering into the ranks of *seonjinguk* before the 1980s (*Chosun Ilbo*, 4 July 1973). Under the headline "The way to win *seonjinguk* is fighting spirit and hard effort," an opinion column written by a business leader emphasized that "as we are catching up with *seonjinguk* including our neighbor [Japan], we have to rapidly improve our level of technology and knowledge daily through more diligent learning, researching, and developing than them" (*Chosun Ilbo*, 1 January 1977).

Being set as a national goal and future, *seonjinguk* provided a reference of comparison in diverse fields. In the modernization process, the Koreans wanted to check their country's position on the developmental path by comparing it with *seonjinguk*. In this regard, one article wrote that "our country's maternal death rate is 317.3 out of 100,000, which is ten times that of *seonjinguk*" (*Chosun Ilbo*, 27 January 1978). Another article published around the same time pointed out that Seoul's traffic fatalities were 44 times those of *seonjinguk* (*Chosun Ilbo*, 24 January 1978). As such, *seonjinguk* played a role as a pivotal reference group in Korea's rapid economic development and national change.

In the newspaper as well, there appeared a tendency to define Korea's identity as being close to *seonjinguk* after the mid-1970s. In an article entitled "The status of the Korean economy has improved to already get into the range of *seonjinguk*," an expert on the economy argued that "Korea's economic development stage is in the process of entering into the circle of *seonjinguk* from the stage of *jungjinguk*" (*Chosun Ilbo*, 12 December 1975). In a similar vein, an article with the headline "Korea in the rank of *seonjinguk*" reported that "a special document of the U.S. Department of State recently revealed that Korea has gone up to the rank of *seonjinguk*, together with Brazil, Taiwan, and Mexico" (*Chosun Ilbo*, 22 June 1978).[12]

Conclusion

This chapter has introduced the forming and unfolding processes of the discourses of development and *seonjinguk* in Korea. Korea's developmentalism emerged as a dominant discourse for Korea's industrialization and modernization in historical circumstances, in which U.S.-led developmentalism emerged globally reflecting U.S. hegemony. In terms of the knowledge-power relationship, the rise of Korea's developmentalism was intertwined with the rise of Korea's developmental regime. In Park Chung-Hee's presidential addresses, there appeared a clear tendency to set development, modernization, and industrialization as the most important national values and goals. Park's addresses showed a departure from the worldview of the discourse of *munmyeong* mainly seen in Rhee Syngman's addresses in the previous period. Unlike his predecessor, who had tended to emphasize Korea's civilizational features, Park thoroughly problematized the poverty of the nation in the past and present, and used this as a main cause for his strong project for the "modernization of fatherland."

The discourse of *seonjinguk* arose as a representative developmental discourse, conceptualizing the goal of national development and modernization as *seonjinguk*. It made a binary distinction between *hujinguk* and *seonjinguk* on a linear developmental path, projecting negative values into the former and positive values into the latter. Based on this, it interpreted economic development and modernization as a transition from *hujinguk* to *seonjinguk*. In this way, the discourse of *seonjinguk* provided a concrete interpretative framework to the abstract developmental notion of the "modernization of fatherland."

The discourse of *seonjinguk* was Eurocentric as it idealized Western countries as *seonjinguk*, setting them as the reference point of Korea's development and social change. In terms of the genealogy of Korea's Eurocentrism, the rise of the discourse of *seonjinguk* accompanied the decline of the discourse of *munmyeong*. The discourse of *seonjinguk* was also nationalistic in the sense that it regarded the achievement of *seonjinguk* as the most important national historical duty. Reflecting the power of the developmental regime notably formed in the Park Chung-Hee era, it played a role of giving political legitimacy to the developmental regime. In practical terms, it contributed to Korea's economic development and modernization by drawing the people's consensus on the goal of *seonjinguk*.

The rise of the discourse of *seonjinguk* brought about a big change in the perceptions of national identity and the world. While Korea's identity had generally been defined as a *munmyeong-guk* of spirit and ethics within the framework of *munmyeong* in the Rhee Syngman era, it degraded to *hujinguk* in the framework of *seonjinguk* discourse. In comparison, Western countries, previously a *munmyeong-guk* of material with a violent propensity, came to be represented as advanced *seonjinguk* with which Korea should catch up. There reappeared a hierarchy between the West and Korea as the former had a temporal precedence in regard to the latter's development process.

The Koreans showed confidence in their achievements of economic development after the mid-1960s. Thus, a dominant perception of national identity in the 1970s was that Korea had entered into the ranks of *jungjinguk*. The frequency of the term "*seonjinguk*" greatly increased in the newspaper during this period, as the discursive focus moved from the "escape from *hujinguk*" to the "entry into the ranks of *seonjinguk*." After the mid-1970s, in particular, a notable national identity was that Korea was an upper-level *jungjinguk* facing the status of *seonjinguk* in the near future. In this context, the 1980s was set as the period of entering into the ranks of *seonjinguk*, and opinion leaders asked the people to make a hard effort to achieve this.

Notes

1 I have obtained 519 addresses by President Park Chung-Hee in the fields of politics/society, industry/economy, and culture/sports/tourism political/social issues, which are archived in the National Archives of Korea (www.pa.go.kr). Along with this, I have gathered 202 articles published between 1961 and 1979 from the *Chosun Ilbo* archive that contained the terms "*seonjinguk*" or "*hujinguk*" in their headlines. The presidential address is the text best showing ruling intent, and the major newspaper circulates mainstream public discourse. The growth of major newspapers including the *Chosun Ilbo* was notable after the late 1960s and their nature changed to media companies pursuing profit rather than "journalism for fair argument" (Kang J.-M., 2007). Thus, the analysis of presidential addresses and the *Chosun Ilbo* articles would show a good slice of the mainstream discursive situation at the time.

2 Lee B.-C. (1999) argues that the import substitution policy had not been replaced by the export-oriented policy but both were operating together in many cases, making the industrial policy of the 1960s the "two-way industrialization policy."

3 Compared with similar concepts such as the "developmental state" and the "developmental coalition," the "developmental regime" is a concept focusing on the overall social structure including various social forces in regard to the promotion of development. As such, it tries to see beyond the role of a certain type of the state or class relation (Cho H.-Y., 2000: 408–409).

4 In regard to this, a representative progressive intellectual, Paek N.-C. (2005: 290, 293), argues that "we do not need to be stingy about admitting Park Chung-Hee's 'intellectual property' as the creator of the 'Korean-style rapid growth model.'" In this sense, he designates Park Chung-Hee as "a contributor to 'unsustainable' development."

5 Park's nationalism as one of his ruling ideologies changed its focus over time. While it was mainly used for the regime's political legitimacy just after the military coup, it tended to be utilized for the cause of economic development in the Third Republic period (1963–1972), and for strengthening national identity to maintain his political power in the Fourth Republic period (1972–1979) (Lee W.-Y., 1991).

6 Lee D.-J. (2009: 105–106) cited foreign research showing that Korea was ranked 16th in a "socio-cultural index" focusing on literacy rate and national homogeneity, while it was ranked 60th in terms of income per capita, among 74 "developing countries" in 1961 when the 16 May coup occurred. Based on this, he mentioned that "there remained a possibility of establishing a totally different system, unlike Park Chung-Hee's negative perception of Korea that 'our 5,000 year old history had been, in short, that of continuous regression, coarseness, and stagnation.'"

7 Park addressed that "16 May was, in a word, a national struggle for this country's modernization" (16 May 1965). For the "modernization of fatherland," he suggested a three-step plan: Establishing grounds for an industrial country until 1966 (the end of the first Five-Year Economic Plan); achieving industrialization until 1971 (the end of the second Five-Year Economic Plan); and opening a period of "mass consumption" and accomplishing the "modernization of fatherland" until the late 1970s (around the end of the third Five-Year Economic Plan) (Heo E., 2007).

8 For discussions about modernization theory as a strategic and ideological discourse supporting U.S. hegemony under the auspices of the U.S. government, please refer to Latham (2000) and Park T.-G. (2004).

9 This contrasted with Rhee Syngman's attitude of designating Korea as a *munmyeong-guk* with a long history, distinguishing it from the newly independent countries after World War II.

10 Lee B.-C. (1998) argues that the Park government's announcement of heavy-chemical industrialization in January 1973 was politically motivated for national security and regime safety rather than following economic rationality. In comparison, Lee D.-J. (2009) interprets it as a kind of import-substitution strategy to overcome the limitations of industrialization centering on light industry. According to Yoon S.-W. (2006), it was mainly the tension in the political-economic relationship between Korea and the U.S., following the Nixon Doctrine and the decline of the U.S. economy, which motivated the launch of heavy-chemical industrialization including the nurturing of defense industry.

11 As in Park's presidential addresses, there appeared in public discourse as well a tendency to define Korea's identity as *jungjinguk* from the late 1960s (*Chosun Ilbo*, 14 January 1968, 21 January 1968).

12 In regard to this, another article introduced a foreign media view as follows: "The Journal of Commerce, a leading economic magazine in the U.S., had reported that Korea was expected to enter into the group of *seonjinguk* in ten years because of its success in economic development, and to join the OECD [Organisation for Economic Co-operation and Development] in five years" (*Chosun Ilbo*, 26 December 1975).

6 Change in the Discourse of *Seonjinguk*

The 1980s and the 1990s

Reflecting power and power relations, discourse pursues its own survival. In order to maintain a dominant status, a discourse has to change in response to the change in external circumstances. In this respect, a dominant discourse of society may be a discursive system best reflecting societal circumstances at a certain historical point. While maintaining its basic structure, the discourse of *seonjinguk* has delicately changed its connotations in the process of Korea's development. While the concepts of *seonjinguk* and *hujinguk* have been central in the discourse, their referents, social roles, and implications have not been the same across different historical periods.

This chapter examines the change of *seonjinguk* discourse in varying historical circumstances from 1980 to 1998. In the political aspect, 1980 was the year when the new military group led by Chun Doo-Hwan seized power, and 1998 was the time when Kim Young-Sam's "civilian government" finished its term amidst the severe "International Monetary Fund Crisis" in Korea.

This chapter aims to explain the delicate change in *seonjinguk* discourse by period, focusing on its main concepts and assumptions, self-national identity and worldview, and Eurocentric implications. It especially looks at how the connotations of the terms "*seonjinguk*" and "*hujinguk*," and the relationship between the two, differed by period. For this, it has analyzed articles in the *Chosun Ilbo* published between 1 January 1980 and 25 February 1998.[1]

This chapter examines, first, the characteristics of Korea's development discourse and *seonjinguk* discourse from 1980 to the early 1990s in the context of the global rise of neoliberalism. Next, it explores the characteristics and social roles of the discourse in the 1990s in relation to the Kim Young-Sam administration's promotion of *segyehwa* discourse.

Internationalism and Idealizing *Seonjinguk*: 1980–1992

In the 1980s, neoliberalism arose globally as a dominant discourse. It was widely promoted by advanced industrial countries, such as Margaret Thatcher's Britain and Ronald Reagan's U.S., and began to earn global significance (Chang H.-J., 2008). Neoliberal principles were adopted by international institutions, such as the International Monetary Fund (IMF) and the World

Bank, for their structural adjustment programs. Neoliberalism was also utilized as a discursive force to drive the transformation of international political economic circumstances. The rise of neoliberalism accompanied the decline of protectionism in the national and global economies (McMichael, 2008). Under the neoliberal ideas of an open market and liberalized trade, the national government was asked to take a back seat in international economic activities. Pressure was put on national economies to open to the international market.

In Korea, the Chun Du-Hwan administration inherited much of the previous Park Chung-Hee's legacy of the pursuit of national economic development tinged with anti-communism and nationalism. In this period, however, international pressure to open up Korea's market intensified, and the international factor greatly affected national economic strategies and policies. As other industrial countries targeted the so-called newly industrializing countries (NICs) for market opening, the Chun regime partly changed its developmental strategy to reflect the open-door policy. For instance, the Chun government launched the "Five Year Plan for the Liberalization of Import" in 1983 to increase the liberalization rate of imports to 95% by 1988, while reforming the tariff system to reduce the protection of domestic industry (Kim J.-G., 2012).

The feature of the Korean developmental state, which was established by the previous Park Chung-Hee regime, gradually weakened with the rise of neoliberalism. The belief spread that national development was to be made mainly by the voluntary economic activities of the private sector, rather than by the state's top-down-style mobilization of resources. A need for strategic transition from "guided" development to privately led development became significant. In terms of the power relationship between the state and capital, the 1980s began to recognize the power of capital. It was the period when capitalists, who had been nurtured and had grown under the auspices of the state, began to ascend to retrieve economic hegemony from the state (Seo J.-J., 1991).

The Korean economy maintained rapid growth in the 1980s as well (Table 6.1 and Figure 6.1). Except for the negative growth in 1980, it maintained 9.9% average growth in gross domestic product (GDP) from 1981 to 1989. This was a very high growth rate comparable to the 10% rate of the 1960s and the 1970s. From 1980 to 1989, the GDP of Korea increased about 3.8 times from $64.9 billion to $243.6 billion, and its per capita income grew about 3.4 times from $1,686 to $5,718. As for the industrial sector, the growth in infrastructure facilities was notable, such as electricity, gas, and the water supply.

In regard to Korea's development discourse, the 1980s witnessed the expansion of internationalism tinged with neoliberalism in the discourse. The consideration of international circumstances and global trends greatly increased in the Korean discourse of national development. Eurocentric universalism connoted in internationalism also intensified in the discourse.[2]

Table 6.1 Korea's Main Economic Indicators in the 1980s

Indicator by year	*1980*	*1981*	*1982*	*1983*	*1984*	*1985*	*1986*	*1987*	*1988*	*1989*
GDP (nominal, $ billion)	64.9	72.4	77.7	87	96.6	100.2	115.5	146.2	197.2	243.6
GNI per capita (nominal, $)	1,686.0	1,842.0	1,957.0	2,154.0	2,354.0	2,400.0	2,742.0	3,467.0	4,653.0	5,718.0
GDP real growth rate (%)	–1.7	7.2	8.3	13.2	10.4	7.7	11.2	12.5	11.9	7.0
Agriculture and fisheries (%)	–16.6	15.7	7.8	9.3	-2.8	6.1	5.4	–4.4	9.5	–0.2
Mining (%)	–1.9	8.7	3.7	16.7	18.8	7.1	15.5	19.2	12.7	4.1
Manufacturing (%)	–1.8	9.2	4.6	17.2	19.5	7.2	15.9	20.0	13.1	4.3
Electricity, gas, and water (%)	7.0	15.5	5.9	29.7	26.0	19.4	26.4	12.1	9.7	11.8
Construction (%)	–2.9	–7.2	15.4	21.4	5.5	5.4	3.4	9.9	8.1	12.2
Services (%)	5.6	5.8	9.3	9.9	9.2	8.7	10.2	12.0	12.4	9.2

Source: Bank of Korea, Statistics Korea

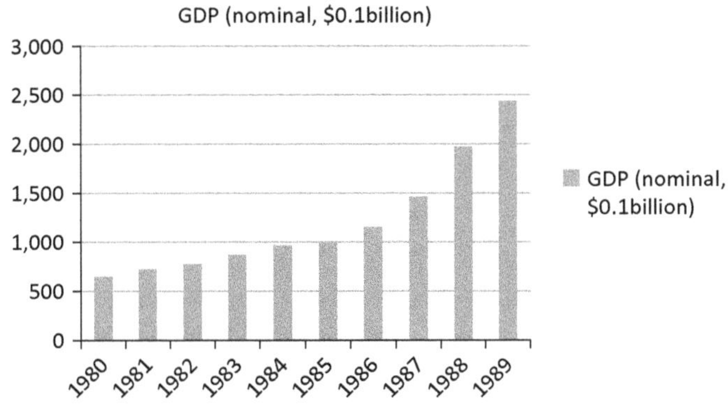

Figure 6.1 Change in Korea's GDP in the 1980s
Source: Bank of Korea, Statistics Korea

Seonjinguk *and the NICs*

With the rise of internationalism, the tendency became notable in Korean discourse to ask whether activities and phenomena in the diverse areas of Korean society were suitable under "international criteria." As for the economic sphere, for instance, the argument for a need to meet "global standards" became conspicuous. The discourse of "global standards" dispersed over the various fields of Korean life. Around the 1988 Seoul Olympic Games, in particular, the argument for becoming "*seonjin simin*" (advanced citizen) came to be widely promoted. That kind of argument asked for a Korean behavioral change to meet the expectations of the "world" in a broad range of social life.[3] In this way, Korea's diverse areas were brought over to the "international" sphere in terms of discourse.

The use of the terms *seonjinguk* and *hujinguk* in the early 1980s was increasingly related to international affairs. In many cases, the concept of *seonjinguk* referred to an international group that was discerned from *hujinguk, gaebal-dosang-guk* (developing country), or *jesamsegye* (the Third World). The Organisation for Economic Co-operation and Development (OECD) and the Group of 7 (G-7) were most frequently referred to as a *seonjinguk* group, in contrast to such groups as the Group of 77, a group of *gaebal-dosang-guk* or *jesamsegye.*

Korea maintained a clear stance as a country of the NICs or *gaebal-dosang-guk* vis-à-vis *seonjinguk*, recognizing different political-economic interests between the two. In this respect, newspaper articles argued that the intentions and practices of *seonjinguk* in international affairs should be approached with caution. They frequently criticized *seonjinguk*'s pressure on Korea in international trade. An article entitled "*Seonjinguk*'s hypersensitivity," for instance, argued:

> However, as the share has noticeably increased, which leading developing countries such as Korea, Taiwan, and Singapore take in the world trade

> volume, the council of the OECD that is a group of *seonjinguk* has shown a move from 1978 to revoke preferential tariffs and trade statuses, which have usually been given to *hujinguk*, from six leading developing countries including Korea by classifying them separately as the NICs.
>
> (*Chosun Ilbo*, 11 March 1984)

This article identifies Korea, Taiwan, and Singapore as "leading developing countries," and distinguishes them from "*seonjinguk.*" It argues that *seonjinguk* made a move to guard against those countries' economic growth, implying a different international development environment from that of the 1950s–1960s when *seonjinguk*'s support of global development was widely proposed. This article indicates that the economic growth of those "leading developing countries" including Korea did not square with *seonjinguk* interests.

In a similar vein, another article criticizes the G-6's Venetian declaration, arguing that the declaration is virtually *seonjinguk* targeting of the NICs for their own interests:

> The "economic declaration" of the summit and the joint declaration of the G-6 must be targeting Korea and Taiwan, Hong Kong, and Singapore, which have been steadily growing in Asia, [...] even though they do not point out the names of newly industrializing countries [...] With this kind of declaration, *seonjin-daeguk* [big *seonjinguk*] have probably demonstrated their solidarity by creating a target.
>
> (*Chosun Ilbo*, 17 June 1987)

Here *seonjinguk* is described as a group of countries, acting together to protect their economic interests.

The cautious approach to *seonjinguk* was not limited to international political-economic affairs. Many articles pointed out *seonjinguk*'s bad behavior towards *hujinguk* or *gaebal-dosang-guk* in environmental and social fields. When a gas leak incident occurred in India, for instance, an article criticized that it was a tragedy related to *seonjinguk*'s intentional transfer of polluter industries into *hujinguk* (*Chosun Ilbo*, 7 December 1984). Similarly, an opinion column argued for Korea's awareness not to import polluted materials from *seonjinguk* (*Chosun Ilbo*, 12 January 1985).

In terms of international trade, *seonjinguk* was considered a group of countries putting pressure on Korea to open up its market. As *seonjinguk*'s pressure on market opening increased, debates about market opening notably appeared in newspaper articles. In this regard, there was a tendency to regard market opening as a kind of necessary condition for entering into the group of *seonjinguk*. This linkage between market opening and the achievement of the status of *seonjinguk* was appropriated by those who tended to think of market opening as inevitable. In this regard, there appeared an attitude in the governmental sector to yield to international pressure and gradually to open up Korea's market to the outside.

However, there clearly appeared criticisms and concerns about the market opening. An editorial entitled "Is it *seonjinguk* only if open?" (*Chosun Ilbo*, 1 November 1985), for instance, reported that the Korean government had set a plan to open its market "at the level of *seonjinguk*" by 1988 due to pressure from the U.S. It expressed a concern about the market opening, saying "opening must not go too far." As such, the discourse of *seonjinguk* was, in some cases, appropriated by the government for its promotion of open-market policy but, as the article above showed, there was a considerable degree of psychological resistance to being open to the international stage.

Yet, this kind of resistance to international pressure and the government's open policy got weaker, and the discourse of *seonjinguk* was frequently utilized for the cause of Korea's "internationalization." As controversies over market opening intensified, the arguments relating market opening to *seonjinguk* also became notable, such as: "*Seonjinguk* has the high level of market opening" or "market opening is a condition for *seonjinguk*."

Chun Doo-Hwan's Political Use

The discourse of *seonjinguk* was utilized by ruling groups for their political interests. Taking power through such bloody events as the 12 December 1979 coup and the Gwangju Massacre, the Chun administration seriously lacked political legitimacy from the beginning. In the process of massive democratic movements against the Chun regime, the discourse of democracy arose as a powerful resistant discourse, enough to override the discursive power of dominant groups' developmentalism (Cho H.-Y., 2003: 66). While the Korean economy maintained high growth through Chun's term, the antigovernment movements for democracy intensified.

By emphasizing the national historical duty of achieving *seonjinguk*, the ruling groups implied that the massive pro-democratic movements were creating confusion and division to weaken national power. The need to achieve *seonjinguk* was more widely promoted by political leaders in the mid- and late 1980s when the pro-democratic movements were getting broader and stronger. They argued that the antigovernment movements were interrupting the nation's pursuit of *seonjinguk*.

Like his predecessor, throughout his presidency President Chun Doo-Hwan continuously mentioned a national need to join the group of *seonjinguk*. He argued that the country was successfully cruising toward *seonjinguk* and its achievement would be possible in the near future. Confronting massive antigovernment movements, he insisted that national unity and harmony, instead of division and conflict, were needed for the nation's journey to *seonjinguk*.

It is interesting to note that his use of the concept of *seonjinguk* became more frequent in 1987 when his power was in a serious crisis. In March 1987, for instance, as many as three articles in our data reported Chun's emphasis on the achievement of *seonjinguk*. In one article, he mentioned that:

> We have now come to grab the doorknob for entering into the group of *seonjinguk* by virtue of the achievements we made in the past six years. Based on these, we have to make more effort this year to become a grand leading part of world history.
>
> (*Chosun Ilbo*, 5 March 1987)

The very next day, he said that "we will necessarily become *seonjinguk* after transferring the government peacefully next year and successfully hosting the Olympics with united power" (*Chosun Ilbo*, 6 March 1987). About a week later, he maintained that "we have now finished the preparation for heading for *seonjinguk*, having overcome various hardships in the past six years by uniting all people's minds and powers" (*Chosun Ilbo*, 13 March 1987). In this way, he utilized the national goal of *seonjinguk* as a cause for national unity at a time when his power was seriously challenged by the people's massive demonstrations.

Facing the people's resistance, Korean ruling groups, which had been historically formed in close relationship with foreign powers, might have had more psychological recourse to *seonjinguk* than to its nationals. However, Chun's utilization of *seonjinguk* discourse to neutralize protests was not as effective as he had expected, and he had to declare in June 1987 the acceptance of many conditions for democratization that were requested by the people.

Idealization of **Seonjinguk** *and Korea's Pride*

While there was wariness in Korean society about *seonjinguk* as a powerful actor on the international stage, *seonjinguk* in the imagination of society became further idealized in this period. The advanced character of *seonjinguk* came to be no longer limited to certain material aspects, such as industry and technology, but was broadened to spiritual aspects. Thus, *seonjinguk* was represented not only as materially prosperous, but also culturally mature. In this way, the *seonjinguk* discourse gradually encroached on the old assumption of Eastern civilization's spiritual superiority vis-à-vis the West. The Koreans' cultural pride vis-à-vis the West became steadily undermined in the idealizing process of *seonjinguk*.

The idealization of the West was promoted by high-profile intellectuals. In an opinion column entitled "Things that we don't have," Kim Dong-Gil, then professor at Yonsei University, wrote about the differences in everyday life between Korea and the West, as follows:

> In the West, men and women in the streets generally dress far better than us. This does not mean expensive clothes but that they dress plainly fitting to their bodies in a fancy way by coordinating colors. What an artistically touching thing is to be fitting well [...] The Westerners also make home better than us. Even if they make home in a one-room apartment, it has all that is needed and all things are positioned in the right place, which is

> both convenient and beautiful [...] Isn't it that we rarely have cultural life? [...] A reason why I somewhat hurt my self-respect in seeing the Westerners is that their rich common sense and rationality are lacking with us who are proud of that, so to speak, "light is from the East." I don't know if light came from the East 5,000 or 3,000 years ago, but it is clearly not the case now.
>
> (*Chosun Ilbo*, 19 January 1986)

This does not mean that there was no resistance to the national aspiration for *seonjinguk*. Rather, the idealizing process of *seonjinguk* or the West was continuously in tension with traditional perspectives valuing spiritual and cultural aspects. The national pursuit of *seonjinguk* was often criticized for its material focus. Various side-effects of material development were also well recognized. In this view, *seonjinguk* was still considered in a limited sense mainly as industrially advanced, e.g., *seonjin gongeop-guk* (advanced industrial country), which carried various negative aspects with it. One opinion column, for instance, pointed out that:

> We frequently hear and see the term "*seonjin*" recently. However, it seems that the "meaning of *seonjin*" is mainly weighed on the criteria of material improvements, such as the increase in national wealth, the growth in national income, export growth, a high level of mass consumption, the improvement in productivity, the promotion of industrialization, the nurturing of the leisure industry, high buildings, the increase in private cars, the expansion of paved roads, and so forth.
>
> (*Chosun Ilbo*, 16 November 1983)

On this basis, this article emphasized non-material values, such as "greed control" and "to practice the wisdom of ancestors to share even a piece of bean."

In a similar vein, an opinion column written by a female artist mentioned that "it is said that when it becomes *seonjinguk*, crimes increase and thus people's concerns deepen while new buildings are going higher and cultural events are getting diverse" (*Chosun Ilbo*, 11 November 1984). Some expressed more direct concerns about Korea's efforts to become *seonjinguk*. A featured article entitled "The culture and things of *seonjinguk* ... are they really all 'good things'?" argued that blind acceptance of foreign materials and cultures should be avoided, and that the recovery of pride in Korean tradition and culture was important (*Chosun Ilbo*, 1 January 1983). It acknowledged that *seonjinguk*, mainly as an industrial being, had both advantages and disadvantages associated with industrialization.

Some articles contested the concept of *seonjinguk* in relation to Koreans' national identity and pride. Under the headline "A country having a lot of traditional cultures is *seonjinguk* ... let's have spiritual pride," an opinion column written by Han Young-Woo, then professor at Seoul National University, pointed out that:

> In regard to a country's level or wealth, one cannot easily designate *seonjinguk* or *hujinguk* just based on visible material. Spiritual wealth should be included in it. A country having a lot of precious cultural traditions cannot be called a *hujin-jeogin* (backward) country even if its material life is somewhat backward [...] We have frequently heard our country is *jungjinguk* or *gaebal-dosang-guk* [...] As long as we have confidence and pride in traditional cultures, our cultural heritage can be globalized to any extent, and this may be the biggest potential wealth that we have [...] [Our country] is a country that has far more historical cultural advantages than the so-called *seonjinguk* that we are now trying hard to catch up with [...] [In the past] we never lost pride even for a moment for ourselves that we were *seonjinguk*.
>
> (*Chosun Ilbo*, 11 March 1986)

The way that this column article views Korea and the West is very different from that of Professor Kim's article above. First of all, it criticizes the tendency to distinguish between *seonjinguk* and *hujinguk* by material criteria. It argues that the country with affluent spiritual resources is not *hujinguk*, although it may be deficient in the material aspect. On these grounds, it expresses discomfort at the tendency to categorize Korea as "*jungjinguk*" or "*gaebal dosang-guk*." The column argues that this kind of identity ignores Korea's "potential wealth" of affluent tradition and culture, which may cause the effect of limiting Korean people's own capacity. On these grounds, it goes on to suggest deconstructing the discursive hierarchy between Korea and *seonjinguk*. It emphasizes that Korea is a country with more historical and cultural resources than *seonjinguk* and, thus, that the Koreans should have the pride of *seonjinguk* for themselves.

Those characteristics of the 1980s *seonjinguk* discourse generally continued until the early 1990s, the period of the Roh Tae-Woo government. It was notable, by the way, that the tendency to idealize and blindly pursue *seonjinguk* gradually strengthened, while the resistance to this weakened. This tendency became clearer in the mid-1990s with the rise of "*segyehwa*" (globalization) discourse promoted by the Kim Young-Sam government.

"*Segyehwa*" and *Seonjinguk* Discourse: 1993–1997

The Korean economy maintained rapid growth in the 1990s (Table 6.2). The real growth rate of GDP from 1990 to 1996, just before the "IMF Crisis," was 8.5% on average. During this period, GDP had grown about two times from \$279.3 billion in 1990 to \$597.9 billion in 1996. Gross national income (GNI) per capita had also grown about two times, from \$6,505 in 1990 to \$13,077 in 1996.

Korea in the 1990s was generally considered to be in need of different national development strategies, as it was regarded as having achieved successful modernization in the past, e.g., both industrialization and

Table 6.2 Korea's Main Economic Indicators in the 1990s

Indicator by year	*1990*	*1991*	*1992*	*1993*	*1994*	*1995*	*1996*	*1997*	*1998*	*1999*
GDP (nominal, $ billion)	279.3	325.6	350	386.3	455.5	556.3	597.9	557.6	374.9	485
GNI per capita (nominal, $)	6,505.0	7,508.0	7,983.0	8,720.0	10,168.0	12,282.0	13,077.0	12,059.0	7,989.0	10,282.0
GDP real growth rate (%)	9.8	10.4	6.2	6.8	9.2	9.6	7.6	5.9	–5.5	11.3
Agriculture and fisheries (%)	–5.6	3.2	9.0	–4.2	0.1	7.0	4.3	4.5	–7.4	5.4
Mining (%)	11.1	12.0	5.6	6.8	11.5	12.7	8.3	5.5	–7.6	21.0
Manufacturing (%)	11.6	12.3	6.0	6.9	11.5	12.9	8.4	5.6	–7.5	21.2
Electricity, gas, and water (%)	16.2	10.6	13.7	12.6	13.2	6.5	10.8	8.8	0.8	10.8
Construction (%)	23.6	11.5	–1.6	8.8	4.6	5.2	6.5	0.9	–11.5	–7.4
Services (%)	9.3	10.2	8.0	8.2	9.5	9.0	7.6	6.7	–2.7	8.9

Source: Bank of Korea, Statistics Korea

democratization. At the global level, the neoliberal trend was intensifying with the popularization of globalization discourse. In these circumstances, there arose a need to "upgrade Korea" to effectively meet the global challenge to go beyond the past achievements of modernization. In this context, the Kim Young-Sam administration was inaugurated with an ambition to drastically reform the country to be globally competitive. It actively embraced the international discourse of globalization and attempted to transform the country to be compatible with the global trend, on the assumption that the preexisting socio-economic system constructed through the rapid modernization period was not suitable for the new era of globalization.

President Kim widely promoted the slogan of "*sinhanguk changjo*" (the creation of New Korea) in his early term for the national goal of *seonjinguk*. He actively employed the discourse of international competition for the purpose of his reform policies. Supposing Korea to face harsh international competition, he insisted that it would collapse just on the threshold of the rank of *seonjinguk* without curing "*hanguk-byeong*" (the problem of Korea) through the strong reformation drive. In this regard, Kang M.-K. (2000: 444) argues that "reformation" and "competitiveness" were the "discourse-constituents of 'New Korea' in 1993."

In terms of governmental policy, the Kim Young-Sam administration accelerated open-door and liberalization policies on the premise that "central planning apparatus was unnecessary and resource distribution was proper to be left to market, given our economy's development phase" (Kim J.-G., 2012: 55–56). The government accelerated the liberalization of imports by drastically lowering tariff rates and removing the measures limiting imports. The Kim government promoted foreign direct investment (FDI) by opening up the service industry, while reducing the number of restricted items for FDI from 195 in late 1995 to 52 in late 1997 (Kim J.-G., 2012). It also tried to deregulate the financial industry and open up its capital market full-scale.

"Global Standards" and Seonjinguk

In his new year address in 1995, Kim Young-Sam promulgated a need for *segyehwa* (globalization) as a way to win international competition by defining the international circumstances as both crisis and opportunity. In this situation, the tendency to judge Korean society by "global" criteria further intensified. While the *segyehwa* discourse was intended as an active response to the global discourse of globalization, it also contributed to accepting various politically charged international neoliberal policies as "global standards," especially those promoted by the U.S. (Seong N.-S., 2001; Cho Y.-C., 2001; Kim Y.-B., 2003).

In this regard, another notable aspect of Korea's development in this period was the change in the nature of its developmental regime into that which was actively willing to meet "global standards." In Cho H.-Y.'s (2003: 84) terms, this was a transition from the old developmental regime to a "neo-developmental regime," which was based upon the discourse of *segyehwa* as a neo-modernization discourse. In terms of the developmental discourse, the transition occurred from protective developmentalism to open-door developmentalism (*ibid.*). Lee G.-I. (2003) designates the transition as that from a developmental state to a "neoliberal competitive state," which prioritized neoliberal values for obtaining competitiveness in international competition. As for the crisis of the conventional developmental state, Yoon S.-W. (2005) notes three main factors: The pressure from the world system, democratization, and the growth in private capital, which reflect the changes in the developmental state's relationships with the world system, civil society, and capital, respectively. According to him, the developmental regime virtually collapsed by the Kim administration's pursuit of liberalization and opening up of the finance sector in the early 1990s (Yoon S.-W., 2005).

The development of the discourse of *seonjinguk* during the 1990s was deeply influenced by the Kim Young-Sam administration's launch of a strong drive for reformation on a broad range of national affairs. In particular, the reformation drive that was promoted under the banner of *segyehwa* played an important role in characterizing the discourse of *seonjinguk* at the time. The government carried out various reformation policies under the cause of enhancing national competitiveness to meet "global standards" in a variety of areas.

In terms of the discourse of *seonjinguk*, the Kim administration approached Korea's domestic and foreign affairs with a national identity of "almost *seonjinguk*." Following the hosting of the Seoul Olympic Games in the late 1980s, a new political, social atmosphere having appeared in the early and mid-1990s characterized by various events gave Koreans confidence in forming the identity of "almost *seonjinguk*," such as the establishment of a democratic civilian government, the plan to join the OECD, the popularization of trips abroad, and so forth. Thus, discursive foci were put on the need to make vigorous efforts to get the nation into the ranks of solid *seonjinguk*.

In the mid-1990s, the desire to achieve the status of *seonjinguk* appeared to be far stronger than at any previous time. More Koreans felt that the aspiration had become supported by substantial national political economic power and thus that the achievement of the national goal came to be a more tangible and realistic historical condition. While *seonjinguk* as a national vision had tended to be promoted mainly by a relatively small number of opinion leaders in previous periods, its necessity was more widely shared by a broader range of the population in the Kim Young-Sam era. Reflecting popular sentiments about the end of the century, such slogans as "achieving *seonjinguk* in the upcoming twenty-first century" became widespread (*Chosun Ilbo*, 24 July 1995). In this situation, the popularity of the concept of *seonjinguk* further increased among the public as it was used in more diverse areas, such as education, labor, environment, health, traffic, etc. Beyond the fields of the economy and technology, virtually every corner of the nation was asked to be engaged in the transformation towards *seonjinguk*. In this respect, the discourse of *seonjinguk* greatly strengthened its hegemonic status as a dominant way to represent the national self and interpret the world.

In those circumstances, the concept of *seonjinguk* underwent some notable changes in its connotation and use. First, its use in the abstract increased, in which the referent of the term *seonjinguk* was not specified. Rather than being a specific entity, it tended to exist as an image and a representation, on which Koreans' various positive values were projected. This was somewhat unique in this period, as the concept of *seonjinguk* in previous periods had tended to be used in the concrete type referring to specific countries, international organizations, or international status in certain limited fields such as international trade. As the scope of the use of the concept expanded, its connotation became more abstract and broader.

Second, in relation to the increase in its abstraction, the image of *seonjinguk* became more idealized. Moving beyond a shortcut for *seonjin gongeop-guk* (advanced industrial country) in a limited sense, it tended to be represented as an advanced country in virtually every field. *Seonjinguk* was not just an advanced country in certain limited fields such as the economy and technology, but an advanced country in every way, including culturally, which had been a sphere in which the Koreans had maintained a sense of pride over Western industrial countries.

The negative aspects of *seonjinguk* or *seonjin gongeop-guk* that had frequently been recognized in previous periods were rarely pointed out in this period, such as dehumanization, damage to the environment, the increase in crime, etc. Challenges to the concept of *seonjinguk* and to the designation of Korea's identity within the discourse of *seonjinguk* relatively weakened and became marginalized. Western countries arose as role models by which various aspects of Korean society were to be evaluated. Western models tended to be regarded as universal, and the historical and contextual differences between them and Korea tended to be ignored.[4] The idealization of *seonjinguk* accompanies the increase of self-dissatisfaction and, thus, Korea's self-respect often shrank vis-à-vis *seonjinguk*.

Third, as national identity had shifted from *gaebal-dosang-guk* or the NICs to "almost *seonjinguk*" in the substantial sense, the perception of conflicting interests between Korea and *seonjinguk* notably abated. There was rather a strong tendency to consider that *seonjinguk*'s demands and expectations should be met in order for Korea to join the *seonjinguk* club. Groups of major industrial countries, such as the G-7, were mainly termed as the group of "*seonjinguk*" instead of other terms such as *seobang-guk* (Western countries).[5]

Criticism of *seonjinguk* policies and strategies in international affairs greatly waned too. Rather, there appeared a tendency to regard *seonjinguk* as the central promoter of the inevitable global trend that Korea had to follow to achieve the status of *seonjinguk*. With regard to the pressure of market opening from *seonjinguk*, for instance, one article argued that "liberalization and opening up to the outside are already irreversible general trends of international society," while emphasizing that "the problem is to quickly prepare policies and institutions for ourselves that are fitting for the era of liberalization and opening" (*Chosun Ilbo*, 29 March 1995). The requests from *seonjinguk* or international institutions, which were often perceived as a kind of "pressure" in previous periods, came to be frequently regarded as "global standards." The "global standards" played a measure to gauge the degree of advancement or backwardness of Korean society.

Korea's Identity and the Perception of a National Goal

As for national identity, many articles assessed that Korea had been moving successfully towards the status of *seonjinguk*. It was the late 1970s when the identity of Korea as "just in front of the *seonjinguk* group" first appeared notably in the public sphere. While this national identity had been presented by a relatively small number of opinion leaders as an optimistic interpretation of national status, it was far more popularized in the general public during the 1990s. In this regard, an opinion column entitled "National character and *seonjinguk*" argued that "the dawn of the era of *seonjinguk* is just about to begin now, clearly separating from the past" (*Chosun Ilbo*, 20 December 1995).

Building a full-fledged *seonjinguk* was considered a more tangible national vision that could be achieved in the near future. This phenomenon became far more distinct after the mid-1990s, when Korea joined the OECD in December 1996. As OECD membership was considered a status of *seonjinguk*, various governmental policies were prepared to cope with Korea's entrance into the rank of *seonjinguk* (*Chosun Ilbo*, 29 March 1995, 6 June 1995). Discursive foci were put on transforming the nation to meet the "criteria" of *seonjinguk*, which were actually created by the Koreans themselves, to push the national move towards a full-fledged *seonjinguk*. In this regard, one article argued that "as Korea has become an economic *seonjinguk* by joining the OECD, shouldn't we become a *seonjinguk* in the field of broadcasting?" (*Chosun Ilbo*, 24 November 1997). As such, even with OECD membership, various areas and aspects of Korea were considered not yet to reach those of sound *seonjinguk*.

Various campaign-style series of articles appeared in the mass media, which argued for learning from *seonjinguk* and upgrading Korea to *seonjinguk*. They covered a broad range of fields including cultural heritage, civil awareness, the environment, energy saving, traffic problems, and so forth. Becoming an upgraded country and *seonjin simin* (advanced citizen) arose as an urgent problem (*Chosun Ilbo*, 1 January 1997). Virtually every corner of the nation came to be compared with *seonjinguk* by the newspaper for the cause of building sound *seonjinguk*. *Seonjinguk* became a stronger reference point by which various aspects of Korea were judged and evaluated, and the authority of *seonjinguk* became far stronger.

An opinion column written by the president of a private university delivers well the national atmosphere in the mid-1990s regarding *seonjinguk*:

> We all are aspiring to become *seonjinguk* in the upcoming twenty-first century, and we should necessarily become *seonjinguk* [...] Our country has reached the threshold of *seonjinguk* by achieving miraculous economic development to have GDP per capita of $10,000 just in front of us in late 1995, from the status of *hujinguk* that had GDP per capita of $80 in the 1960s. However, *seonjinguk* does not only mean to have big trade amount economically, to have a lot of productive facilities, or to have affluent mineral resources. Rather, a country that can create new technology and invent new products, and which has the capacity to raise high-tech industries competitive worldwide is a true economic *seonjinguk* [...] After all, it is impossible for our country to head for *seonjinguk* without the reformation of technology, living [standards], and education. It would be the right way to solidify the road for *seonjinguk* to nurture human resources that have fair personality valuing frankness for one's life, diligence and the spirit of sacrifice serving for neighbors, language ability to meet the high-tech era of international competition, and computer ability.
>
> (*Chosun Ilbo*, 24 July 1995)

The writer of this article argues that the reformation of Korean society is required in technology, life, education, etc., while defining *seonjinguk* as the country that "can create new technology and invent new products, and which has the capacity to raise high-tech industries." In this respect, *seonjinguk* in Korean society is not just a country that is rich economically but a country that has various features that are desired by Korean society in its development process. With a perception that reformation in the areas external to the economy is closely related to the improvement of the economy, the article reflects the assumption of modernization theory that society's cultural aspects, such as values and beliefs, decide economic modernization. Furthermore, the writer of the article endorses the status of *seonjinguk* by implying that frankness, fair personality, and the spirit of sacrifice are the virtues of *seonjinguk*. As such, the Koreans' aspired values are projected into the concept of *seonjinguk*.

On the other hand, the aspiration for *seonjinguk* strengthened a perception of increasing competition in the "globalizing" world. As for a weakness of Korea's products in international trade, one article worried that "foreign products are rapidly driving away national products with the opening of the domestic market that has been closed" (*Chosun Ilbo*, 4 April 1993). In terms of Korea's performance compared with its main competitors in a race for *seonjinguk*, another article reported that "our country recorded the lowest growth among the Asian NICs last year," and that "only we failed to enter into *seonjinguk* among the four Asian dragons, and now fell into a situation of being classified in the same group as Malaysia and Thailand" (*Chosun Ilbo*, 11 March 1993).

Conclusion

This chapter has examined the change in the discourse of *seonjinguk* from the 1980s to the 1990s. In the 1980s, neoliberalism emerged globally and the pressure on the national governments increased to open up their markets to the outside under the cause of free trade. Under international pressure, the Korean developmental regime centered on the Chun Doo-Hwan administration began to consider the inevitability of opening up Korea's market. With a national identity as one of the NICs, Korea considered the group of *seonjinguk* as having different interests from Korea's in international affairs. The promoters of market opening utilized the discourse of *seonjinguk* by arguing in such a way that "market opening is a condition for *seonjinguk*," which incurred controversy over neoliberal policies.

On the other hand, the concept of *seonjinguk*, an advance mainly in the field of industry in the previous period, broadened to include other fields beyond industry. With the increase of internationalism, there appeared a tendency to idealize *seonjinguk*. Around the 1988 Seoul Olympic Games, in particular, there were arguments that various fields of the nation should meet the expectations of the world, and the mass media launched various series of articles to learn from *seonjinguk*.

However, challenges to and criticism of *seonjinguk* also appeared notably. Some intellectuals criticized the national pursuit of *seonjinguk* for being biased towards material aspects, while pointing out that *seonjinguk* was not a desirable state as it resulted in serious problems accompanied by industrialization. In this regard, they argued that the Koreans should take pride in their cultural heritage, instead of having a deficient identity vis-à-vis *seonjinguk*. Yet, this critical attitude about *seonjinguk* gradually weakened. Meanwhile, the Chun Doo-Hwan regime tried to utilize the discourse of *seonjinguk* for its political interests to ask for the nation's unity and harmony amidst the intensifying massive antigovernment demonstrations in the mid-1980s.

The 1990s witnessed the intensification of Eurocentric universalism in the discourse of *seonjinguk* as the Korean developmental regime actively adopted the global discourse of neoliberalism and globalization. Under such slogans as "*sinhanguk changjo*" and "*segyehwa*," the Kim Young-Sam administration vigorously promoted the acceptance of "global standards" as a way to achieve *seonjinguk*. This was premised upon the past-style national development not being suitable to Korea's current status in a globalizing world.

The developmental regime boosted the drastic reformation of Korea for *seonjinguk*, and every corner of the country came to be compared with *seonjinguk*. With Korea's membership of the OECD in 1996, the Koreans felt as if their country had become almost *seonjinguk*. Reflecting the sense of the end of the century, opinion leaders strongly promoted national aspiration for achieving sound *seonjinguk* in the upcoming twenty-first century. In this process, the concept of *seonjinguk* became greatly abstracted and idealized, and an epistemic hierarchy between Korea and *seonjinguk* appeared to be manifest.

Notes

1 For analysis, I have used articles in the *Chosun Ilbo*, the oldest leading conservative newspaper in Korea, which has reflected mainstream developmentalist voices. Using the search function of the *Chosun Ilbo* archive, I have obtained 642 articles containing the term *seonjinguk* in the headline (257 cases for 1980–1992; 385 cases for 1993–1998), and 55 articles with *hujinguk* in their headline from 1980–1998 (22 cases for 1980–1992; 33 cases for 1993–1998). In these periods, the increase in the term *seonjinguk* is especially noticeable in the Kim Young-Sam era.

2 In the context of criticizing Eurocentrism contained in universalism, Wallerstein (2006) distinguishes "European universalism" that reflects European values and interests, from "universal universalism" for the whole of humankind.

3 To become *seonjin simin* was a major issue in the 1990s as well. For instance, the *Chosun Ilbo* (1 January 1997) featured a series of articles under the headline "Let's become *seonjin simin*." In this series, the newspaper campaigned for a sense of public order, such as keeping traffic order, showing restaurant etiquette, etc.

4 With regard to this, it is interesting to see that an article interpreted a low turnout of Korean voters in an election as "*seonjinguk-hyeong* (*seonjinguk*-style) voting tendency" (*Chosun Ilbo*, 21 June 1991).

5 Until the 1980s, such groups of countries as the G-7 and the OECD were often referred to as groups of "*seobang-guk*" (Western countries), "*seonjin gongeop-guk*" (advanced industrial country), or "*seonjin gaebal-guk*" (advanced country in development). For instance, an article of international news in 1985 called the G-7 "*seobang 7 guk*" (seven Western countries) (*Chosun Ilbo*, 2 May 1985).

7 The Discursive Structure of Korea's Developmentalism and the Mobilization of Nation

Geundaehwa (Modernization), *Segyehwa* (Globalization), and *Seonjinhwa* (Becoming Advanced)

Discussions about East Asian countries' "development" have been made in relation to the "developmental state." The developmental state and developmentalism are closely interconnected as the former is discursively justified by the latter. The developmental state is a type of state having intent and capacity to effectively mobilize all national resources for the goal of national economic growth, while maintaining "autonomy" or "embedded autonomy" from the market and civil society (Kim Y.-T., 1999b, 2007).

In the case of Korea, many researchers point out that the developmental state, which had led rapid national development and economic growth in the 1960s and the 1970s, began to retreat in the 1980s undergoing neoliberalism and democratization, and eventually transformed into the "post-developmental state" or the "market-oriented state" in the 1990s (Lee B.-C., 2000; Kim Y.-T., 2007; Yoon S.-W., 2009; Park S.-Y., 2012; Kim I.-Y., 2013). The decline of the Korean developmental state became further manifest through the neoliberal restructuring of the Korean economy after the "International Monetary Fund (IMF) Crisis" in late 1997. In the wake of this incident, the market capacity greatly increased in relation to the state, as the belief spread that economic development would be more effective when led by the free activities of capital.

Then, what would be the status of Korea's developmentalism at the present time, which is generally understood as the period of the post-developmental state? Would developmentalism have declined according to the decline of the developmental state? In regard to these questions, some researchers discuss the change of developmentalism in the post-developmental state era in relation to neoliberalism. Yoon S.-W. (2009), for instance, conceptualizes Korea's developmental experience after the "IMF Crisis" as "developmental neoliberalization," by emphasizing that neoliberalism in Korea has basically pursued an open-door policy, liberalization, and deregulation while bearing a characteristic of developmental intervention when necessary. This kind of discussion is notable as it recognizes the possibility of the combination of developmentalism and neoliberalism, which seem to be somewhat contradictory with each other in their foci on the central agent of the economy. In this regard, it observes a possibility that developmentalism, a discourse having appeared in support of the developmental state, still exerts its influence on Korea in the post-developmental state era.

Yet, Yoon S.-W.'s discussion is weak as it basically treats developmentalism and neoliberalism as discourses at an equal level, by arguing that the era of developmentalism as a discourse for the developmental state has basically changed to the era of neoliberalism for the post-developmental state. In this regard, he mentions, on the other hand, that "neoliberalism was utilized as a mobilizing strategy for national competitiveness and developmental goals such as a high growth rate, increase in exports, and catch-up" (Yoon S.-W., 2009: 55). If neoliberalism is utilized for the goal of national development in developmental terms, as he mentions, could we not consider neoliberalism as a strategic sub-discourse for developmentalism? In this regard, Cho H.-Y. (2002) notes that developmentalism can appear in various forms, such as "protectionist developmentalism" valuing state intervention and "open-door developmentalism" oriented to the self-regulation of the market.

We may refer to both Yoon S.-W. (2009) and Cho H.-Y. (2002) in understanding Korea's development, as both intend to grasp the complicated nature of Korea's developmental experience by conceptually combining developmentalism and neoliberalism. A difference between the two, by the way, may be that the former focuses on the diversity of neoliberalism, while the latter attends to the diversity of developmentalism.

This chapter employs a structural approach to developmentalism, assuming that it contains a broad range of discursive inclinations or discursive systems supported by various sub-discourses and discursive elements. If neoliberal policies in the post-developmental state era of Korea ultimately pursue the goal of developmentalism, Korea's neoliberalism can be fairly regarded as a strategic discourse of developmentalism. In this view, the era of developmentalism may be still going on even if the era of the developmental state has ended with its transformation into the post-developmental state.

Both the developmental state and neoliberalism can basically be understood as a strategic institution and idea for developmentalism. That is, while developmentalism and a developmental goal have been constant in Korea, the methods for achieving the developmental goal have changed from the idea of state intervention to neoliberalism, from protectionism in trade to open-door policies, or from the developmental state to the post-developmental state. In this respect, developmentalism in Korea is not necessarily combined with the developmental state, but developmentalism without the developmental state is possible at any rate.

In fact, developmentalism in Korea has been presented in various slogans in different historical periods. While the slogan of "*geundaehwa*" (modernization) was promoted by the developmental state in the Park Chung-Hee era (the 1960s and 1970s), "*segyehwa*" (globalization) was publicized by the Kim Young-Sam government in the 1990s in response to the change of international trade circumstances. On the other hand, "*seon-jinhwa*" (becoming advanced) was propagandized by the Lee Myung-Bak government in the late 2000s reflecting the strengthening of the government's neoliberal stance.

This chapter aims to demonstrate the structure of developmentalism in Korea through the analysis of discourses centered on those slogans. For this, it analyzes the presidential addresses of Park Chung-Hee, Kim Young-Sam, and Lee Myung-Bak, in which each of the discourses of "*geundaehwa*," "*segyehwa*," and "*seonjinhwa*" is notable, respectively.[1]

The foci of analysis are put on the following questions: First, what national identities and visions Korea's developmentalism has presented; second, what developmental strategies Korea's developmentalism has emphasized; and third, how Korea's developmentalism has secured its legitimacy. Through the analysis, this chapter will explain what structure Korea's developmentalism has maintained and in what context it has secured its legitimacy, by paying special attention to discursive elements having commonly appeared in different historical periods.

Developmental Perceptions of a National Goal and Problem

National Goal: Seonjinguk

The change in dominant discourse in society induces a change in its dominant worldview, and in its identity and vision. Since the change in dominant discourse to the discourse of development in the Park Chung-Hee era, Korea has been pursuing the "developed" status as its national goal and vision. The Koreans have generally termed the "developed" status as "*seonjinguk*," and projected their developmental aspirations into this concept in their national development process.

The analysis of presidential addresses confirms that a tendency to set *seonjinguk* as the national goal commonly appeared in all periods.

> I am sure that we will certainly join the rank of *seonjinguk*, overcoming any difficulties when we become one entity and make hard efforts for building up national power [...] This is the historical duty of our generation.
>
> (Park Chung-Hee, 26 February 1979)

> We should win this competition. Thus, we must achieve entry to the rank of *seonjinguk* that we all are aspiring to.
>
> (Kim Young-Sam, 30 October 1996)

> We should realize the dream of *seonjinguk* by reflecting on some countries' failures [...] Change is not an option but a necessity for entering into the ranks of *seonjinguk*.
>
> (Lee Myung-Bak, 18 May 2008)

The appearance of the national goal of *seonjinguk* in presidential addresses indicates that the goal has not been achieved yet. While *seonjinguk* was pursued in all periods, its connotation varied according to the change in the perception of domestic and international circumstances in regard to development. *Seonjinguk* in the Park era tended to be assumed as a "strong and wealthy country" at the advanced level of industrialization. In the Kim and Lee eras, in comparison, it was mainly represented as a "first-class country" having "world-level" national competitiveness enough to compete internationally. Reflecting these subtle differences in the connotation of *seonjinguk*, the presidents often termed it differently from one another, such as "*seonjin* industrial country" (Park) and "world first-class country" or "*seonjin* first-class country" (Kim and Lee).

Nonetheless, an important criterion for *seonjinguk* was the level and scale of the national economy, such as per capita national income. For instance, the achievement of per capita national income of $1,000 was congratulated in the Park era, and the accomplishment of $10,000 was boasted in the Kim era, while these levels were regarded as not yet reaching the level of *seonjinguk*. In the Lee era, the achievement of $20,000 was recognized as an index showing Korea's status close to *seonjinguk*, and the per capita income of $30,000 was suggested as the next goal for sound *seonjinguk*.

> Now our economy has just passed over the level of $1,000 in national income per capita. We have to go up to the level of $3,000 or $5,000 in order to rise to the level of *seonjinguk*.
>
> (Park Chung-Hee, 27 March 1979)

> We have leapt up to the top 12th trade country in the world by virtue of the lead of export industry, becoming a country with the top 11th economic scale and $10,000 national income per capita [...] We should become true *seonjinguk* with a great economy by the early twenty-first century.
>
> (Kim Young-Sam, 30 November 1995)

> We have to look for a way to achieve *seonjinhwa* and advance towards the world first-class country. We have to open the era of $30,000 in national income per capita and necessarily achieve the *seonjinhwa* of quality of life in a pleasant environment and an active welfare system.
>
> (Lee Myung-Bak, 11 July 2008)

In Kim's address above, the national goal is "*seonjinguk* with a great economy" (*seonjin gyeongje daeguk*). It emphasizes the importance of advancing national status by using the expression "leap up" for the increase in national trade to become the top 12th trade country in the world. It suggests economic indices, such as exports, economic scale, and national income, as important criteria for judging *seonjinguk* with a great economy. In Lee's address, in a similar vein, the national goal of "world first-class country" is combined with the expression "advancing towards," implying that achieving the national goal is a progressive movement.

The goal of *seonjinguk* has been set as an ultimate national goal since the 1960s with the rise of developmentalism in the Park Chung-Hee era. However, the discursive focus of national development tended to be put on the "escape from *hujinguk*" in the early 1960s as Korea's self-identity was mainly defined as *hujinguk*. It was the late 1970s when the nation was considered just in front of the rank of *seonjinguk*, and this was the time when the goal of entry to the rank of *seonjinguk* began to be manifestly pursued. In this context, President Park seemed to have set the 1980s as the actual era of entering into the rank of *seonjinguk*.

It is interesting to note that Korea's identity has remained "on the threshold of *seonjinguk*" for nearly 40 years since its rise to that status in the late 1970s. Although Park promised the achievement of *seonjinguk* in the 1980s, Korea has remained, in the Koreans' perception, as a country not yet reaching true *seonjinguk*, and the goal of entering into the ranks of *seonjinguk* still plays a role as a main discursive element of Korea's developmentalism.

National Problem: From "Hujinguk" *to "Incomplete Success"*

In Korea's developmentalism, "underdevelopment" and "development" are expressed in the binary distinction between "*hujinguk*" and "*seonjinguk*," and "development" is considered as a movement from the former to the latter. In Korea's development process, positive and negative values have been projected into the concepts of *seonjinguk* and *hujinguk*, respectively. An economically rich *seonjinguk* tends to be represented as an ideal country having rational and mature systems in all national areas, while a *hujinguk* is contrastingly imagined as the "marginalized" other to *seonjinguk*.

In Korean developmentalism, the "problem of underdevelopment" is recognized in relation to the goal of *seonjinguk*. In many cases, it is considered that the level of Korea's development is in the status of "relative underdevelopment" not reaching the level of *seonjinguk*. By the way, the target to be problematized has varied by period in relation to the change in Korea's national identity. The developmental "problem" of Korea in the early Park Chung-Hee era was mainly the status of "underdevelopment" that was the level of "*hujinguk*." President Park did not hesitate to call Korea *hujinguk*, while criticizing the tendency to consider it as *munmyeong-guk* for being narcissistic as "a frog in the well." In mentioning *hujinguk*, he often used negative terms, such as poverty, retrogression, stagnation, weakness, while employing for *seonjinguk* such terms as "self-effort," "self-reliance," "honorably," "dream," "confidence," and "courage" (2 May 1965). In this way, the contrasting image between *hujinguk* and *seonjinguk* was clear in his addresses, and so was the hierarchy between the two. For Park Chung-Hee, the main reason for Korea to be designated as *hujinguk* was "poverty."

> It is needless to say that the instability and confusion Korea is facing today derive mostly from "poverty." The escape from poverty and the improvement of people's lives are urgent problems that should be solved prior to anything else.
>
> (Park Chung-Hee, 15 August 1964)

President Park's early term (the early 1960s) was the only period when the underdeveloped status of Korea was termed as "*hujinguk*" with the features of absolute poverty and backwardness. As the achievements of the national development project were recognized afterwards, the focus of problematization moved to the status of "relative underdevelopment" in relation to developed *seonjinguk*. In the eras of Kim Young-Sam and Lee Myung-Bak, for instance, Korea's problematized status was mainly the status of "incomplete success" that was usually termed as "*seonjinguk munteok*."

Accordingly, the perception of the process of "going over *seonjinguk munteok*" also varied in the periodical change. For Park, there was a tendency to perceive it as a matter of time, that is, it would be eventually achieved in time if the current developmental process continued. In the eras of Kim and Lee, in comparison, going over the "threshold" tended to be considered as requiring the "qualitative improvement" of the nation. The process was perceived as a qualitative leap of the nation to a higher level, rather than as a continuation of the previous developmental process. As the "qualitative leap" was an ambiguous notion, the criteria for judging the accomplishment of *seonjinguk* had become more obscure in Kim's and Lee's periods.

Presidents Kim and Lee often problematized that insufficient elements for *seonjinguk* still remained over the nation, identifying them as the main cause of holding Korea on the "threshold" of *seonjinguk*. Kim in his early term, for instance, perceived that the nation was infected with the "disease of Korea":

> The most serious disease of Korea is collective egoism arguing only for "my share." We can never reach *seonjinguk* without curing this disease of Korea.
>
> (21 September 1993)

Here Kim considers collective egoism as a "disease of Korea" obstructing Korea's reach for *seonjinguk*. As such, the putative problems of Korea are raised in relation to the national goal of *seonjinguk* and, in this case, *seonjinguk* is implicitly assumed as the country free of those problems that Korea currently has.

President Lee showed a similar perception:

> Now the conflicts of the old era are reviving and social trust is collapsing in our society. And, the economic situation is getting worse as the oil

> price rapidly increases, and the leap and development towards a *seonjin* first-class country is being delayed.
>
> (12 July 2008)

The gap between the urgent developmental goal (*seonjinguk*) and the lacking status of not reaching this (*hujinguk* or *seonjinguk munteok*) necessarily raises a need for national change. The stronger the negative perception of the current national situation is, the greater the need for national change becomes. For a thorough reformulation of the nation, presidents even asked for a strong and drastic level of change in people's minds, such as "human transformation" (Park), "mindset revolution" (Kim), and "*seonjinhwa* of mindset" (Lee), along with the extensive governmental reform policies.

In those respects, Korean society has been constantly in the "wind of rapid change" since the launch of the modernization project. The wind was especially strong when the new government appeared, and the development discourse and the discourse of *seonjinguk* played a significant role in justifying it. In this regard, a widely promoted developmental logic had been that the change was inevitable for Korea's advancement to *seonjinguk* and the pains accompanying it should be endured for happiness in the future.

The Mobilizing Mechanism of Developmentalism

Crisis Construction: The Survival of the Fittest, Transitory Status, and the Last Chance

Korea's developmentalism creates a sense of "crisis" to facilitate the developmental mobilization of people by maintaining tension for the goal. In presidential addresses, the ways of raising the consciousness of crisis mainly appear in two ways: First, the recognition of the harshly competitive international circumstances; and second, the perception of Korea's "in-between" status on the international stage ("on a forked way," "sandwiched status," or "a nut in the nut-cracker"). These reflect, in a way, an assumption of linear evolutionism that countries are "chasing and being chased" for the "survival of the fittest" on the same developmental path.

The argument that every area of the nation should be mobilized for the enhancement of national competitiveness is justified on the assumption that the nation will be in danger without people's efforts for constant national change. The entry to the rank of *seonjinguk* is considered as the way for national survival. In the perception of harsh international circumstances, national unity and solidarity are emphasized and the sacrifice of people's current life is asked for future national honor. In this regard, Park Chung-Hee, for instance, argues as follows:

> We are living in an international society in which keen competition, amazing change, and endless development are continuing. That is, we are living in an international circumstance in which the competition for the survival of the fittest is fiercer than at any other time. In order for our nation to maintain its life and achieve the honorable future in this era of severe competition, we have to keep on progressing with firmer unity and effort.
>
> (Park Chung-Hee, 2 February 1967)

Koreans' sensitivity to international change has, in part, derived from their historical experience of colonialism in the early twentieth century. The Koreans' experience of victimization has appeared as a historical trauma in Korea's developmentalism to repeatedly remind people of the harshness of international circumstances. In this regard, Korea's developmentalism tends to emphasize that the past experience of colony had been caused by people's complacency and insensitivity to the international trend.

This kind of historical perception gives justification to the argument that the nation should catch up with the world trend through constant change and effort for reform, or that the nation will retrogress if it does not sensitively respond to the change in global circumstances. In regard to this, President Kim mentioned:

> The historical duty is not to repeat the failure of ignoring and wrongly responding to the historical current in the *gaehwa* period 100 years ago. The historical necessity is to change for survival as the world is undergoing rapid change. Today's world is changing into a very different world from the world so far through the information revolution and the scientific-technological revolution, and each nation is competing hard to take a lead in those changes. We will again be a straggler in history if we do not actively respond to this era of civilizational change.
>
> (27 February 1995)

In Lee's addresses, the victim mentality and the tone of social evolutionism appear relatively weak. Rather, they tend to show somewhat stronger confidence in the national future than do the others' addresses. Especially after the Seoul Summit of the G-20 in 2010, Lee enhanced confidence in the nation as a "central country of the world," and a perception was relatively strong that the world stage was operating by fair rule. Nonetheless, Lee still perceived the world as a place of keen competition.

> Now Daegu city should advance towards the world as well as the nation. It should be able to win the competition with the world. As the open society competes with the world, it cannot win with its door closed.
>
> (21 May 2008)

The second way of creating a sense of crisis is to empathize that Korea is on a forked road in its journey for *seonjinguk*. The presidents attempted to maximize the mobilization effect by arguing that the nation was on a forked road either to enter into *seonjinguk* or to retrogress to *hujinguk* and, in this situation, that the national fate was up to what people would do in the next few years. A popular perception was that whether they were to advance to *seonjinguk* or to retrogress to *hujinguk* depended on their own efforts. In this regard, President Park argues as follows:

> We are truly on a tense forked road whether we are to endlessly wander suffering poverty and sorrows under the label of backwardness or to create a new history of freedom and prosperity bravely escaping from this stagnant reality.
>
> (15 August 1964)

In this address, Korea's current position is likened to being on a "tense forked road." The forked road is assumed to lead to two situations: One is to "endless wandering" and the other is to the "creation of a new history." The former is the direction of "suffering poverty and sorrows under the label of backwardness" and the latter is that of "freedom and prosperity." By contrasting the two directions, Park naturally creates a sense of urgency for the developmental goal.

Similar perceptions appear in addresses by Kim and Lee as well:

> We are now on a critical national forked road either to progress or to retrogress [...] It is up to what we do now whether the nation will rise as a central country in the world or will fall onto the backside of world history.
>
> (Kim Young-Sam, 12 December 1995)

> The chance may not come again if we do not enter into the ranks of *seonjinguk* at this very point. Now we are on a forked road of history whether we enter into the ranks of *seonjinguk* or not.
>
> (Lee Myung-Bak, 22 May 2008)

In regard to the sense of crisis, another notable perception shows the "in-between" mentality in regard to Korea's identity: For instance, that Korea is in a "sandwiched" situation or in a status of a "nut in the nut-cracker" between *seonjinguk* and developing countries. In this regard, addresses by Kim and Lee argue that Korea has constantly been on the "threshold of *seonjinguk*" without reducing the gap with *seonjinguk*, while being rapidly chased by latecomer developing countries. A transient national identity, such as being "on the threshold" or being "in between," creates mental instability and anxiety across the nation.

Furthermore, the presidents intend to maximize the sense of crisis with a perception that this is the last chance and the next few years will decide whether the nation enters into *seonjinguk* or not. For instance, Lee mentions that:

> It is said that there is no country having succeeded in entering into the ranks of *seonjinguk* among countries newly independent after World War II. It is also said that not a small number of countries collapsed just on the threshold of *seonjinguk* and fell down. This is why the next five years are important. These five years will be a period determining the success or failure in entering into *seonjinguk*.
>
> (11 July 2008)

This address argues that the crisis may occur in reality, by mentioning the historical cases of failure on the threshold of *seonjinguk*.[2] On this ground, Lee sets his term, the next five years, as a "critical period" determining whether or not to enter into the rank of *seonjinguk*.

In those respects, the Koreans have kept on living with the "last chance" for entering into the ranks of *seonjinguk* since the emergence of developmentalism and the launch of the national developmental project in the 1960s. They have been constantly asked to make efforts to grab the "last opportunity" to achieve the "national mission" of entering into *seonjinguk*, with a transient national identity of "being on the threshold of *seonjinguk*" especially since the late 1970s.

Reminder of National Potential

The aforementioned discursive elements – developmental goal, problem, and crisis construction – weigh down on people's shoulders. The heavy burden could bring about defeatism, an attitude of evading the developmental goal. To handle this, Korea's developmentalism employs an element, the "reminding of national potential." While the aforementioned elements imply the imperativeness of the goal, the "reminder of potential" hints at its likelihood. That is to say, while Korea's situation is tense as it should achieve *seonjinguk* as soon as possible amidst competitive international circumstances, the "reminder of national potential" enhances national confidence by implying that the likelihood of achieving the goal is high as the nation has great potential.

While Korea is perceived as requiring urgent change, its prospects for a better future are also recognized in light of its long historical heritage and the achievement of rapid modernization. Park Chung-Hee, for instance, emphasized the national potential as follows.

> Do we have any reason for being poor? We have many reasons for being better than others, as a people living on the fertile land and in a precious natural condition, having a long history, beautiful traditions, and

> the ground of wisdom that can be comparable to those of any other people.
>
> (1 March 1965)

In the 1970s, Park promoted confidence in the nation mainly by emphasizing economic achievements.

> Export has passed $10 billion due to the development of the heavy-chemical industry. The nation has become a one-day life zone by virtue of the development and organization of land and the expansion of a highway network. The urban and rural areas together have kept on making amazing developments [...] We will achieve a high industrial society and rise to the rank of *seonjinguk* in the early 1980s, the near future.
>
> (13 January 1978)

This kind of perception also appeared in Kim Young-Sam's addresses that the nation had achieved boastful developmental achievements in the past.

> Today's Korea has become the most successful country in democracy among developing countries [...] Our economy has kept on growing at the fastest speed in the world, now facing entry into the ranks of *seonjinguk* just ahead.
>
> (25 June 1993)

In this context, Kim emphasized that "our country has to reach the level of the top seventh *seonjinguk* in the fields of politics, economy, culture, and ethics" (17 June 1993).

In the Kim Young-Sam era, on the other hand, there sometimes appeared an opinion that Korea had already entered into the ranks of *seonjinguk* with moments such as the achievement of $10,000 per capita income and the joining of the Organisation for Economic Co-operation and Development, reflecting the Koreans' confidence and pride in the nation's past successful modernization. In Lee Myung-Bak's addresses, a perception is relatively more notable that Korea has already entered into the ranks of *seonjinguk*. This perception appears strong especially around the year 2012, near the end of his term.

> Korea has now become a central country in global society. It has developed into a country giving aid, from a country receiving aid [...] It has become the seventh country in the world, which entered into the ranks of *seonjinguk* with a population of 50 million and over $20,000 per capita income.
>
> (2 July 2012)

Meanwhile, the opinion also appears contradictorily that Korea is not yet true *seonjinguk*. In this regard, Lee has suggested a per capita income of

$30,000 as a condition for *seonjinguk* as follows: "Per capita income of our country will exceed at least $30,000 in 2018. We will hold the Pyeongchang Winter Olympics [in 2018] at the exact time when we are entering into *seonjinguk*" (1 June 2012).

In those respects, the goal of *seonjinguk* is mainly set on the two pillars of "change" and "hope." The perception of "incomplete success" raises a need for change and effort, while pride in the past promotes hope that the goal can be realized eventually. In regard to "hope," the presidents also emphasize that crisis and hardship can be an opportunity. For instance, Kim Young-Sam states that "today's world has gotten into an era of endless competition without border. This endless competition is a hardship to us, but is also an opportunity for leaping to *seonjinguk*" (30 April 1996).

The Strategic Sub-discourses of Developmentalism: *Geundaehwa, Segyehwa*, and *Seonjinhwa*

In his early term, Park Chung-Hee suggested "*geundaehwa*" (modernization) as a strategy for escaping from the status of *hujinguk*. For him, "*geundaehwa*" was the very process of dispelling poverty and ultimately reaching the status of *seonjinguk*.

> We need only do another Five-Year Economic Plan that will be the third one. Then, we will be able to catch up with the rank of *seonjinguk* as a sound modern industrial country. This is what we are now referring to as the modernization of fatherland.
>
> (18 April 1967)

This address sets "modern industrial country" as the national goal, identifying it with the status of "*seonjinguk*," and refers to *geundaehwa* as the process of catching up with the rank of *seonjinguk*. Here the nationalistic feature of Park's developmentalism clearly appears as it relates the strategic slogan of "*geundaehwa*" to the term "*joguk*," e.g., "*joguk geundaehwa*" (the modernization of fatherland). It also demonstrates a proposition of then-popular modernization theory by expressing *geundaehwa* as a process of catching up with *seonjinguk*.

In terms of the subject of development, "*geundaehwa*" featured a slogan for a state-led developmental strategy, i.e., the "developmental state." The discourse of *geundaehwa* had provided discursive justification to the export-oriented national development strategy since Park's early term, and was embodied in such developmental policies as the Five-Year Economic Plan. In relation to global discourse, the *geundaehwa* discourse in the Park era reflected the hegemony of modernization theory that buttressed US global hegemony (Latham, 2000; Kim C.-G., 2002; Park T.-G., 2004).

In comparison, the *segyehwa* discourse in the Kim Young-Sam era reflected a different perception of Korea's situation from that in the Park era. Above all, Korea's position on the developmental path was generally defined as being on the "threshold of *seonjinguk*" ("*seonjinguk munteok*") in this period, as the nation had achieved a considerable level of industrialization with the strong state-led developmental drive. This putative status of Korea was somewhat similar to that in the late 1970s, but people's confidence in the level of national development was far stronger than that time.

Along with the change in national developmental identity, there were diverse internal and external factors that induced the emergence of *segyehwa* discourse in the Kim era. These include the decline of the state's relative autonomy with the growth of capital internally, and the retreat of the state with the globalization of capital externally (Kim I.-Y., 2013: 33). The analysis of Kim's addresses shows that the recognition of the changing international circumstances was one of the most important factors for the emergence of the *segyehwa* strategy. A perception became notable in the Kim era that trade barriers among nations were being lowered and the world economies were being unified into one economy. The launch of the World Trade Organization (WTO) in 1995, which followed the Uruguay Round of the General Agreement on Tariffs and Trade, was a critical event that strengthened Korea's recognition of the restructuring of the world, i.e., globalization.

The Kim era was also the time when neoliberalism reflected in the "Washington Consensus" expanded its influence around the globe. Much of the restructuring of the world economy or globalization at the time took place according to neoliberal ideas and policies. While there were the expansion of globalization and the rise of neoliberalism at the global level, there was a notable change in power relations between the state and capital in Korea, which was usually characterized as the rise of capital in relation to the state.

In terms of the state-business relationship, it was the period when the state notably lost its predominance over business and the latter tried to "discipline" the former, with the Kim Young-Sam administration's financial liberalization and the opening-up of the capital market as momentum (Yoon S.-W., 2005). The pressure on the Korean state to liberalize Korea's economy came from multiple directions, domestically and globally. In this regard, Crotty and Lee (2007: 73) argue that "the structures of Korea's state-guided economy were dismantled [in the decade preceding 1997]."

In those respects, the rise of *segyehwa* discourse in the Kim Young-Sam era can be understood as reflecting various internal and external conditions: Internally, the weakening of the developmental state in relation to the rise of capital; and externally, the restructuring of the world economy and the rise of neoliberalism. Raising a need for actively responding to the global change, President Kim presented the *segyehwa* strategy as the only way to catch up with the global current and eventually win the competition in the new global setting.

The *segyehwa* discourse asked all subjects in the nation to be suitably competitive in the world. For this, it emphasized that the governmental sector should lead the policies of deregulation, openness, and reform. At the new year press conference in 1994 (6 January 1994), Kim Young-Sam emphasized that "we have to change our narrow sight in the well into a wider sight towards the world," arguing that "*segyehwa* and international competition have become our reality." In this address, he mentioned that *segyehwa* was an important tool for increasing the nation's international competitiveness, and suggested its three main directions: Liberalization, opening, and rationalization.

President Kim raised a need to align people's mindset and various national customs with the "world level." For this, he asked people to broaden their range of vision "to the world and the future." As a way to justify the *segyehwa* strategy, he associated "*segyehwa*" with the new "era of informationization and globalization," while equating the "authoritarian era" with "*geundaehwa*" of the past. As for the cause and urgency of *segyehwa*, Kim mentioned as follows:

> *Segyehwa* is a shortcut leading us to the "first-class country of the twenty first century" [...] We aim for *segyehwa* in every field, such as politics, diplomacy, economics, society, education, culture, sports, etc. For this, our sight, mindset, institution, and custom should leap to the world level [...] *Segyehwa* cannot be achieved just in a day. It asks all of us for painstaking effort and endurance, and true courage. This is the only way for us, and there is no alternative. Thus, I want to present "*segyehwa*" as the national goal of this year.
>
> (6 January 1995)

Segyehwa was distinguished from the similar concept of "*gukjehwa*" (internationalization) in the sense that the former intended a more systematic and broader range of change than the latter (6 January 1995). In those respects, the *segyehwa* discourse in the Kim era promoted two main ideas in regard to Korea's vision. One was that *segyehwa* was a required strategy for enhancing national competitiveness enabling all national fields to be able to compete with the world in the era of endless competition. The other was that it was the only way to win the international competition to ultimately achieve "twenty-first-century *seonjinguk*."[3]

The perceptions of the level of national development, national identity, and international circumstances in the Lee Myung-Bak era had much in common with those in the Kim era. In regard to this, a common perception in the Lee era was that Korea was a great economic power ranked around the top ten in the world and a high-income country with $20,000 per capita income. These national achievements tended to be attributed to the successful full-out economic development project in the past. Meanwhile, the international circumstances were still considered to be very competitive, in which every nation-state pursued its own practical interests.

In those perceptions, President Lee's *seonjinhwa* discourse emphasized a need for every field of the nation to be advanced to reach the "world level," to go beyond past developmental achievements. For this, it promoted neoliberal ideas highlighting market freedom and the roles of non-governmental subjects for national competitiveness and development. It argued that the goal of *seonjinguk* could be achieved when subjects in all national fields, both in the economic and non-economic spheres, had the ability to compete with the world.

Lee Myung-Bak presented the slogan of *seonjinhwa* from his early term on the assumption that "*geundaehwa*" had been successfully achieved in the fields of the economy and politics, e.g., industrialization and democratization. In this regard, he suggested *seonjinhwa* as the project both to inherit the achievements of past *geundaehwa* and to make Korea accomplish the sound status of *seonjinguk* in the twenty-first century circumstances. For this, he emphasized the enhancement of national competitiveness centered on the autonomy of the private sector, rather than a governmental lead, while promising governmental policies of deregulation and openness. In the discursive aspect, this developmental model was a great departure from the state-led model, e.g., the developmental state, in the Park Chung-Hee era or the era of *geundaehwa*.

Conclusion

This chapter has examined five main elements constituting Korea's developmentalism since the Park Chung-Hee era: A developmental goal, problematization, crisis construction, reminders of national potential, and strategy. While the goal of *seonjinguk* was pursued in all periods, the escape from *hujinguk* was especially targeted in the early Park era as the nation was defined as *hujinguk*. The connotation of *seonjinguk* varied over time. While it referred mainly to an "advanced industrial country" in the Park era, it tended to mean a "first-class country" with "world-level" national competitiveness in the Kim and Lee eras.

Developmentalism problematizes the status of underdevelopment. In Korea, the main developmental problem was the status of *hujinguk* in the early Park era, and the status not reaching *seonjinguk* or the status of "*seonjinguk munteok*" afterwards. As such, Korea's developmentalism has been supported by the discourse of *seonjinguk* assuming the distinction between *hujinguk* and *seonjinguk*.

The perceived gap between the goal of *seonjinguk* and the reality of not reaching it raises a need for national change and justifies developmental policies for this. To secure its legitimacy, Korea's developmentalism spreads a sense of crisis that Korea is on a forked road either to enter into *seonjinguk* or to drop out of it, being chased by latecomer developing countries. It maximizes the need for change with a continuing perception that the next few years are the last opportunity to enter into the ranks of *seonjinguk*. Since the rise of developmentalism, the Koreans have constantly been living in a "critical period" for the goal of *seonjinguk*. They have been asked to respond promptly to global changes and always to move and reform themselves to follow the global currents.

While those discursive elements are relevant to the urgency of achieving the goal, the reminder of national potential is related to its prospects. To give confidence in the goal's achievement, Korea's developmentalism highlights the nation's long, rich history, along with its achievements of industrialization and democratization in a short period. While the perception of "incomplete national status" induces the negative aspects of Korea's identity, the reminder of national potential attends to its positive ones. The former raises a need for change, while the latter stresses prospects and hope for the goal's achievement.

Korea's developmentalism has strategically promoted the slogans of *geundaehwa, segyehwa*, and *seonjinhwa* in varying historical circumstances. *Geundaehwa* in the Park Chung-Hee era took on the feature of strategic discourse for the state-led industrialization project. In the Kim Young-Sam era, the *segyehwa* discourse focused on the enhancement of national competitiveness enough to win the world, as it arose in the perception that the world economy was being unified into one zone.

Amidst the rise of neoliberalism as a global hegemonic discourse, Korea's *segyehwa* discourse advocated the policies of deregulation and openness in regard to national development, on the basis of the national identity of *seonjinguk munteok*. The *seonjinhwa* discourse in the Lee Myung-Bak era had many aspects in common with the *segyehwa* discourse, as it aimed for a world-level first-class country through neoliberal policies. Those features of Korea's developmentalism can be summarized in Figure 7.1.

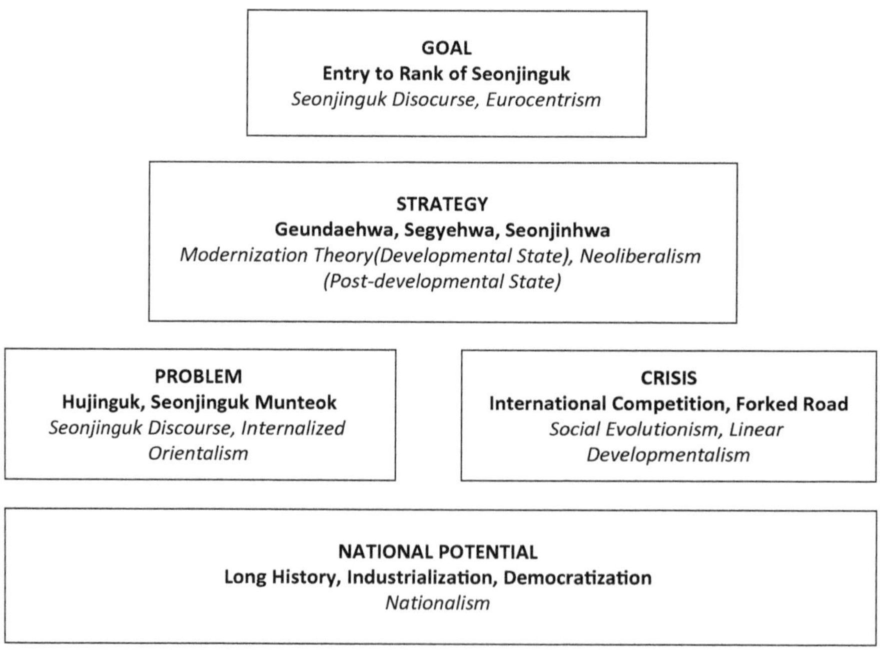

Figure 7.1 Discursive Structure of Korea's Developmentalism

Notes

1 For analysis, I have obtained 1,164 presidential addresses in the fields of politics/society, industry/economy, and culture/sports/tourism from the National Archives of Korea: 521 addresses for Park Chung-Hee, 292 for Kim Young-Sam, and 351 for Lee Myung-Bak.

2 In regard to this, the development experiences of Latin American countries, such as Argentina, are usually referred to by the Korean mass media as "actual" historical cases showing failure just on the threshold of *seonjinguk* in entering into the ranks of *seonjinguk*.

3 Kim Young-Sam had attributed the "IMF Crisis" in his late term to the lack of efforts for *segyehwa*: "In retrospect in current economic hardship, it is revealed that our efforts for reform were greatly insufficient. That is, we did not catch up with the change of the world" (11 December 1997).

Part III

National and Regional Identities and Mutual Perceptions in the Development Era

8 A Comparison of Development Discourses in Korea, China, and Japan

National Identities and Mutual Perceptions

The discourse of *seonjinguk* is a dominant discourse in Korean society, which constructs the identities and representations of various countries in the world. To designate a country as "*hujinguk*," for instance, is not merely to refer to its objective status, but contains the negative perception of the country in regard to "underdevelopment," "poverty," "backwardness," "irrationality," "immaturity," etc. On the contrary, to define a country as "*seonjinguk*" contains a degree of respect and praise for it as a country having already achieved what Korea has been aspiring to.

The Korean discourse of *seonjinguk* generally calls the U.S., Western European countries, and Japan representative *seonjinguk*. It tends to perceive them as the countries having led modernization early and undergone a long modernization process to accumulate great wealth, make good material and economic infrastructure, and establish rational and mature national systems.

This tendency is not unique to Korea, as development discourse has been a global hegemonic discourse since the mid-twentieth century. Many countries in the world have constructed their versions of development discourse and perceived countries through these discursive frameworks.

This chapter examines how Korean development discourse perceives neighboring China and Japan, and defines self-national identity in relation to them. It investigates how those three Northeast Asian countries are identified and represented in the Chinese and Japanese discourses of development from a comparative perspective. For the Korean discourse, it analyzes the texts of major Korean newspaper editorials.[1] The foci of analysis are put on the following questions: First, how the identities and representations of Japan are constructed in relation to "*seonjinguk*" and "*hujinguk*"; second, how the identities and representations of China are constructed in relation to the concepts of "*seonjinguk*" and "*hujinguk*"; and third, how the identities and representations of Korea are constructed in relation to those of China and Japan. For the introduction of Chinese and Japanese development discourses, I have referred to the research conducted by Jeong I.-J., Park J.-H., Kim J., and Song B.-G. (2015).[2]

The Koreans' Perceptions of China and Japan: Review of Previous Studies

Previous research on the Koreans' perceptions of China and Japan tended to focus on the historical images of those countries, or favorable and unfavorable feelings about them, typically based on the analysis of historical texts or survey methods. As for China, negative images were dominant in Korean society during the Cold War, such as "totalitarianism, a satellite of the Soviet Union, anti-traditional, anti-civilizational, dictatorship, and aggressive expansionism" (Jeong M.-S., 2012: 220). Another notable image of China in the Cold War period reflected modernization theory, e.g., "an aberrant, temporary political group, which deviated from the path of modernization" (*ibid.*).

However, as the Cold War order in East Asia was shaken in the 1970s by such events as the establishment of the Sino-U.S. diplomatic relationship and the Sino-Soviet disputes, a tendency appeared to consider China in somewhat positive ways. In this period, China was perceived by some intellectuals even as "a model for Korea's reform," or as "a partner for solidarity and cooperation" (Jeong M.-S., 2007, 2012).

The Koreans' perception of China changed dramatically after their establishment of a diplomatic relationship with China in 1992. With this as momentum, the Koreans' view of Chinese history changed "from the Taiwan-centered one to the Mainland China-centered one" (Kim J.-H., 2006: 385–386). Accordingly, the Koreans began to consider China basically as "a country to closely cooperate with" while, at the same time, still having a feeling of fear towards it (*ibid.*). Through a survey on Korean businessmen working in China, Jang S.-G. (2011) argues that the Koreans currently have complicated images of China, as a country "fearful, attractive, and barbaric."

Some studies discuss the source of the Koreans' negative images of China in relation to the change of global order. Lee W.-Y. (2004: 60), for instance, argues that as the traditional hierarchical order of China-Korea-Japan in East Asia in the pre-modern period changed to the capitalist world-systemic hierarchical order of the U.S.-Japan-Korea-China in the modern era, there appeared a tendency for the Koreans to "look down on China with a sense of superiority that Korea was more civilized and economically developed." Lim C.-S. (2009) also attends to Korea's incorporation into the U.S.-centered world order to explain the spread of negative perceptions of China in Korean society. He argues that "unfavorable feelings are prevalent in Koreans' perception of China due to Americanization" and raises a need to look at China from a perspective of its civilizational history (Lim C.-S., 2009: 290).

As for Japan, the Koreans' perceptions have also been multiple and complicated. Previous studies show that there have been diverse attitudes among Koreans towards Japan, such as hatred and a victim mentality as a result of Japanese colonial rule, and a sense of competition and cooperation with Japan being a rich and developed country (Park J.-H. and Kim D.-H., 1997; Park J.-H., 2008).

According to Park J.-H.'s (2008) survey on high school students in Seoul, the first thing that respondents recalled about Japan was "the issue of *Dokdo*," followed by "Japanese colonial rule." This indicates that territorial and historical issues strongly affect Korean students' perception of Japan. In regard to the question, "What kind of country is Japan to us?" the highest number of respondents answered that it was a "country in a constantly competitive relationship." In Park E.-H. and Seong H.-J.'s (2008) survey on Korean college students learning Japanese language, the proportion of respondents considering Japan "very good" or "good" was 60.3%, while those who considered Japanese people to be "very good" or "good" was 42.6%. Favorable feelings about Japan and the Japanese were relatively higher among Korean students learning Japanese language than among other Koreans.

In a survey conducted by the East Asia Institute of Korea (2013) in cooperation with Japanese Genron NPO, a dominant number of Korean respondents (76.6%) had a "bad impression" of Japan, while only 12.2% had a "good impression" of it. Main reasons for the bad impression were the "issue of *Dokdo*" (84.5%) and "Japan's lack of regret for its colonial history" (77.0%). This showed the significance of territorial and historical issues in Koreans' perception of Japan.

While those studies have provided knowledge about the Koreans' general perceptions of China and Japan, there is a lack of insight into what discursive frameworks the Koreans use to define those countries' identities and representations in certain ways. In this respect, this chapter examines how the identities and representations of Korea, China, and Japan are constructed in relation to Korean *seonjinguk* discourse. It also introduces how those three countries are identified and perceived in the Chinese and Japanese dominant discourses of development, e.g., Chinese discourse of "*fādá guójiā*" (developed country) and Japanese discourse of "*sensinkoku*" (*seonjinguk* in Korean).

Japan's Identities and Representations in Korean Discourse

The status of Japan greatly changed with the rise in the discourse of *seonjinguk* in the Park Chung-Hee era, as it began to be identified as *seonjinguk* that was advanced in capitalist industrialization and economic development. Its image of *munmyeong-guk* as an invasive civilization began to be replaced by the image of *seonjinguk*. Currently, Japan is very frequently mentioned as *seonjinguk* in Korea's public discourse, and is generally represented as socially and economically more developed and mature than Korea.

Japan in International Issues

In the analysis of the terms directly referring to Japan in international issues, it finds that "*seonjinguk*," among others, is by far the most frequent term referring to Japan (30 cases). Given that Western countries are generally referred to as *seonjinguk*, Japan is assumed to have national characteristics similar to those of the countries in North America and Western Europe. The next most frequent term for Japan is "great economic country" (*gyeongje daeguk*; five cases), followed by "powerful neighboring country" (*jubyeon gangguk*) and "competing country" (*gyeongjaeng-guk*) (four cases each). While the identity of *seonjinguk* is dominant with Japan, those related identities are based on the perception of Japan as a country having great economic and political power on the international stage. Additionally, the terms "member country of the G-7," "neighboring country" (*jubyeon-guk*) and "major country" (*juyo-guk*) have been used twice each.

In addition to those direct references, this chapter has analyzed the main characteristics of Japan appearing in the sentences of the newspaper editorials. In analysis, the highest number of cases (14) mentions Japan as a country possessing "advanced technology." The most dominant characteristic of Japan in this regard is a country of "advanced technology," "core first-class technology," and "original technology." The second most frequent characterization is "distortion of history" (nine cases), e.g., politicians' thoughtless remarks, the distortion of school textbooks, the glamorization of past history, and the glamorization of invasive war, especially in regard to history related to Korea.

It is important to note that the two most frequently mentioned characteristics of Japan are in stark contrast with each other. That is, while Japan is generally regarded as showing the features of *seonjinguk*, as a possessor of advanced technology and a producer of high-quality products, it is also perceived as having the image of distorting history, e.g., the glamorization of past colonial history. With the former case, Japan is a country for Korea to "catch up" with, bringing about a sense of competition for the Koreans. With the latter case, however, Japan induces a sense of superiority for the Koreans, along with a sort of victim mentality, as the Japanese historical consciousness is considered as a distortion of or digressing from normal conscientious historiography.

The image of "distorting history" greatly interrupts Japan's image of *seonjinguk*. In this regard, some editorials criticized Japan as "having not yet reached the sound rank of *seonjinguk*" or as "lacking qualifications for a permanent member of the UN Security Council [that has been pursued by Japan]" (*Dong-a Ilbo*, 3 November 2003; *Seoul Shinmun*, 23 September 2004). The Koreans' perception that Japan distorts history is a main source making Japan's status of *seonjinguk* imperfect. In this respect, Japan does not receive much respect from the Koreans, which ordinary *seonjinguk* deserves. In Korean public discourse, the Japanese attitude over their invasive history is often compared with the Germans' regretful attitude for their war crimes. This is a point, in Koreans' mind, that makes Japan's rank of *seonjinguk* somewhat lower than other *seonjinguk* in the West.

In the narratives of the newspaper editorials, the negative aspects of the Japanese economy have been also highlighted. A frequent characterization is that the Japanese economy has been in "low growth" or in "long-term depression," and has undergone a "lost decade" in the 1990s due to the collapse of the bubble economy (six cases).

In short, the image of Japan as an "advanced country" is strong in the field of science and technology. In terms of history and international politics, however, it tends to be represented as a country provoking its neighboring countries, or a "brazen and threatening" country distorting history and showing the conservative swing in its foreign policy. In regard to the economy, two contrasting images appear simultaneously: While positive images are strong, such as a great economic country ranked second or third in the world and a "big rich country" with high national income, there are also the negative images of "recession" or "instability" as a country struggling with low growth and a credit crunch after the long-term depression in the 1990s.

On the other hand, three tendencies are notable in the perceptions of Japan in regard to its relationship with Korea. The most notable is its competitive relationship with Korea. Japan as a *seonjinguk* is generally perceived as going ahead of Korea in the competitive developmental race, and is considered a country that Korea should catch up to in the fields of economy and technology. One editorial, for instance, argues that the Korean economy "can find a way out between advancing Japan and chasing China, to any degree" (*Kyunghyang Shinmun*, 7 August 2003).

The second is a cooperative relationship. In this case, Japan is considered as Korea's neighboring partner collaborating for common goals in such fields as the environment. In this regard, one editorial notes that "the minister meeting among Korea, China, and Japan is currently running as a collaborative channel for solving the problems of yellow dust and pollutants contained in it" (*Dong-a Ilbo*, 11 January 2010).

The third is the inflictor-victim relationship in historical terms. There is a notable perception that Japan victimized Korea in past colonial history, without sincerely regretting it in the present.

Japan in Domestic Issues

The analysis of Japan's identity regarding its domestic issues finds that Japan is generally better perceived in domestic issues than in international ones. The tendency to see Japan as a country more advanced and mature than Korea is more notable in regard to its domestic issues. In this analysis as well, the most frequent term for Japan is overwhelmingly "*seonjinguk*" (18 cases), which is followed by "member of OECD [Organisation for Economic Co-operation and Development]" (three cases), "a country of longevity" (two cases), and "*seonjinguk* of high-speed railroad" (two cases). All of those terms give positive identities to Japan. There is one case calling it negatively, a "*hujinguk* in history."

Japan's positive identities are well reflected in its representations appearing in the narratives of the editorial sentences. The most frequent representation is "mature political culture" (eight cases). In regard to this, the editorials introduce Japanese politicians' efforts for self-reform in contrast with the putatively self-preserving Korean political circle in such issues as the reduction of lawmakers and of their annual allowance, the decisive response to corruption of their colleagues, the normal operations of the parliament, and so forth. For instance, an editorial characterizes the Japanese Diet as follows:

> [The Japanese Diet] reduced lawmakers' annual allowance by 14% before raising taxes last year. The parliaments of *seonjinguk* at least show gestures to share the pain. Korea's National Assembly is in stark contrast to them.
>
> (*Segye Ilbo*, 5 January 2013)

As such, Japanese politics is perceived as having the *seonjinguk*-style mature culture internally, while it is considered as taking on a rightist tendency externally, threatening its neighboring countries.

The next most frequent representation is "lost decade" (five cases). This is a perception that the Japanese economy has lost much of its momentum, having gone through the recession of the 1990s. Given that the *seonjinguk* economy is usually considered as advanced, efficient, and having high technology, this is a factor in the economic field undermining the *seonjinguk* status of Japan. However, this still reflects a perception that Japan is an "advanced country." Japan's "lost decade" is mentioned mainly in the context of warning of the possibility of Korea's negative future, and is utilized to raise a need for Korea to make constant efforts to avoid what Japan has undergone. This is based on a perception that Korea in the future could go down the same path of recession.

The next most frequent characterizations of Japan are the "policy allowing retail stores to sell medicines" (four cases) and the "good management of old citizens' welfare as a country of longevity" (four cases). Those cases portray Japan as a "rational" society allowing retail stores' sale of medicines, and as an exemplary country of longevity, which have been issues recently raised in Korea. As such, the editorials use the Japanese cases as good examples to refer to in handling various issues in Korea. For instance, Japan is mentioned as a reference case of longevity for Korea rapidly undergoing population aging. In this respect, Japan's features of *seonjinguk* are better recognized in its domestic issues, that is, it is more rational and mature than Korea, having many aspects for Korea to learn from.

China's Identities and Representations in Korean Discourse

Before the mid-twentieth century, China's identity in the Koreans' perception generally went in line with the Koreans' self-national identity, as the two countries were in a similarly marginalized position in the Eurocentric global colonial order. With the advent of the Cold War afterwards, however, the identities of China and Korea in Koreans' perception became very different from each other. In the newly emerged discursive frameworks such as anti-communism and the *seonjinguk* discourse, the Koreans made a clear boundary in national identity between the two. China was designated a communist country within the anti-communist discourse, an aberrant contrasted with liberal democracy such as Taiwan. It was also identified as *hujinguk* within the framework of the discourse of *seonjinguk*, a country struggling with poverty at the low level of industrialization.

The Koreans' perception of China drastically changed again with Korea's establishment of a diplomatic relationship with China in 1992. With this as momentum, China's image greatly improved, from a communist enemy to a communist neighboring country that Korea had to communicate and cooperate with for regional peace and prosperity. However, negative perceptions of it are still notable amidst the dominance of the discourse of *seonjinguk* and the lingering anti-communist ideology in Korea.

China in International Issues

The analysis of this study shows that the current images of China are somewhat complicated in Korean discourse, going beyond the simple image of *hujinguk* in *seonjinguk* discourse. In regard to international issues, the most frequent terms for China are not "*hujinguk*," but "*sinheung gyeongje-guk*" (newly emerging economic country) and "*juyo-guk*" (major country) (six cases each). These are followed by "*gaedoguk*" (developing country; five cases), "*sinheung gyeongje daeguk*" (newly emerging great economic country; five cases), "*gyeongje daeguk*" (great economic country; four cases), "*jubyeon 4 gang*" (neighboring four powers; four cases), "Asian country" (four cases), and "*hubal juja*" (latecomer; three cases).[3] In those terms, the images of "emerging country," "powerful country," "major country," and "developing country" are notable. In them, China is mainly represented as a country "great, powerful, and newly or lately emerging."

As those terms have appeared in the editorials containing the term "*seonjinguk*" or "*hujinguk*," it is notable that there is no case directly designating China as *seonjinguk* or *hujinguk* in regard to international issues. Rather, there is a tendency to define China as an "emerging" or "developing" country, a developmental status between *seonjinguk* and *hujinguk*. In this sense, China is generally perceived as having escaped from the status of *hujinguk* in international issues, but is still distinguished from the advanced and mature images of *seonjinguk*.

It has also analyzed how China is characterized in the narratives of editorial sentences as to international issues. It shows that China is most frequently characterized as a country "rapidly chasing" Korea (15 cases), which is followed by the "emergence as a new economic power," the "reduction of the technological gap," and the "expansion of influence on international order" (11 cases each). Combining the representation of the "reduction of the technological gap" with that of "rapidly chasing" Korea, we can see that 26 editorials in total represent China as a country chasing Korea, reducing the technological gap with it. This perception reflects that Korea has advanced so far. However, it also raises a sense of crisis for the Koreans about their possible loss of competitiveness over China. In terms of the international order, China's representation is notable as an emerging great power rapidly expanding its influence on the international stage. In those respects, the two most notable images of China appearing in the narratives of the editorials in regard to international issues are "chasing" and "emerging." All of the representations mentioned above make dynamic and potential images of China.

Overall, China is perceived as a "developing country" in the discourse of *seonjinguk*, which is yet at a lower level of development than Korea, but is also recognized as an emerging large economy threatening Korea's current economic and technological status, and a country of the "G-2" rapidly expanding its influence in the world. In this respect, China appears to the Koreans as a very significant country that is greatly different from ordinary developing countries in international issues.

China in Domestic Issues

China's national image is somewhat negative in its domestic issues. In China's domestic issues, the identity of "*hujinguk*" is notable, as the most frequent term identifying China is a "*hujinguk* of human rights" (six cases). An editorial entitled "China is a great country when it escapes from the *hujinguk* of human rights," for instance, criticizes that "the country cannot clear its name of the *hujinguk* of human rights, if a person goes to jail because he has asked for the end of the Communist Party's dictatorship and the freedom of expression and association" (*Kyunghyang Shinmun*, 12 October 2010). The terms with the next highest frequency are "G-2" (four cases) and "socialist country" (three cases).

In regard to China's representation, the analysis of the narratives of editorial sentences shows that the most frequent one is the "backward level of human rights and democracy" (11 cases). The identity of China as a *hujinguk* of human rights is greatly notable in its domestic issues, and the image of a powerful emerging country shown in international issues is rarely seen in the data. The two most notable domestic issues making China's *hujinguk* image are "human rights" and "democracy." In this regard, China tends to be perceived as a country moving behind Korea on the path of political modernization – the path of democratization that Korea has already undergone in the 1980s.

As for China, an identity of *hujinguk* is well combined with an identity of a communist country usually represented as a dictatorship and totalitarian. This reflects that the discourse of *seonjinguk* and the lingering anti-communist ideology are the two most notable discursive sources of the negative perceptions of China. Those negative identities and representations entail the Koreans' sense of superiority over China and, at the same time, their sense of fear over the emergence and expansion of China.

In short, China's images are better in international issues than in its domestic issues. While China is perceived as a powerful emerging country rapidly chasing

Korea in economic and technological aspects and expanding its influence on the international stage, it is regarded as *hujinguk* in its domestic affairs. The identity of *hujinguk* represents China as socially and politically immature, having a low sense of human rights and democracy, producing low-quality products, and polluting the environment. In this regard, China is sometimes perceived as doing harm to its neighboring countries, including Korea.

Korea's Identities and Representations in Relation to Japan and China

Korea in International Issues

In regard to international issues, the analysis of this study has found various terms referring to Korea in relation to China and Japan. The most frequent terms are "great economic country ranked around tenth in the world" and "the chair country of the G-20" (six cases each). The next most frequently used term is "*sinheung-guk*" (emerging country; five cases). In this respect, Korea tends to be positioned in the world as a country with economic power ranked around tenth and political power deserving the chair of the G-20.[4] In terms of the level of economic development, however, it is considered an "emerging country" not reaching the level of *seonjinguk* yet. This identity of Korea is somewhat similar to that of China rather than Japan.

On the other hand, Korea is designated as *seonjinguk* or *hujinguk* in certain contexts. Some editorials call Korea *seonjinguk* of "historical record," "free trade agreement," "utilizing nuclear power," or "satellite" (one case each) in specific contexts, but others designate it as *hujinguk* of "free trade agreement," "tourism," "sea garbage," or "rocket" (one case each). Here the positive evaluations of certain events or phenomena occurring in Korea are projected into the concept of *seonjinguk*, while the negative ones are associated with the concept of *hujinguk*. In regard to the free trade agreement (FTA) with the U.S., it is interesting to see that Korea is called *seonjinguk* or *hujinguk* depending on a newspaper's position in agreement or disagreement with it.

The analysis of the narratives of the editorials has found that Korea is most frequently characterized as a country in "a sandwiched situation or a status of a nut in the nutcracker, between Japan and China" (15 cases). One editorial, for instance, mentions Korea's economy: "It is in a sandwiched status between *seonjinguk* and *gaedoguk* or China and Japan, as in a foreign media report that 'export champion Korea has lost its way'" (*Dong-a Ilbo*, 21 March 2007). Next frequent representations associated with Korea are the "period of low growth" (14 cases), the "host of G-20" (13 cases), the "economic power around tenth in the world" (12 cases), and the "expansion of FTA" (11 cases).

The perception of Korea's "sandwiched" status reflects that *seonjinguk* of Japan is going ahead of Korea with high technology and the *sinheung-guk* of China is chasing it rapidly with an advantage in product price, which is a typical developmentalist perception that Japan, Korea, and China are running a race on a linear universal path of development. Korea's in-between status raises a sense of crisis that Korea is being caught up to by China, while not reducing the gap with Japan. Thus, there often appears a perception that Korea is on a forked road either to enter into the ranks of *seonjinguk* by catching up with Japan, or to fall into the ranks of *hujinguk* being caught up to by China.

In this context, editorials ask for Korean people's hard efforts to overcome the "sandwiched situation" to survive in the competitive global order. In relation to this, there is a perception that Korea is playing a role of bridging or mediating *seonjinguk* and *gaedoguk* on international issues.

Korea in Relation to the Domestic Issues of China and Japan

Korea's in-between identity is also reflected in the narratives of editorials on the domestic issues of Japan and China. In general, Korea tends to be perceived as lacking in comparison with Japan, but as having desirable features in relation to China. For Korea, Japan as *seonjinguk* is mainly considered as its "reference point of comparison," "exemplary case," or "reference case," while China is regarded as a "negative reference case" for Korea.

For instance, the editorials mention Japan's domestic issues in relation to Korea in such ways as: While *seonjinguk* Japan made disaster safety systems mandatory, had fewer insurance crimes, and showed efforts for self-reform by the political circle, Korea as a country not reaching *seonjinguk* had "the *hujinguk* level of disaster safety systems" (*Dong-a Ilbo*, 4 October 2010), was suffering from "widespread insurance crimes" (*Kukmin Ilbo*, 27 January 2011), and had the "political circle displaying a typical case of high cost and low efficiency" (*Dong-a Ilbo*, 30 January 2012; *Segye Ilbo*, 23 May 2012). As such, the contrast between *seonjinguk* Japan and non-*seonjinguk* Korea is manifest in regard to Japanese domestic issues.

In relation to China, however, Korea's features appear very differently. In terms of human rights and democracy, in particular, Korea tends to be regarded as a country having achieved democratization ahead of China, being more "advanced" than China in terms of credibility, clarity, and predictability of government policies. When they are to criticize Korea, however, the features of Korea tend to be perceived as somewhat similar to those of China. One editorial, for instance, mentions that "nepotism is widespread in China […] Korea can move towards *seonjinguk* only when it overcomes *hujinguk*-style nepotism" (*Dong-a Ilbo*, 4 September 2010).

National Identities and Mutual Perceptions in Chinese and Japanese Development Discourses

Chinese Development Discourse

In the Chinese public space, development discourse is formed around such concepts as "*fādá guójiā*" (發達國家, developed country), "*fāzhǎn zhōng guójiā*" (發展中國家, developing country), and "*zuìbù fādá guójiā*" (最不發達

國家, least developed country). Each of these is somewhat equivalent to the Korean concepts "*seonjinguk*," "*gaebal dosang guk*" (*gaedoguk*; developing country), and "*hujinguk*," while there are notable differences in connotation between those Chinese and Korean concepts.

The economy of "*fādá guójiā*" that China pursues is never a capitalist economic system as is suggested in Eurocentric developmental discourse. China interprets the achievement of "*fādá guójiā*" ultimately as the way to accomplish "socialism with Chinese characteristics," utilizing a socialist market economy. The Chinese discourse of "*fādá guójiā*" gives justification to the Chinese national goal of accomplishing Chinese socialism. In this respect, the Chinese developmental goal of "*fādá guójiā*" postulates a different developmental path from the "developed countries" of Western capitalism.

In the discourse of "*fādá guójiā*," China defines itself as "*fāzhǎn zhōng guójiā*" (developing country). On this assumption, China aspires to development for the level of "*fādá guójiā*," while being careful not to be caught in the "middle-income trap." For this, it asks for constant technological innovation and national reformation. However, China stresses that its development path should naturally be different from those of current "*fādá guójiā*" as it has been developing in different historical circumstances from those of "*fādá guójiā*" that have experienced early capitalist industrialization. It is also recognized that China is currently in a historical situation in which those "*fādá guójiā*" are leading the world order.

In the Chinese discourse, "*fādá guójiā*" is presumed to be temporally advanced over "*fāzhǎn zhōng guójiā*," but this does not necessarily mean that the former is superior to the latter. Here is reflected China's development situation in two senses. First, it reflects Chinese confidence that China will be a leading country exceeding current "*fādá guójiā*" as it can utilize the latecomer's advantage. Second, it is to emphasize the Chinese sense of difference not only in their developmental path but also in dealing with the problems accompanying a rapid development process: For instance, the Chinese solution is "socialism with Chinese characteristics."

There is a perception that China as "*fāzhǎn zhōng guójiā*" is yet lacking in many ways compared with "*fādá guójiā*." On the other hand, other perceptions are also notable, such as: That China has become the second greatest economy in the world; that China is rapidly chasing current "*fādá guójiā*" with the latecomer advantage; and that China is an important country in the world market, as the world's greatest manufacturing country. In particular, there also appears a perception that China has quickly escaped from the 2008 global financial crisis, which was caused by "*fādá guójiā*," to stabilize the world economy and has greatly contributed to the world economy.

Having chosen the path of socialism since its national establishment in 1949, China admits that Western countries are advanced in terms of economy and industrialization. However, it has adopted Eurocentric discourse of development to a limited degree, by pursuing economic development for "socialism with Chinese characteristics," rather than the "catch-up"-style capitalist economic development. The "revolutionary modernity" that had been pursued by China showed a characteristic of enhancing the combination of nationalism, socialism, and developmentalism altogether, each of which respectively aimed for: National unity, sovereignty, and autonomy; equality and social justice; and overcoming of economic backwardness (Lin, 2006).

In this context, Chinese socialist development discourse neither accepts Eurocentric linear evolutionism nor suggests Western countries as the ideal model of development. It rejects Eurocentric modernization theory that tries to equate modernization with capitalist development.

The perception of the West appearing in the Chinese dominant discourse is very different from that reflected in the development discourses of the capitalist world. The "Western learning fever" of anti-traditionalism in the 1980s, which arose with Deng Xiaoping's reform and opening policies, had been seriously criticized by the New Left's "new nationalism" that emerged in the early 1990s. Chinese new nationalism, which emphasizes Chinese identity by highlighting the values of Chinese tradition and Chinese socialism, tends to perceive the West as having achieved economic prosperity but lacking in cultural aspects. It argues that capitalist modernity of the West contains conflictive, discriminating, and exploitative socio-economic relations and, thus, the West-led international order is studded with competition, conflict, and war, leading humankind to disaster (Zhao, 1997).

In this context, Chinese new nationalism highlights the values of equality and distribution, and reevaluates Chinese traditional thought and culture, e.g. Confucianism, and the spirit of harmony and equality contained in socialism, in order to achieve harmonious modernity. In this discursive framework, China is perceived as the leader of alternative modernity to the capitalist modernity of the West.

An identity dilemma for the Chinese in their discourse of development is that China as "*fāzhǎn zhōng guójiā*" is in an inferior position to "*fādá guójiā*" of Western capitalism, but the Chinese have overcome this with confidence that China can create a better development model through its unique path of development. Beneath the Chinese confidence is a perception that China can achieve the level of "*fādá guójiā*" through its own development path, which denies the assumption of linear developmentalism that China is following the development path of current "*fādá guójiā*." In the Chinese development discourse, the China that has arrived at the level of "*fādá guójiā*" through its path of socialism will be a developed country that is more equal, peaceful, and harmonious than are Western developed countries. In this respect, the Chinese solution to the identity dilemma of China as "*fāzhǎn zhōng guójiā*" is a serious challenge to the hegemony of Western development discourse.

Japanese Development Discourse

Like Korea, the discourse of "*sensinkoku*" (先進國, せんしんこく, advanced country) circulates widely in the Japanese public space, which is based on a dichotomy between "*sensinkoku*" and "*gosinkoku*" (後進國, こうしんこく, backward country). Japanese society had generally perceived itself as a middle-advanced country just after the defeat in World War II, and began to consider itself as on the "threshold of the rank of advanced country" in the 1950s. In the 1960s, Japan tended to define itself as an advanced country, reflecting confidence in its economic development in the post-war period.

Japanese self-identity as an advanced country echoed a global tendency to perceive Japan as a "developed country" in the framework of development discourse after the war. Despite their differences with one another in various aspects, Japan and the West shared the historical experiences of early industrial and military modernization through colonialism, and of competing with one another as "civilized countries" on the international stage. In this respect, it can be said that Japan and the West had a sense of kind over the former colonized countries in the non-West.

While Japan generally considers itself an advanced country today, it also perceives itself as having backward aspects in some parts. In the Japanese discourse, thus, awareness sometimes appears that Japan's position as an advanced country could be shaken if it does not overcome partial backwardness.

As for Japan's perception of others, Korea in the Japanese discourse began to be generally considered as a middle-advanced country from the 1980s. Korea was perceived as having advanced to the threshold of the rank of advanced country in the early 2000s, having overcome the financial crisis, and was regarded as having secured the level of advanced country in some areas. However, it was also pointed out that Korea had structural problems to reach the level of advanced country.

In the 2010s, there generally appear three main perceptions of Korea in Japanese discourse. First, Korea has already entered into the rank of advanced country or is an advanced country in some parts. This tendency is to recognize Korea's upward movement from "emerging country" to "advanced country," or to observe Korea's advance in diverse areas, such as "human rights," "credit cards," "talent education," "smart technology," "environment," "network voting," etc.

Second, there appears attention to new problems that Korea should face as an advanced country. It points out that Korea as an advanced country has come to face problems other advanced countries have. For instance, it introduces Korea's situation of facing agricultural problems as an "advanced country in free trade agreements," while reviewing Korea's FTA with the U.S.

Third, there is an attitude of not admitting Korea as an advanced country. It tends to intentionally denigrate Korea in such a way that Korea has failed on the threshold of advanced country status and is currently "unenlightened," or to evaluate Korea cynically as an "advanced country in surveillance" or being backward in politics after democratization. This reflects a degree of anti-Korean sentiment among some Japanese.

As for China, the Japanese discourse tends to consider it an "emerging country" or "middle-advanced country" in the 2010s and, in this regard, some writing has analyzed China's agony about the "middle-income trap." The Japanese discourse often distinguishes the case of China from that of an advanced country by mentioning such terms as "the response of an advanced country to China," "China's response to an advanced country," etc. These presume that China is not an advanced country yet.

In relation to this, there is also a perception that China is moving towards the status of advanced country. Some consider China a partially advanced country in such areas as "space," "software," "electronic journals," "environment," etc. Others perceive it as a country pursuing the status of advanced country or a country having arrived on the threshold of advanced country. On the other hand, there are also arguments that, as there are for Korea, China is a country that can never be an advanced country, which reflects some anti-Chinese sentiment among the Japanese.

Conclusion

This chapter has examined how Korean major newspapers identify and represent Korea, China, and Japan in relation to the discourse of *seonjinguk*. The analysis of international issues has shown that Japan is generally defined as "*seonjinguk*" having "advanced technologies" with a tendency to "distort history." In comparison, China is mainly considered as "*sinheung-guk*" or "*juyo-guk*" with the images of "chasing" and "emerging," e.g., "reducing technological gaps with Korea," "emerging economic power," and "expanding its influence on the international political economy."

As for Korea, the most frequently used terms are "economic power ranked around tenth in the world" and the "chair country of the G-20," which are followed by "*sinheung-guk*" (emerging country). The most notable representation of Korea in the narratives of editorial sentences is "a sandwiched status or a status like a nut in a nutcracker, between Japan and China," followed by the "era of low growth."

In domestic issues, Japan is perceived as *seonjinguk*, having the features of both "mature political culture" and a "lost decade." It is mainly referred to as an "exemplary case" or the "reference point of comparison" for Korea. Japan tends to be better perceived in its domestic issues than in international issues. By contrast, China is most frequently identified as the "*hujinguk* of human rights" in its domestic issues, followed by the "G-2." The most notable representation of China in editorial narratives is a "low level of human rights and democracy." In contrast to Japan, China tends to be better perceived in international issues than in domestic ones.

The identities and representations of Japan and China are somewhat multi-layered in the Korean discourse. As for Japan, the identity of *seonjinguk* is manifest but the representation of distorting history undermines its status of *seonjinguk*. In comparison, China's identity is notable as an "emerging country" or "*hujinguk* of human rights," but it also has another notable identity of a "major country" rapidly emerging on the international stage. These multiple identities and representations bring about complicated feelings for the Koreans: For instance, Japan is *seonjinguk* that is not much respected, while China is an "emerging country" that should not be disregarded, as a major country in the world.

This chapter has shown that the Chinese dominant development discourse presents an alternative development path and vision that are a serious challenge to the developmental hegemony of Western capitalist countries. It has also introduced the Japanese development discourse as having a somewhat similar perceptual tendency to the Korean discourse, making a hierarchy among Japan, Korea, and China according to their levels of economic development.

Notes

1 This chapter analyzes the editorials of nationally read Korean newspapers published over a recent ten-year period. For this, the search was for editorials in ten newspapers published from 30 June 2003 to 29 June 2013, which were available in the Korea Press Foundation database (www.kinds.or.kr). First, the search obtained the editorials that contained the terms "Korea," "China," and "Japan" in their contents, and then selected among them those containing the terms "*seonjinguk*" or "*hujinguk*," which were 201 in number (material for "international issues"). A review of this material found that it did not show much about the characteristics of each country. To compensate for this weakness, another group of editorials were obtained (material for "domestic issues"), which contained the terms either "Japan" and "*seonjinguk*" or "Japan" and "*hujinguk*" in their contents (192 cases), and the terms either "China" and "*seonjinguk*" or "China" and "*hujinguk*" in their contents (141 cases). The search for each country's domestic issues was limited to three years (30 June 2010–29 June 2013).

2 The two sub-sections of this chapter about Japanese and Chinese development discourses are a revision of part of the report (2015–22, in Korean) for the National Research Council for Economics, Humanities and Social Sciences. I am grateful to my co-authors of the report, Professors Jeong Il-Jun, Park Jeong-Hyeon, and Song Byeong-Gwon, for their permission to reuse the contents of the report. For a deeper discussion about Chinese development discourse, please refer to Park Jeong-Hyeon and Kim Jongtae (2015, in Korean).

3 Reviewing the result with a focus on the identities of "*sinheung*" (emerging) and "*gyeongje daeguk*" (great economic country), it finds that the number of cases referring to China as "*sinheung*" (*sinheung gyeongje-guk* or *sinheung gyengje daeguk*) is 11, and those identifying it as "*gyeongje daeguk*" (*sinheung gyeongje daeguk* or *gyeongje daeguk*) is nine.

4 The frequent identification of Korea as the chair of the G-20 reflects that the newspaper data for this study include those at the time when the G-20 Summit was held in Seoul in 11–12 November 2010.

9 A Comparison of Regional Identities between Northeast Asia and Europe

The Constructions of "Self" and "Others"

Discussions have been had about the importance of geographical proximity in the studies of region and regionalism. To explain regionalism in terms of geography is quite a usual attempt, which tends to argue that regionalism takes place through the interactions among neighboring countries, or that it is the outcome of political decisions among geographically proximate countries.

Recent studies, however, tend to emphasize a constructivist perspective assuming region or regionalism as the outcome of "imagination." They argue that subjective elements, such as values, worldviews, and identities shared by countries are far more important than geographical proximity in constructing region or regionalism. For instance, Asian countries, such as Korea and Japan, have constructed a region of "Asia-Pacific" with those in the far-away American continent, such as the U.S. and Mexico, and a total of 21 countries in Asia, Oceania, and America constitute the Asia-Pacific Economic Cooperation (APEC). Thus, researchers consider "region" or "regionalism" as the outcome of international politics (Katzenstein, 2002), or of perceptive practices constructed by discourses (Jayasuriya, 1994).

Countries' interests collide with one another in the construction of region and regionalism. The region imagined by East Asian countries after the 1990s Asian financial crisis, for instance, might have been different from "Asia-Pacific" envisaged by the U.S. The East Asian countries' interest in region was institutionally reflected in the launch of the Association of Southeast Asian Nations (ASEAN) + Three pursuing regional interests quite different from those of APEC. As such, each country imagines region to maximize its interests, and regionalism or regional institutions reflect countries' power dynamics surrounding the imaginations of regions.

Regional identity is a process of making boundaries between "us" and "them," by constructing homogeneity of the "in group" distinguished from the "out group." Intraregional "sameness" and its "difference" from outside are imagined on such elements as regional cultures, common memories, shared values and worldviews, and political-economic interests. In this respect, a region is an "imagined community" and, in the dimension of discourse, is a "discursive community."

Regionalism is premised on "intersubjective structures," a combination of shared interests, expectations, and knowledge at the regional level, through which intraregional countries and societies define their identities and interests (Wendt, 1994). In this respect, a "region" can be understood as an imagined space in which diverse social groups including countries interact with one another at the transnational level in a variety of dimensions, based on a degree of shared identities.

A process of defining the area of self is, on the contrary, that of defining the area of the other. In identity construction, the "other" plays positive or negative roles, as the positive other is the other that self pursues to resemble, while the negative other is the one that self refuses to simulate. Self pursues assimilation with the positive other while dissimilation with the negative other. In constructing the other, the subject tends to idealize the positive other, by projecting his/her/its aspiring values and attributes onto it, while marginalizing the negative other by projecting onto it values and attributes to refuse. The boundary between self and other strengthens when the former perceives that its interests are infringed by the latter. The perceived "threat" or "enemy" from outside intensifies the internal unity of group and accelerates its internal homogeneity (Adler, 1997; Tsoukala, 2008; Carpentier, 2011).

The subject interprets self and objects through discourse and, thus, the identities of self and objects vary according to discourse. As knowledge or discourse reflects power relations, identities constructed by it also reflect power relations. Thus, a dominant identity of a group can be regarded as reflecting power dynamics supported by the group's dominant power.

A society's dominant discourse appearing in a certain historical period provides it with dominant world views and identities at the time. The global hegemony of the West has been supported by Eurocentric discourses justifying its material power in terms of such elements as race, culture, social structure, etc., which is actually rooted in wealth accumulated after 1492 (Blaut, 1993). Under Western hegemony, societies in the world have constructed the identities of self and others through the frameworks of Eurocentric discourses.

There have recently been discussions about the regional identity of Northeast Asia, with the increase in intraregional interactions. However, research is somewhat rare that approaches it in terms of discursive construction of self and others, given that regional identity is closely related to the region's dominant discourse. In this respect, this chapter examines the discursive elements of Northeast Asian identity in comparison with European identity, considering that a regional identity is a process of demarcating self and others in the region's dominant discourse.

This chapter focuses on two aspects regarding the construction of regional identity. First, it investigates whether there are "primary" and "practical" conditions for regional identity construction: The "primary condition" refers to a regional consciousness based on the elements related to the "primary group," such as culture, emotion, kinship, etc., and the "practical condition" is a regional awareness mostly created by the concerned countries' practical interests such as economic development, defense, etc. Second, it attends to the regional constructions of "self" and "others," reflected in dominant discourses in Europe and Northeast Asia. It looks into, in particular, whether "self" and "others" of the two regions have been constructed positively or negatively, and inside or outside the region, in regard to the historically dominant discourses of "civilization," "development," and the "Cold War" in the modern era.

The following is organized in three main sections. First, it examines the genealogy of the construction of European "self" and "others" in the modern era. Second, it investigates the conditions for regional identity, reflected in the European Union (EU). Third, it discusses the Northeast Asian case: Its ways of constructing "self" and "others," and the primary and practical conditions for regional identity.

History and Reality of Europe's Constructions of "Self" and "Others"

A Genealogy of Europe's Construction of "Self": The Discourses of "Civilization," "Development," and the "Cold War"

The Christian identity of Middle Ages Europe was possible because of its construction of the Islamic world as the "other." To Middle Ages Europe, the Orient was generally a fearful entity, in which "violence, cruelty, and fanatic idolatry were prevailing" (Ahn B.-J., 2001: 14). Europe after the Renaissance still constructed the Orient with a "negative image of unfamiliar and mismatching to European values" and perceived it as "a society dominated by despotism, servility, extravagance and hedonism, and sexual indulgence" (Ahn B.-J., 2001: 14).

One of the main concepts in modern Europe to distinguish between Europe and non-Europe was "civilization." Based on the barbarism–civilization dichotomy and the belief in progress from the former to the latter, the discourse of civilization projected Europeans' positive values, such as rationality, humanity, activeness, maturity, and moderation, into the concept of "civilization," while contrary negative values into that of "barbarism." Europe raised a sense of superiority and solidarity over non-Europe by defining itself as "civilization." Europe "categorized, measured, and evaluated non-European societies through European values into which Europe had given universal attributes for itself," and "created the image of non-Europe according to its own needs and prejudices" (Ahn B.-J., 2001: 16). Thus, "Europe confirmed its self from a sense of superiority over the non-European world, and found out its identity through the denial and rejection of non-European cultures" (*ibid.*).

"Race science" in the nineteenth century transformed European history into a "natural history" (Nederveen Pieterse, 1995, 2001). In this respect, Europe's identity was based on the sense of superiority as civilization in terms of social evolutionism, and on the sense of superiority as "whites" in terms of biological evolutionism. Since the modern era, Eurocentric discourses have tended to distinguish between the "prototype" and the "emulator" on the evolutionary path, by assuming the sequential relationship between the two (Greig et al., 2007).

After the world wars, the discourse of development led by the U.S. emerged as another notable global discourse supporting the hegemony of the West. The development discourse homogenizes the West into the "developed" or the "advanced," while constructing the non-West as the "other" of the "developed." While the "duty of civilization" in the colonial era was a kind of unilateral project, the "duty of development" reflected the economic aspiration of newly independent non-Western countries. In the development era, Non-Western countries launched national projects to "catch up" with the West, seeing their developmental future from the "already developed" Western countries (Sikkink, 1991; Ndlovu-Gatsheni, 2012).

The Cold War was another historical circumstance that promoted the formation of Europe's regional self. In this regard, political modernization theory is a political development discourse as it dichotomizes politics into "pre-modern politics," characterized by despotism or authoritarianism, and "modern politics" featured by mature democracy. It defines transition from the former to the latter as "political modernization." In the historical circumstances of the Cold War, political development theory highlighted the political superiority of Western capitalism over communism, getting support from anti-communist discourses.

By setting Soviet communism as its great threat or enemy, Europe raised a need for regional unity and strengthened its regional solidarity. As Kang W.-T. and Cho H.-S. (2009: 42) noted, European countries had to unite internally to defend themselves against the external threat of communism in the Cold War intensifying. The U.S. supported Europe's unity in security to construct it as the "ideological community" or "political community" of the bastion against the communist power of the Union of Soviet Socialist Republics (USSR) and Eastern Europe (Lim W.-T., 2012). As was reflected in the launch of the North Atlantic Treaty Organization (NATO) in 1949, the formation of Europe as a "defense community" was possible because of the existence of Soviet communism. In terms of political development discourse, Europe strengthened its self-consciousness of superiority as the politically "developed" sharing the values of liberty and democracy in relation to the "other" of Soviet and Eastern European communism as the politically "underdeveloped."

In short, European societies shared a series of regional identities in different historical periods from the Christian identity in the Middle Ages, the identity of "civilization" in the modern era, to that of the "developed" after World War II, while constructing negative others corresponding to each historical period. Those historical processes were significant discursive elements for Europe to imagine itself as a homogenized region in different historical periods.

The "Primary" and "Practical" Conditions for the Formation of the EU

Having experienced two big wars through the early and mid-twentieth century, Europe came to reflect on its wars in the past, keenly realizing the need for regional unity as a way to maintain peace. Europe set its past as the "other" to overcome, in which it was nationally divided to use violence against one another, and imagined a regionally unified future as its ideal self. In this respect, the idea of unified Europe in the post-war period was promoted for three main practical goals: To prevent war and promote peace; economic cooperation and prosperity; and security (Jin S.-W., 2003).

Europe utilized common historical experiences and memories as resources for forming regional identity, such as humanism, scientific techniques, industrialization, economic development, democracy, etc. These various elements were related to "civilization," "progress," and "modernity," the main concepts representing modern Europe. As of 2016, Europe maintains an official regional community at the level of "union," consisting of 28 member countries. The EU officially claims to be an open community centering on the values of democracy.

The regional consciousness and identity of the EU are reflected in discussions about the qualifications for its member countries. For instance, Turkey, as previously an associate member of the European Economic Community (EEC), has continuously asked for membership of the EU. Some argue that Turkey's putative heterogeneity from Europe has been an obstacle to membership, regarding various elements constituting the European identity, such as religion, geography, race, and culture (Yoon T.-W., 2014). It is considered that Turkey is religiously an Islamic country, mismatching to Europe's Christian identity, geographically on the borderline between Europe and Asia, and racially the descendants of Central Asian Huns and Gokturks, distinguished from peoples in the European races. As for culture, Turkey has not shared modern European thoughts, such as the Enlightenment and rationalism.[1]

On the other hand, the identity of the EU is based on diversity. In the consciousness of the European community are the perceptions of diversity in religion, culture, and people within the region, and there is a tendency to highlight common values to pursue regional unity in diversity (Lee W.-G., 2011). European identity assumes multiplicity based on multilateral relations among countries and, in this respect, "one Europe" does not necessary mean "one European culture" or "one European identity."[2] Europe's identity is the "identity in which nations' identities are reconstructed at the European level, rather than an identity transcending the nations" (Lee O.-Y., 2011: 133).

It is also noted that power dynamics and conflicts of interest have existed among member countries in the process of constructing Europe's regional unity. The unification of Europe has been led mainly by Western European countries, such as France and Germany, and in this respect, the construction of the EU is considered the "process of inclusion and exclusion practiced by Western Europe's criteria," or the expansion of the EU as the "process of expanding Western Europe's identity" (Passerini, 2002; Jin S.-W., 2003: 156). The United Kingdom's withdrawal from the EU, known as

"Brexit," well reflects the interests conflict among Western European countries over the EU.

Betraying the hopes of the EU, furthermore, the European identity among the member countries' citizens is not that strong, compared with national identity. According to Eurobarometer surveys from 2010 to 2015, about 30–40% of European respondents replied "no" to the question "Do you feel you are a citizen of the EU?" The expansion of EU roles in member countries causes an effect, rather, of strengthening national consciousness, contrary to the regional expectation that the unification of Europe in politics and the economy will naturally spread the sense of European consciousness (Choi J.-W., 2006). Responding to this, the EU has implemented various policies in education and culture to expand the senses of community and identity. For this, the creation of "shared memories" among countries is utilized as the EU highlights the regional context in the education of history while making efforts to reconstruct national spaces as regional spaces (Lee W.-G., 2011).

Overall, the EU can be regarded as a transnational regional community whose launch has reflected the member countries' various political and economic interests on the grounds of a historically formed sense of regional identity. The construction of its identity has been based on the sense of kind in geography, culture, and race, which derived from historically shared experiences and thought in the region. It has also been a process of pursuing regional unity on national diversity to meet the emerged need for peace, economic prosperity, and security. In those respects, the European regional community is the result of the combination of the "primary condition," reflecting the regional sense of kind, and the "practical condition" for achieving regional peace and prosperity by overcoming the "other" of Europe's conflictive past as well as that of Europe's outside.

History and Reality of Northeast Asia's Constructions of "Self" and "Others"

In recent discussions about regional identity in East Asia is reflected East Asia's confidence in its economic success after the 1980s.[3] The theories of Asian values and Confucian capitalism arose in the studies of East Asian development, and the discourses emphasizing the distinctiveness and uniqueness of East Asia were raised by Asian leaders and intellectuals, such as Malaysian Prime Minister Mahathir and Singapore Prime Minister Lee Kuan Yew. The discourses of East Asian community emphasized that East Asia could construct a cultural community based on its unique and distinctive culture while pursuing the construction of a political-economic system reflecting regional specificities.

The discourses of East Asian community can be discerned between the discourse of "cultural homogeneity" and that of "East Asian specificity" (Park S.-W., 2011). While the former focuses on the common cultural characteristics in East Asia, such as Confucianism and Chinese letters, as essential elements for the construction of regional identity, the latter tends to emphasize the distinctiveness of East Asia compared with other regions such as the West.[4] While giving insights into the values of Asian commonality and uniqueness, those Asia-centric discourses, however, tend to oversimplify the relations between cultural homogeneity and uniqueness on the one hand, and the construction of regional identity on the other hand. In this respect, they show a degree of "cultural determinism."

This chapter pays attention to whether there has been either the experience of constructing regional identity or, in relation to this, a constructive process of "self" and "others" in Northeast Asia. It discusses the current state of Northeast Asian identity by examining intraregional countries' ways of constructing "self" and "others" in terms of dominant discourses.

Northeast Asia in the Discourse of Civilization: From the Mid-nineteenth to Mid-twentieth Centuries

The international order in Asia was established centering on Chinese civilization before the expansion of the West in the nineteenth century, which was justified by the Sinocentric discourse of civilization. In this discourse, the "other" was "barbarism," not meeting the criteria of civilization, and was considered as existing both inside and outside Asia. As the distinction between "civilization" and "barbarism" was the matter of observing the "Tao" of civilization or not, rather than of making essential hierarchy among societies or regions, its influence on constructing regional identity was not great. Furthermore, China's consciousness of self in relation to "others" was not very strong as it tended to consider itself as the world itself.

The expansion of Western colonialism to Asia after the Opium Wars (1839–1842; 1856–1860) was, in discursive terms, a collision between the Eurocentric discourse of civilization designating the West as the most advanced and the Sinocentric one perceiving the West as "barbarian." When different discursive systems collide with each other, truth is generally decided by the power of its supporting group. In the newly emerged "threatening" international order dominated by the logic of power, Asian countries came to realize their modern selves in relation to the West, which they had to resemble although they might not have been willing to resemble them.[5]

In Northeast Asia, it was Japan that recognized the seriousness of Western power the earliest. Witnessing the defeat of China in the first Opium War, followed by the experience of shocking intrusions by U.S. Commodore Perry's fleet in the mid-nineteenth century, Japan aggressively pursued transformation to a modern country through the Meiji Restoration. For Japan at the time, the West was the "other" not only to confront, but also to learn about in order to confront. The idea of accepting Western civilization was vigorously suggested by modern Japanese intellectuals (Hahm D.-J., 2004; de Bary et al., 2006; Park Y.-S., 2008).

In terms of identity, Japan's civilizational view basically pursued assimilation to the West, whereas constructing Asian countries as the "other." For Japan, the West was the entity to overcome, learn about, and assimilate, while the East was the object to civilize as the inferior "other" whose level of civilization did not reach Japan. In this respect, Japan's various discourses on regional community in the late nineteenth to early twentieth centuries showed a limitation as they contained Japan's strategic intention to justify the domination of its Asian others. That is, Japan's discourses on regional community at the time did not truly assume a sense of homogeneity and solidarity with the countries in the region, such as Korea and China, which was the essential element of regional identity.[6]

In the case of Korea, intellectuals for *gaehwa* and *munmyeong* (enlightenment and civilization) also argued for a need to accommodate Western civilization as a way to maintain national sovereignty. In their discourse of *gaehwa* and *munmyeong*, the West was represented as an entity to constantly threaten Korea's sovereignty with its physical power, but it was also the object to resemble for national sovereignty (see Chapter 2). As the Eurocentric discourse of civilization took hegemony in Korea, the West was considered as an entity for Korea to assimilate, while Korea and China were identified as entities not reaching the West. In the framework of Korea's modern civilization discourse in the late nineteenth century, the "other" was nothing but Korea and the East themselves. Korean modern intellectuals set modernization modeling after Western civilization as the urgent mission for the nation, and this was actually a process of overcoming the negative "other" in itself.

Asia still had the "other" in itself even after World War I. In the non-Eurocentric discourse of civilization, the East was perceived as the possessor of spiritual, moral, and peaceful civilization, but it did not include Japan. The dominant discourse of civilization in the Korean public space in the 1920s and 1930s notably raised a need to resist against Japan, in such ways as: "Rise, the youth of Korea, who are infringed by the civilization of invasion" (*Chosun Ilbo*, 13 November 1925). It utilized civilization discourse to criticize Japanese colonial rule by, for instance, questioning whether there was torture in the legal system of the "civilized" country, i.e., Japan, while asking for the "civilization" of the Japanese police (*Chosun Ilbo*, 9 March 1923, 12 July 1924, 9 September 1924).

In short, as the West was set as the center of civilization in the late nineteenth and early twentieth centuries, Northeast Asia constructed its "positive self" outside it, while its "negative self" inside. In a situation where the aspiration for the "other" outside and the negation of self inside were crossed, the conditions for constructing regional identity were greatly lacking. Although Northeast Asia had overcome the negativity of its self, to some degree, with the rise of non-Eurocentric discourse of civilization after World War I, it was not in a situation of recognizing regional identity, as Japan was still perceived somewhat similar to Western civilization, a civilization of invasion. That is, geographical Northeast Asia still contained the "other" within itself.

Northeast Asia in the Discourse of Development

It was the U.S. that saved the West from its hegemonic crisis in global power relations. The U.S., having risen in relation to Europe after World War II, self-claimed as the new driving force of Western civilization, hardening the ground for its global hegemony (Patterson, 1997). In a new evolutionary interpretive framework that was promoted by the U.S., the areas previously designated as "barbarian" began to be re-conceptualized as "under-development." The superior status of "civilization" over "barbarism" began to be transferred to the superior status of "development" over "under-development." In this way, the discourse of development emerged as a hegemonic discourse supporting the global hegemony of the U.S.

In regard to East Asian identity, national identities and perceptions reflected in the development discourses of Korea, China, and Japan show notable heterogeneity with one another (see Chapter 8). For Korea and Japan, the "positive other" that they aspire to resemble is the West, rather than Asia. Korea designates the West as "*seonjinguk*" (advanced country), aiming for the nation's "entry into the ranks of *seonjinguk*." Meanwhile, Japan designates itself as the "advanced" in its discourse of development, while designating Korea and China as not reaching its developed status. In this respect, the statuses of Korea, China, and Japan are not at the same level in the dominant development discourses of Korea and Japan.

In China's development discourse, Japan and Korea are generally designated as "developed" countries, and China as a "developing" one. However, the identity of "developing" in the Chinese discourse does not contain as much inferiority as potential and advantage as a latecomer, which is very different from that in Korean and Japanese discourses. In this discursive framework, China as the leader of the "developing" world presents a vision of the "developed" in the future, which has overcome the weaknesses of current capitalist "developed" countries. For this, the Chinese emphasize the need for taking different development paths, such as "socialism with Chinese characteristics," to go beyond the Eurocentrism manifestly appearing in the Japanese and Korean discourses.

As such, in terms of dominant development discourses in Northeast Asia, heterogeneity is notable in mutual perceptions and identities of Korea, China, and Japan. The Korean and Japanese discourses of development, in particular, continuously produce the perception that those three countries are not in the same rank by assuming the hierarchy between the "developed" and the "developing" (or "underdeveloped"). The Chinese discourse also pursues a different development path from the capitalist paths of Korea and Japan, while emphasizing China's advantageous status as "developing." In this respect, development discourses in Northeast Asia are not greatly conducive to the construction of regional identity.

Northeast Asia in Cold War Discourse

As the Cold War intensified globally especially after the Korean War (1950–1953), a confrontational regional structure was established in Northeast Asia between Korea-the U.S.-Japan and North Korea-China. As part of Northeast Asia had been put under the military-security hegemony of the U.S., Northeast Asia was imagined and embodied as a region reflecting U.S. political intent and interests. As U.S. global hegemony was maintained by the perceived threat from the USSR (Wallerstein, 2000), its hegemony in Northeast Asia was sustained by the constructed threat from North Korea and China. In the confrontation between North Korea and South Korea, a divided system of "hostile interdependence" was formed in both Koreas (Paek N.-C., 1998; Lee N.-J., 2013).

The security regime of Korea-the U.S.-Japan is a great obstacle to the construction of Northeast Asian identity, as it is a regional system constructed by setting North Korea and China as the enemy. In the sense that China, in particular, is a main concerned country in the discussions of Northeast Asian community, the Cold War discourse or security discourse in Northeast Asia tends to heighten regional heterogeneity, rather than homogeneity.

The Cold War in Northeast Asia is still going on as the extreme confrontation between the two Koreas plays a role at the forefront. Thus, the discussions of Northeast Asian community often express the intention of overcoming the Cold War system reflected in the existent regional order led by the U.S. For instance, the region of "Northeast Asia" appearing in the idea of the "era of Northeast Asia" led by the Roh Moo-Hyun government of Korea in the 2000s, intended to "get over the preexistent military-security perceptions as well as U.S.-centric and Japan-centric perceptions" (Lee S.-H., 2004: 134).

In terms of international politics, current Northeast Asia has difficulty in perceiving internal homogeneity as the intraregional countries are confronting one another being divided into "us" and the "enemy." This is contrasted with the European situation in which the sense of internal homogeneity strengthened as the Soviet Union and Eastern Europe were assumed as the main "threat" to the region.

In Korea-the U.S.-Japan's perception of "regional threat," furthermore, appears a tendency for moral essentialism that is based on the sense of their moral superiority over North Korea and China. An exemplary perception is that the most serious factor threatening the peace of Northeast Asia is North Korea's hostile and rogue nature. This entails another perception that regional peace and stability are entirely dependent upon the effective containment of the aggressiveness of North Korea.

In terms of security, the "threat" is socially constructed rather than is existent "out there." As Wendt (1995) mentions, the Americans can feel more fear from just two North Korean nuclear weapons than from 200 British nuclear weapons. In a similar vein, North Korea may feel threatened more by U.S.

nuclear capacity around the Korean Peninsula than by hundreds of Chinese nuclear weapons.[7] As such, "threat" derives from "meanings" socially constructed rather than naturally arising from physical destructive power. In this respect, there arose a need to pay more attention to the "construction of enemy" between the concerned countries in Northeast Asia, and to the ways of deconstructing the hostile discourse and relationship between them (Kim, 2016).[8]

The Cold War discourse in Northeast Asia led by Korea, Japan, and the U.S. accompanies anti-communist discourse, which distinguishes between communism and liberal capitalism, and making the "other" with the former. In this discourse, communism is designated as a deviated ideology denying political freedom and national tradition. The Korea-U.S.-Japan military alliance centering on the U.S. is based on anti-communist ideology, which assumes the communist powers of North Korea, China, and Russia as the main threat or the enemy.

In the Rhee Syngman period of Korea, national self-identity based on anti-communist discourse was the "anti-communist country," and the West was assumed as the countries of liberal democracy in contrast with communism. In this discursive situation, "pro-American perception and the perception of the U.S. as a blood alliance took a solid position" in response to the "hostile other" such as North Korea and China (Cho H.-Y., 2003: 53; Kim D.-C., 2011).

The perception of China in Korea's anti-communist discourse in the 1950s was well reflected in the designation of the Kuomintang's Taiwan as "free China" (*jayu jungguk*) in relation to the Communist Party's mainland China as "Chinese communists" (*junggong*). In the Korean society in that period, mainland China was generally imagined as a hostile country threatening the "free world" (Jeong M.-S., 2007, 2011, 2012). Thus, the Chinese Communist Party was perceived in negative images, such as despotism, oppression, hostility, menace to peace, inhumanity, etc., and China and the Chinese military were sometimes called the "Chinese communist barbarians" (*junggong orangke*).

Anti-communist discourse came to be combined with development discourse in the Park Chung-Hee era. The idea that "development was a way to win against communism and ultimately to achieve the reunification of the Koreas" provided discursive grounds for the anti-communist developmental state. Developmentalism after the late 1960s, in particular, got along more notably with anti-communism in such slogans as "national defense on the one hand and industrial construction on the other hand" (Kim J.-H. and Cho H.-Y., 2003). The association of anti-communist and development discourses created a perceptual framework of "liberal democracy = development = *seonjinguk*" and "communism = underdevelopment = *hujinguk*." Thus, North Korea and China were generally represented as countries of hostile communism, underdevelopment, and *hujinguk*.

In post-Cold War Korean society, China has often been perceived in a negative light, although it has escaped from the image of "hostile enemy." In the current popular discourse in Korea, China is notably identified as a "great economic country" or a country of the "G-2" in the aspects of international economy and international politics, while it is frequently designated as "*hujinguk*" in human rights and democracy in regard to its domestic affairs. Here the Chinese identity of *hujinguk* reflects, in part, an identity of a communist country that tends to be associated with "despotism" in the framework of anti-communism.

Conclusion

This chapter has examined the conditions and realities of Northeast Asian identity in comparison with Europe, focusing on dominant discourses' construction of self and others. In constructing regional community, Europe utilized what it had experienced and constructed in the modern transition as common values for regionalism, such as humanism, industrialization, economic development, and democracy. In those values were reflected European senses of kind in culture, emotion, and race. The EU can be considered an official regional community having successfully combined "primary conditions" – the sense of kind in culture and emotion reflected in the discourses of Christianity, civilization, and development in changing historical periods – with "practical conditions" in which concerned countries' various interests are reflected in the aspects of peace, economy, and security. In terms of identity, Europe has created conditions conducive to regional community by constructing a positive "self" inside and, in relation to this, negative "others" outside.

Diverse discourses on regional community currently appear in Northeast Asia, but both primary and practical conditions for it are greatly lacking. The Japanese and Korean discourses of civilization in the nineteenth century constructed their positive others outside it by perceiving the West as the center of civilization. As Japan joined the ranks of imperial countries, it tended to perceive its neighboring countries as the objects to colonize, while the colonized countries designated Japan as the civilization of invasion. After World War II, development discourse set an international hierarchy of Japan–Korea–China according to the level of economic development, and the Cold War and anti-communist discourses set North Korea and China as "hostile others." In those respects, Northeast Asia's negative others have existed within the region throughout the modern period. As there has been no emotional sense of kinship to contribute to constructing regional self-awareness in Northeast Asia, it lacks the "primary conditions" for regional community.

In regard to "practical conditions," Northeast Asian countries have not made an effort to mutually cooperate and unify for practical interests such as peace and security, only to construct "others" inside the region. The confrontations among Northeast Asian countries are ongoing in security, military, and ideological dimensions under the influence of the U.S., an extra-regional country. The discussion above can be summarized in Table 9.1, Table 9.2, and Table 9.3.

Table 9.1 Comparison of Europe and Northeast Asia in the Construction of Self and Others

	Europe		*Northeast Asia*	
	Self	*Other*	*Self*	*Other*
Discourse of civilization	Civilization (Europe)	Barbarism (non-Europe)	Mix of half-civilized, civilization of spirit and ethics, civilization of invasion, etc.	Civilization (civilization of invasion): the West Barbarism (such as Africa)
Discourse of development	The developed (Europe)	The under-developed or developing (non-Europe)	Mix of the developed, developing, underdeveloped, etc.	The developed: the West The under-developed (or developing): Africa, Latin America, Asia, etc.
Discourse of the Cold War	Democracy (Europe)	Communism and dictatorship (non-Europe)	Mix of capitalism, democracy, socialism, etc.	"Threatening others" are located inside the region

Table 9.2 Comparison of the Conditions for Regional Identity: Primary and Practical Conditions

		Practical condition	
		No	*Yes*
Primary condition	No	Superficial exchange	Practical cooperation or alliance (e.g. U.S.-Korea alliance)
	Yes	Division or confrontation (e.g. South Korea and North Korea)	Regional community (e.g. Europe)

Regional unity appears as a result not only of official conversations and consultations between the governments but also of the increase of transnational interactions in the non-governmental sectors. The case of the former can be called "regionalization from above" or "formal regionalization," while that of the latter "regionalization from below" or "informal regionalization" (Breslin et al., 2002). While regionalism is the idea of pursuing common regional order, regionalization is a process of regional interaction and interdependence.

In Northeast Asia, the tendency towards "regionalization" appears more notably than does "regionalism," which is led by an increase of interactions in

Table 9.3 Comparison of the Conditions for Regional Identity: Positive, Negative Self, and Others

		Other	
		Negative	*Positive*
Self	*Negative*	Violence, deconstruction	Dependency, catch-up strategy (e.g. Korea in *seonjinguk* discourse)
	Positive	Ethnocentrism, colonialism (e.g. Europe)	Equal communication and exchange (e.g. inside Europe)

various socio-economic fields. In the international economic aspect, Korea's trade with China takes the highest 23.4% of its total trade, while its trade with China, Japan, and ASEAN combined reaches as high as 44.6% (financial year 2016). In terms of personal exchange, Asia's regional exchange is greatly increasing in tourism, business, education, training, immigration, and so forth. About 90% of outbound Korean passengers head for East Asian countries annually, while 80% of foreigners currently living in Korea are from East Asian countries (Park S.-W., 2011: 91). Thus, "East Asia is not a discourse, but is becoming a social fact and reality," given "East Asia's intra-regional exchanges and mutual dependence, and gradual community construction, occurring in the real world" (*ibid.*: 92).[9]

However, the increase in transnational interactions in Northeast Asia has a limitation as a "regionalization without regional identity." There is almost no regional self-awareness in Northeast Asia regarding primary and practical conditions for regional community. In this respect, current discussions on East Asian community have a serious weakness of lacking specificity and reality (Shin J.-H., 2014: 254).

The construction of a regional community in Northeast Asia is possible when there are common goals of regional peace and economic prosperity based on a sense of homogeneity. This study suggests a need for Northeast Asian countries to suspect existent discursive frameworks regarding development and security, and to go further to deconstruct and reconstruct them for regional peace and prosperity.

Notes

1 Due to the attempted coup by the Turkish military on 15 July 2016, followed by domestic political instability, Europeans' sense of difference from Turkey will seem to further increase.

2 The attitude of embracing multiple identities "rejects hierarchical relations based on the rankings of inferiority and superiority and, further, rejects political pressure on unitary identity asking for assimilation to dominant identity" (Lee O.-Y., 2011: 138).

3 Voices for regional community increased in Northeast Asia after the mid-1990s, reflecting various historical events such as the end of the Cold War, the demise of the socialist bloc, the intensification of globalization, the Asian financial crisis, the rise of China, the intensification of regionalism including the EU and North American Free Trade Agreement, the increase of interdependence in the East Asian regional economy, and the increase of attention to Asian values as an alternative to Western modernity (Han S.-I., 2005; Park S.-W., 2011; Shin J.-H., 2014).

4 For instance, theorists for Asian values emphasize that Confucian communitarianism has an alternative value to Western individualism, by arguing in such a way that "Asian societies have maintained ordered healthy societies because of their cultures, traditions, values, and norms, such as familism, Sinocentrism, communitarianism prioritizing society over individual, respect for authority and social order, respect for consensus and harmony rather than competition and confrontation, etc." (Jeon J.-G., 1999: 196).

5 In this respect, to designate the "other" as an entity not to resemble is an attitude based on the experiences of the West. For the weaker in the competitive international order, the "other" can be not only the entity not to resemble but also one that it must resemble.

6 Japanese theory of Asian solidarity in the late nineteenth century, that of East Asian community in the 1930s, and that of Greater East Asia in the 1940s actually presumed that Korea and China were "objects to dominate," and these discourses were utilized to justify Japan's invasion of Asia (Han S.-I., 2005: 11).

7 North Korea had already experienced ruthless attacks of the U.S. during the Korean War, such as its "ruthless bombing on the people in white clothes" and "burn to the ground policy" (Kim T.-W., 2013).

8 In a situation where part of Northeast Asia is imagined by the lead of the U.S., the Americans' hostile perception of North Korea is well reflected on Fox News, the most-watched TV news in the U.S. (Kim, 2016).

9 Hettne and Söderbaum (2002) distinguish five stages of regionality by level of integration, from "regional space" to "regional complex," "regional society," "regional community," to "regional state."

10 Conclusion

Beyond the Discourse of *Seonjinguk*

This book has examined the characteristics, historical unfolding, and genealogy of the discourse of *seonjinguk*, which has provided a dominant worldview to Korean society during its developmental era. The discourse of *seonjinguk* is one of the most popular discursive systems premised upon the conceptual dichotomy between *seonjinguk* and *hujinguk*, which has led a main strand of Korea's developmental and Eurocentric worldviews.

The discourse of *seonjinguk* is developmental as it sets growth-oriented national development as a main condition for *seonjinguk*, while it is also Eurocentric as it imagines the West as paragons of *seonjinguk*. In terms of the genealogy of Korea's Eurocentrism, the discourse of *seonjinguk* is in line with the discourse of *munmyeong* in the *gaehwa* period. A genealogy of Korean and global Eurocentric discourses since the late nineteenth century are summarized in Table 10.1.

"Deficient" Identity and the Imitation of *Seonjinguk*

In *seonjinguk* discourse, the West is idealized as "*seonjinguk*," while the non-West is marginalized as "*hujinguk*." This tendency takes place not just regarding the country's general image but also concerning its diverse aspects such as language, custom, institution, ways of thinking and behaving, and so forth. In relation to this, the Koreans have been considering that the paragon of modernity exists outside their society, in *seonjinguk*.

Thus, a tendency appears in Korean society to imitate *seonjinguk*, often out of context. Their respect for the English language and following of foreign customs, such as Halloween, Valentine's Day, etc., are not irrelevant to the discourse of *seonjinguk*. The Koreans tend to perceive "something Western" as "something polished." When visiting good places in Korea, they sometimes make comments such as, "Oh, this is like Europe," or "Oh, this is like New York," regardless of their actual experience of visiting Europe or New York. Koreans rarely express their positive feelings in such phrases as the "scenery

Table 10.1 Historical Change of Eurocentric Discourses in Korea and the World

		Colonial era (1880s–1940s)	*Post-colonial era (1950s–present)*
Global discourse	Main concept	Civilization	Development
	Dichotomy	Civilized/ uncivilized	Developed/ underdeveloped
	Hegemony	Europe	U.S.
Korean discourse	Main concept	*Gaehwa* (enlightenment), *munmyeong* (civilization)	*Baljeon* (development)
	Dichotomy	*Gaehwa/mi-gaehwa* (un-enlightened); *munmyeong/yaman* (barbarism)	*Baljeon/jeo-baljeon* (underdevelopment); *seonjinguk* (developed country)/*hujinguk* (underdeveloped country)
	Hegemony	Modern *gaehwa* and *munmyeong* elites	Developmentalists
	Representation of the West	*Gaehwa-guk* (enlightened country), *munmyeong-guk* (civilized country)	*Seonjinguk*
	Self-identity	Traditional *munmyeong-guk* → half *gaehwa* or half *munmyeong* → *munmyeong-guk* (of peace, spirit, ethics, etc.)	*Hujinguk* → *jungjinguk* (developing country) → *sangwi jungjinguk* (high-level developing country, newly industrializing country) → *seonjinguk munteok* (on the threshold of *seonjinguk*)

of Southeast Asia." Thus, there is imitation of Western places, persons, and organizations in Korea, such as "Korea's Napoli," "Korea's Central Park," "Korea's Elvis Presley" etc.

Since the mid-twentieth century, the Koreans have had "deficient self-identity" in relation to "*seonjinguk*." This means, on the other hand, a sense of superiority over *hujinguk*. For instance, the discourse of *seonjinguk* is a main source of Koreans' discriminative perceptions of foreigners, incurring their respect for those from "*seonjinguk*" while disregard for those from "*hujinguk*" (Kim J. and Han G.-D., 2013). In this respect, the Korean discourse of *seonjinguk* is an interpretive system akin to the Orientalism of the West.

Korean society currently identifies itself as "*seonjinguk munteok*," setting entry into the ranks of *seonjinguk* as its historical duty to achieve in the near future. The discourse of *seonjinguk* presents the national goal and vision for Korea, and designates the direction of national change. Under the hegemony of *seonjinguk* discourse, Korea's present time is mobilized for the achievement of *seonjinguk* in the future.

The genealogical study on discourse enables us to suspect a taken-for-granted interpretive framework in a certain historical period. The *seonjinguk* discourse currently taken for granted in Korea is not a universal interpretive framework applicable to any historical time or space. Rather, it is the historical and social creation of the Park Chung-Hee period when the Korean developmental state aggressively pursued rapid national reformation under the slogan of "*joguk geundaehwa*." The national project of "*joguk geundaehwa*" was, after all, to achieve the goal of entering into the ranks of *seonjinguk*, and this has remained an "incomplete mission" in Korea.

The fact that *seonjinguk* discourse is still taken for granted in Korea means that the country has yet to escape from the interpretive framework of the Park Chung-Hee period. In the global context, the global developmentalism of the 1950s–1960s, the heyday of U.S. hegemony, is still exerting its influence strongly on Korean discursive situation. The Eurocentric feature of *seonjinguk* discourse has, rather, strengthened since the Park era. The nationalistic feature of *seonjinguk* discourse has gradually come to connote Eurocentric universalism more strongly since the global rise of neoliberalism in the 1980s.

It is undeniable that the discourse of *seonjinguk* has historically contributed to Korea's rapid economic development and the improvement of people's living standards to some degree. However, it can be wondered how the discourse of *seonjinguk* is appropriate to evaluate the diversity of the world and to enhance the maturity of Korean society when the goal of "development" is quite vague globally. From a post-colonial perspective, the discourse of *seonjinguk* is well caught up in the "colonial power matrix" of the dominating West and the dominated non-West, while disregarding the "decolonial turn" for the diversity and subjectivity of the non-West (Quijano, 2000; Grosfoguel, 2007; Ndlovu-Gatsheni, 2012). From a post-developmental viewpoint, the discourse of *seonjinguk* is still stuck in the "unsustainable" Eurocentric game of development (Sachs, 1992; Escobar, 1995).

Bob Dylan and Korea's Self-Respect

Rapidly catching up with *seonjinguk*, Korean society has abandoned much of its thinking ability. It seriously lacks the capacity for independent thought and judgment, and its ability to create its own stories and narratives is quite limited. Instead, it is prone to talk about foreign narratives. Korean society is accustomed to seeing the world through the viewpoint of the West. Famous people in *seonjinguk* have to be famous in Korea, and popular theories in *seonjinguk* have to be popular in Korea as well.

The discourse of *seonjinguk* reflects Korea's lack of self-respect. A way for Korea to resolve this problem is to rely on the external authority of *seonjinguk*. One of the important judging criteria of social phenomena in Korean society is how the case is in *seonjinguk*. As it had its babies adopted abroad in the past, Korean society is currently insensitive to the situation where talented young Koreans go to *seonjinguk* for their diplomas and successes to be raised there as Korea's intellectuals and experts.

Those who have earned their doctoral degrees in the U.S. are currently dominating Korean academia and Korean society, enjoying the authority of the "dominated dominator" (Kim J.-Y., 2015). Thus, Lee S.-H. (1997: 184) questions: "What is the difference between parvenu madam, who are gratified by blindly buying imported products, and scholars who regard Western thought as universal truth and blindly imports it?"

Korea does not have the adequate level of critical awareness about the cultural hegemony of Western *seonjinguk*. Korea's willingness to accept Western cultural products is stronger than any other country in the world. Korean society is pleased to trust American journalism, such as CNN, *The New York Times*, or even Fox News.[1] The visits of Hollywood movie stars or the Most Valuable Player of the National Football League to Korea draw national attention. Korea is sensitive to how it is evaluated by others, especially by the West. A critical report by a British correspondent in Seoul about Korea's taste in beer has made the whole country agonize about this. Koreans are excessively curious whether foreigners, especially those from *seonjinguk*, like "*kimchi,*" "*hanbok*" (Korean traditional dress), or "Gangnam style."

Korean society aspires to Western prizes, such as the Nobel Prize, Academy Awards, etc., more than do any others. Its enthusiasm for international sports events, such as the World Cup and the Olympic Games, reflects its aspirations to be admitted by the West. It does not understand American singer Bob Dylan's cynical attitude towards the Nobel Prize. Korea's level of self-respect may not reach that of Bob Dylan.

Korea makes a hard effort to win the ranking competition constructed by *seonjinguk*. This is often considered "internationalization" or "globalization." Korean universities, for instance, encourage Korean scholars to write papers not particularly relevant to Korean society in order to publish them in foreign journals. Due to this, many urgent problems in Korea do not draw Korean researchers' attention adequately, while the affairs of foreign interests tend to get excessive attention in the Korean academia.[2]

Reality of the U.S., and Malaysia's Imagination

The discourse of *seonjinguk* circumscribes Korea's imaginative capacity for "development." In its framework, Korean society imagines the world as more simplified, divided, and hierarchical than it actually is. The discourse of *seonjinguk* disrupts the contextual understanding of each society by providing people with the tinted glasses of the *seonjinguk-hujinguk* hierarchy. It deludes the Koreans into the perception that the institutions, social phenomena, and behavioral patterns of *seonjinguk* are the archetypes of modernity and, thus, are applicable to Korean and other societies.

The country most frequently referred to as *seonjinguk* is the U.S. The Korean elites, which were historically formed through U.S. military rule, the Korean War, and the developmental era, presented the U.S. as the model for Korea's development. However, the U.S. is struggling with various problems of its own, such as severe socio-economic inequality and polarization, excessive consumerism, embedded violence, a strict surveillance and control system, racial and ethnic conflicts, and unilateralism and military expansionism externally.[3] The U.S. is occasionally called "jungle capitalism" for its very competitive political-economic system and is always at war with other countries or political groups. Having created numerous people's deaths and suffering through its invasion of Iraq under the delusive cause of removing "weapons of mass destruction," for instance, the U.S. lacks a humane nature when it justifies the invasion as the gift of freedom to the Iraqis.[4]

As of early April 2017, a crisis is heightening around the Korean Peninsula because of the U.S. Donald Trump government's mention of the possibility of a preemptive attack on North Korea. The Korean media are reporting that U.S. high-tech military weapons, such as carrier flotilla, are arriving one after another around the Peninsula. There is even a report that it is the greatest crisis since the Korean War. While there is a viewpoint that the current sense of crisis is exaggerated, an important problem is that the Korean Peninsula is constantly exposed to the possibility of such an extreme situation (in fact, the crisis reappeared in August 2017).

With Pyeongyang's recent development of an inter-continental ballistic missile as momentum, the possibility of "war" with North Korea is being occasionally mentioned by U.S. governmental officials and so-called "security experts." There is an estimate that millions will die at the beginning in the case of war in the Korean Peninsula. However, is North Korea really a threat to the U.S., the world's strongest power? Anyway, it is regrettable that the Koreans' fate is dependent upon the Americans in the sense that the U.S. is currently the most probable country to bring about war, if any, in the Peninsula.[5]

Despite its confrontation with North Korea, the Koreans are somewhat insensitive to the possibility of war in their lives. For the Koreans, war is mostly considered something likely to appear in a book or movie. However, it is a matter of everyday life for the Americans. Accounting for about half of world military spending, the U.S. has been waging numerous wars under the cause of "freedom and democracy," and this is ongoing today. A large part of the U.S. media's everyday reports are about war, and "war culture" is rampant in U.S. cultural fields, such as movies, games, TV, etc. (including wars against aliens, monsters, and machines). The U.S. military-industrial complex, which U.S. President D.D. Eisenhower worried about, has been exerting great influence around the world as well as in the U.S.

Korean society should be alert to the fact that it is sharing the problem of the Korean Peninsula with the U.S. The U.S.-Korea alliance should not be a goal in itself, nor be blindly pursued, but should be a strategic tool for the peace and reunification of the Peninsula. The hardliners in Korea as well as the U.S., who raise their voices for military solutions under the cause of "security," will not take any responsibility for numerous people's lives and suffering that could be caused by any real military conflict. It is time for Korean society to sincerely think about the true way to strengthen its "security," as the ultimate goal of security is "peace." Korea should also recognize that the deep-rooted cause of the North Korea problem does not lie as much in Pyeongyang's nuclear or missile program, as in an antagonistic relationship with it (Kim, 2016).[6]

It is to be considered that the extreme military totalitarian system of North Korea has been formed and internally justified in the process of confronting the U.S.-Korea alliance, the world's strongest level of military power. Insofar as war is not an option for the Korean Peninsula, is there any method other than the establishment of peace through "reconciliation" and "communication," no matter how "strange" a nation North Korea is? Furthermore, the North Koreans are members of the Korean people with whom they should pursue coexistence, peace, and ultimately reunification. In this respect, the Koreans' attitude towards "strange North Korea" is to be different from that of the Americans, who have no racial, cultural, and emotional solidarity but an "antagonistic relationship" with it. The biggest victim of the extreme confrontation between the two Koreas will be the Korean people themselves.

In regard to the tension in the Korean Peninsula surrounding North Korea's nuclear weapons and missiles, the responsibility of the U.S. is not small. The U.S. has been refusing serious communication with North Korea only to ask for the "dismantlement of the nuclear program" as a precondition that is actually unacceptable to North Korea. The series of North Korea's nuclear and missile experiments can be understood basically as a self-defense measure and protest against the U.S. which is not willing to admit it as an equal counterpart for negotiation (Sigal, 2002).[7] North Korea's nuclear project proceeded rapidly after the early 2000s when the U.S. George W. Bush government labeled North Korea a member of the "axis of evil" and invaded Afghanistan and Iraq consecutively. The hardline U.S. policies against North Korea afterwards have only provided a cause for nuclear and missile development to Pyeongyang.

The attitude in Korea to hesitate to point out the U.S. strategic mistake, being afraid of the possibility of a "fracture in the U.S.-Korea alliance," is not helpful for Korean as well as U.S. security. Furthermore, various ungrounded arguments such as that attributing North Korea's nuclear development to the "ladle out" policy of the former "leftist Korean regimes" are also harmful to Korea's security as they obscure reality. The irresponsible attitudes and behavior of the "confrontationists" in the two Koreas and the U.S. are threatening the "security" of the Korean Peninsula.

At least, the Koreans should not lose leadership in their relationship with concerned countries in regard to the matter of the Korean Peninsula. This is because the biggest stakeholders of the matter of the Peninsula are the Koreans, and they are most knowledgeable about this matter. For the Koreans, the ultimate goal of "security" in the Korean Peninsula should be "peace" and *there is no alternative.* They have to be alert to the situation in which U.S. President Trump and Chinese Premier Xi Jinping discuss the "problem of the Korean Peninsula." Tragic history should not be repeated with the Korean Peninsula becoming a battlefield for foreign powers.

The Koreans should be able to perceive the U.S. in an objective manner and, for this, they have to remove their mental dependence on the U.S. Those who are mentally dependent on the U.S. and *seonjinguk* should no longer be the mainstream of Korean society.

The Koreans also have to overcome the illusion about the U.S. The validity and practicality of U.S.-led developmentalism and modernization theory were seriously challenged by post-development theorists who argued, for instance, that "[i]f all countries 'successfully' followed the industrial example, five or six planets would be needed to serve as mines and waste dumps" (Sachs, 1992: 2). The main culprit of global climate change, the U.S. lacks reflexivity on self and modernity to notify the United Nations of its withdrawal from the Paris Agreement. Global civil society has been asking for a focal change of "development" from "growth" to "sustainability," "quality of life," "solidarity," "diversity," "equality," etc. (International Forum on Globalization, 2004).

In *seonjinguk* discourse, countries are to lose their unique identities on being designated as "*seonjinguk*" or "*hujinguk*." The discourse of *seonjinguk* does not pay enough attention to countries' own unique efforts for development, such as the Bhutanese pursuit of "gross national happiness." The Costa Rican highest level of happiness tends to be disregarded as a story somewhat irrelevant to Korean society. The discourse of *seonjinguk* precludes the possibility that Korea can learn from those non-Western countries.

Each country's vision of development is not unitary. For instance, Malaysia made a plan of "Vision 2020" under the leadership of Prime Minister Mahathir in 1991, suggesting a national vision of achieving a fully developed country by 2020 (Mahathir, 1991). However, the concept of "a fully developed country" in "Vision 2020" connotes somewhat different things from those of "*seonjinguk*" in the Korean discourse.

> What, you might rightly ask, is "a fully developed country"? Do we want to be like any particular country of the present 19 countries that are generally regarded as "developed countries"? Do we want to be like the United Kingdom, like Canada, like Holland, like Sweden, like Finland, like Japan? To be sure, each of the 19, out of a world community of more than 160 states, has its strengths. But each also has its fair share of

> weaknesses. Without being a duplicate of any of them we can still be developed. We should be a developed country in our own mould.
>
> (Mahathir, 1991)

As such, Malaysia presents an alternative route to Eurocentric developmentalism. The nine challenges that the Malaysian "Vision 2020" suggests meeting are:

> (1) establishing a united Malaysian nation with a sense of common and shared destiny; (2) creating a psychologically liberated, secure, and developed Malaysian Society; (3) fostering and developing a mature democratic society, practising a form of mature consensual, community-oriented Malaysian democracy; (4) establishing a fully moral and ethical society; (5) establishing a matured, liberal and tolerant society; (6) establishing a scientific and progressive society; (7) establishing a fully caring society and a caring culture; (8) ensuring an economically just society; (9) establishing a prosperous society, with an economy that is fully competitive, dynamic, robust and resilient.
>
> (Mahathir, 1991)

Malaysia aspires to be a country evenly developed in the aspects of economy, politics, society, psychology, and culture, focusing on the needs arising in its own historical and social contexts.

Things that the Koreans Have Lost

Korean society has lived in high tension for the past half-century for the pressing national goal of *seonjinguk*. It has achieved material affluence in the goal-oriented way of living, but has lost precious social values, such as humanity, leisureliness, communalism, and so forth. The happiness level is low across all age groups in Korean society while the suicide rate is high. In fact, developmentalism has driven Korean society hectically. Pursuing "globalization" without serious reflection on itself and the world, Korea has come to undergo the severe financial crisis in the late 1990s. As Korea lacks serious self-reflection, somewhat radical but empty slogans such as "national reformation," "national transformation," or "national reset" are still rampant there. In regard to what the Koreans lost in the national fever of development, a Buddhist monk points out as follows:

> It was our long tradition not to trample even on fallen flowers, and was our ancestors' moral way of life to refrain from carrying off hot water in the ditch, caring about living organisms in there. The customs of "*go-su-re*" (scattering some food on the ground) and "*kka-chi-bab*" (leaving some fruits on the tree for birds) also derive from the thought of life-respect embedded in our living. But, modern material civilization did not just

> cause environmental destruction but went further to make our respect for life and the virtue of nature disappear altogether. There is a need now to reevaluate current development and nature destruction through tiny living things that we call "*mimul*."
>
> (Jiyul, 2004)

Korean developmentalists are still obsessed with developmental slogans, such as Lee Myung-Bak's "747 pledge" (7% annual economic growth; $40,000 income; and the seventh greatest country). They create a sense of crisis that the nation may perish without the achievement of its developmental goal. As the financial crisis in the 1990s showed, however, their strategies are sometimes hollow and can even lead the nation to a serious crisis. The "bold" controversial idea and behavior of pouring the national budget of more than $20 billion into the development of rivers were also justified by developmentalism. Nonetheless, developmental slogans still exert big influence in Korean society. Having experienced rapid economic development since the 1960s, the Koreans have still been expecting another developmental miracle.

Developmentalism and *seonjinguk* discourse disrupt Koreans' quality of life, as the pursuit of rapid social change increases social stress. Those discourses demand ceaseless national change by setting the present identity as a transitional one, while the future goal as the historical duty to surely achieve. National stress goes up in this constant wave of national change. In this respect, developmentalism and *seonjinguk* discourse contribute to maintaining Korean society as a "mobilized system" for the historical duty of achieving *seonjinguk*.

Developmentalism marginalizes humans. It prioritizes the interests of the state, capital, and organizations, by setting their achievements as a kind of sacred duty to justify the marginalization of humans. In this regard, it tends to vindicate the sacrifice of people by emphasizing the "future" and "hope" of the nation. Korean society is accustomed to excessively mobilizing people for the goals of the government, capital, and organizations. It asks people for enduring extreme work. The values of humans are judged by their instrumental value rather than their intrinsic value. In this respect, Korea's developmentalism contains nonsense, abnormality, and inhumanity within itself.

The low level of happiness in present-day Korea, which has succeeded in achieving the status of "developed," may derive largely from the perceptual gap between the goal of *seonjinguk* and the reality of an "incomplete mission." In this sense, the way to "true *seonjinguk*" may perhaps begin from breaking away from the imperative worldview of developmentalism.

Having run ceaselessly for the past half-century, Korea now needs thoughtful consideration for each of its citizens' intrinsic values, life quality, and happiness, instead of such slogans as "*geundaehwa*," "*segyehwa*," and "*seonjinhwa*." Korea should now recover humanity and leisureliness, escaping from developmental nationalism that began with the project of the "modernization of fatherland." While maintaining a sense of tension in the harsh modern international order, Korea should not let this infringe on the quality of people's lives.

To pay attention to humans is also a process of recovering common sense, normality, and humanity, which have been neglected in the process of national economic development. It is the time for Korea to be mature enough to go beyond the illusion and instigation of developmentalism.

The "Illusion" of *Seonjinguk* and "True" *Seonjinguk*

Given the ideal image of *seonjinguk* in Korea, it is close to a developmental "illusion" that can be barely caught. That is, "*seonjinguk*" in Koreans' imagination does not exist in reality. Various social problems in Korea, such as socio-economic polarization, egoism, material fetishism, success-ism, a lacking leisureliness, high suicide rate, and low happiness, derive not as much from Korea not yet being *seonjinguk*, as from Korea still being obsessed with developmentalism.

The importance of economic growth should vary according to society's material needs. The material base of Korea today greatly differs from that in the 1960s when the escape from "*hujinguk*" was vigorously aspired to. Development for economic growth may be useful in a certain historical situation with a weak material base, but is not a universal value in itself. Development prioritizing economic growth is not a sufficient condition for national or societal development. Development that sacrifices other important values for economic growth is, basically, not a true development

Korean society should now move towards a mature society to make true *seonjinguk* of its own. For this, it should be able to create a new vision of development based on close examination of its strengths and weaknesses. Korean society should break the conventional perceptual framework that was constructed under Western hegemony to establish an alternative vision and strategy through precise examination of the things that the society truly needs at this historical point.

In the new vision for development, economic growth and national income should be treated not as the goal in itself, but as one of various elements for national development. True development at this point should enhance diverse social, cultural, and economic values in balance, rather than sacrificing one for the others. The logics of economics, growth, and competition should not dominate all areas of the country.

Whereas developmental *seonjinguk* discriminates against and excludes the weak from the strong's position, true *seonjinguk* at this historical point may be a country that can warmly care about people, things and values that have been marginalized thus far amidst developmental obsession with the "growth" of nation and capital. Thus, it is a country where humanity is full, leisureliness is widespread, and people are living satisfied with their own life-styles. The level of national economy may be suitable as far as it suffices for people to enjoy their leisureliness and happiness. It is true *seonjinguk* when even easy-going people, lazy people, or people intrinsically unfitting to capitalism are able to afford their own happy lives. True *seonjinguk* may be a country where, as Moore (1972) notes, its members do not have to experience "useless suffering."

As a Korean monk mentions, there are "things visible only when we stop" (Hyemin, 2012). Since Park Chung-Hee's "modernization of fatherland" project, developmentalists have always asked people "not to stop," but how dreary would the world be if there were only people "not stopping"? Those who make our society warm and mature would be those who have experienced "things visible when we stop." In this respect, people "stopping" plays an important positive role in society and, thus, they also deserve due social reward.

Appreciating Korea's Modernity and the "Human-centered" World

Korea needs to recover a sense of self-respect for its own modernity. There are not many metropolitan cities whose size is comparable to Seoul, where people can enjoy a relaxed walk in their neighborhood at dusk and night. As is shown in the candlelight rallies in late 2016 and the transition of political power afterwards, Koreans' civic awareness is far more mature than they thought. In this process, the Koreans have recognized that many of the problems in Korea, which they had thought as the essential problems of Korea's modernity, were actually the problems of national leadership or the "level" of its privileged and ruling classes.

The Koreans scrambled to criticize the contradiction of Korea's modernity in regard to such incidents as the tragedy of the *Seongsu* Bridge collapse and the financial crisis in the 1990s. While they are to learn serious lessons from those incidents, it should also be noted that such kinds of incidents are not unique to Korean modernity but also happen in *seonjinguk* like the U.S. As Beck (1992) points out, modernity contains "risk" in itself. The Koreans should be alert to a type of modernity that is running without break on the blind belief in science and technology and insatiated greed for wealth.

Korea has achieved its modernity through rough historical experiences, such as foreign powers' oppression and intervention, and developmental dictatorship. Given the historical misfortune of modern Korea, its current form of modernity based on successful industrialization and democratization can be considered as quite a fortunate achievement.

A hybrid of Eastern and Western civilizations, Korea's modernity is distinguished from others. Accordingly, it would be to disregard the unique feature of Korea's modernity if one were to consider it a "compressed" version of Western modernity or converging into the modernity of *seonjinguk*. The interest in "modernities" is to recognize that each society's modernity is the construct of its own historical, social conditions (Featherstone et al., 1995). This is to criticize the Eurocentric view of modernity, which tends to assume the archetype of modernity as a yardstick with which to judge societies, creating a hierarchy among them. Korea has to go beyond the Eurocentric concepts of "development" and "modernity," if it is to move forward to a mature society. The directions and routes of development and modernization are diverse, open, and multidimensional. Koreans should care about what kind of development and modernity to pursue.

Neoliberal developmentalism has hit Korea since the late 1990s financial crisis. Developmentalists argued that neoliberalism was a condition for *seonjinguk*. With the spread of neoliberal developmentalism, Korea has become a stage for more intensive competition for its members, and socio-economic polarization has accelerated in the mood of justifying the "winner takes all." The gap in socio-economic reward is too big between the weaker (or the unlucky) and the stronger (or the lucky), and the gap is widening in the popularity of the slogan of "entering into *seonjinguk*." The sufferings of the former tend to be treated as natural in the competition for survival, or as conducive to national competitiveness, and the sense of justice is weakening around the country. In this situation, everyone tries desperately to be the winner.

Korean society should reduce the gap in reward between winner and loser in any competition, e.g., that in schools, the workplace, or the lottery for apartment ownership. It should be a society in which its members compete in a rather relaxed atmosphere, and the loser can pleasantly admit the properness of the reward for the winner. For this, the winners or the "lucky" persons have to be willing to yield their "luckily" earned privileges and rewards in order to reduce the gap with the losers or the "unlucky" persons. This is also for the winners themselves because it is a very competitive situation, in which winners can become losers at any time.

Korean society seems to have lost its developmental direction. It seems just to pursue the illusion of *seonjinguk*. The world is in a similar situation. Eurocentric developmentalism emerged as global hegemonic discourse under U.S. global hegemony, but a new alternative discourse has not appeared in the present situation where U.S. leadership is seriously suspect and the world is going multipolar (Nederveen Pieterse, 2017). The world is now in need of new orders, new discourses.

In regard to the direction of development, Korea should throw away passivism. It actually has much to contribute to the creation of new discourses and orders in the world. The world will be better if the wisdom and peaceful spirit of the East are combined with the material scientific propensity of the West, as was argued in the Korean non-Eurocentric discourse of civilization in the past. The world should no longer be Eurocentric.

In those respects, the pursuit of the "human-centered world" by the current Korean Moon Jae-In government, which was inaugurated on 10 May 2017, gives an important implication to the development of the world as well as Korea. Having been marginalized for the interests of the state and capital amidst the global expansion of capitalism, "humans" should now retrieve the position of "center" escaping from the position of "instrument." Humans are no longer to be mobilized for economic growth but, as the Moon administration advocates, the economy should be a "human-centered economy," serving humans. Now the "development" of society and nation should be judged not by economic indices, but by the value of humans and their quality of life.

It draws attention if the Moon Jae-In government's pursuit of a "human-centered world" will change the features of Korea's "post-developmental state." It is generally agreed that the Korean developmental state, having led rapid economic growth in the 1960s–1970s, made way for the post-developmental state in the 1990s with the rise of neoliberalism. The post-developmental state is now about to change its character to a "human-centered" one. If the Moon government's "human" paradigm is stabilized as a long-term trend in Korea, its development experience could be conceptualized as having moved from the 1960s "developmental state" to the "neoliberal post-developmental state" in the 1990s, and eventually to the "human-centered post-developmental state" after 2017.

The "human-centered world" can also be a universal value for a world that is in a "developmental dilemma." If Korea, a country having achieved unprecedented economic development with the world's strongest developmentalism and national development project, can succeed in making a "human-centered" society, it would be able to provide a new development model to the world.

The Deconstruction and Reconstruction of *Seonjinguk* Discourse

Korea as a former colonized country has achieved rapid economic growth and democracy, which are considered the most successful in the post-war world, to have become a country aspiring to the "*seonjinguk* club." In this respect, the discourse of *seonjinguk* is an important research topic for comprehending Korea and its development.

It is, however, the dilemma of *seonjinguk* discourse that Korea may not be true *seonjinguk* insofar as it maintains the current discursive framework. First, the image of *seonjinguk* is no more than a developmental illusion, which tends to justify growth-oriented development in Korea. This is reflected in the fact that Korea has been perceived as remaining on the "threshold of *seonjinguk*" for about 40 years, since the late 1970s. Second, a country obsessed with Eurocentric linear developmentalism may not be true *seonjinguk* for its immaturity in thought and consciousness. True *seonjinguk* should be a country that is able to understand various phenomena in various societies in their contexts, to fairly appreciate the values of each society.

Third, methodologically, the society that is running at breakneck speed for the goal of *seonjinguk* cannot be true *seonjinguk* as it hardly takes the time to take care of its weak and sore parts. True *seonjinguk* might be a country that is able to reflect on and care about itself continuously. In this respect, what is considered as the status of *seonjinguk* is not to "achieve" but may come to the Koreans unwittingly while they are faithful to themselves. *Seonjinguk* is not "out there," but inside Koreans themselves.

That a country whose per capita income is about $27,000 (i.e., Korea) is to run for the goal of $30,000 is nothing but to play around with numbers. Korean developmentalists have been tightening Korean society, by presenting the arbitrary number of $30,000 as a condition for *seonjinguk* since the 2000s. The per capita income of $10,000, or $20,000, not to mention $30,000, is also enough for *seonjinguk*. The real matter is its members' quality of life. What on earth would the per capita income of $30,000 or $300,000 be useful for if everyone severely competed with one another to be a winner in the situation of a wide socio-economic gap, in which the "winner takes all" is justified and the loser lives a hard life in shame and resentment?

If Korea wants to be true *seonjinguk*, it may have to go beyond the current discourse of *seonjinguk*. This is to overcome the conventional perception of development and the era of development. This is not only to break the colonial interpretive framework and Korea's deficient identity over the West, but also to recover Koreans' confidence and subjectivities. The discourse of *seonjinguk* needs to be deconstructed and reconstructed to reflect the post-colonial, post-developmental epistemic turns.

The Koreans have to critically approach the current concept of *seonjinguk* that is growth-oriented, developmental, and Eurocentric, to think about the concept that is humanistic, post-developmental, and post-Eurocentric. They have to deconstruct the concept of *seonjinguk* that justifies bipolarization and severe competition, to reconstruct the concept that attends to coexistence and harmony. They have to escape from the system that mobilizes humans and civil society for the interests of the state and capital, to create a system in which the state and capital serve the interests of humans and civil society. New discourse should appreciate the diverse ways of life in the world, and pay more attention to humans. This is the time to imagine a more humane, equal, and peaceful world.

For the deconstruction and reconstruction of *seonjinguk* discourse, it needs first to bring down *seonjinguk* from the status of imagined country to real country. We may call Western countries "*seonjinguk*" in the sense that they started capitalist industrialization in advance. However, it is also to be noted that their accumulation of wealth was not necessarily the result of their own rationality, entrepreneurship, and maturity, as was argued by Eurocentrists. The rise of the modern West was historically possible because of modern colonialism having accompanied war, conquest, exploitation, and community destruction after 1492.[8] The process of Western industrialization and modernization, which were based on the philosophy of "controlling nature" instead of "harmony with nature," also brought about various problems in the modern world.[9]

The current modernities of the West are distant from idealized *seonjinguk* imagined by the Koreans. As Korea has its own various problems, every country is to have its own problems. Mistakenly considering the problems in Korea as not existent in *seonjinguk* is to give *seonjinguk* the status of imagined country.

Conceptually, "*seonjinguk*" is a blanket term disregarding differences and diversity among countries. We may categorize them into "*seonjinguk*" in the sense that they started industrialization in advance, but the features of modernity appearing in those countries are not unitary. It is a misunderstanding to think that the so-called "*seonjinguk*," such as European countries, the U.S., and Japan, have similar social structures and phenomena with one another. To argue that "using a cell phone is prohibited in *seonjinguk*" is to commit the fallacy of generalization to exaggerate the feature of *seonjinguk* in a few cases. In a similar vein, the concept of "*hujinguk*" is also a blanket term. The Koreans are to contextually understand the uniqueness and specificity of each of the countries, and diversity among them.

Korea may now want to imagine what true *seonjinguk* is to pursue. While assessing its modern achievements as they are, Korean society should be able to recognize what it truly needs at this historical time. Korea has to envision a nation embracing social, cultural, economic, and political values in balance. Especially, it has to be able to highly regard humans. Through this, Korea should pursue true development and move towards true *seonjinguk*. This will eventually be to contribute to the true development of the world.

Notes

1 Curran (2011) gives a critical discussion about the commercialism and political conservatism of the U.S. media, in regard to the media's duty for mature democracy.

2 It is especially serious that Korean society's independent thinking ability is weak even in the fields of international relations and international politics. Some researchers point out that dependency on foreign academia, the U.S. one in particular, is so heavy that Korean political science is currently in an identity crisis (Kang J.-I., 2013; Kim H.-N., 2013).

3 Moore (1966, 1972) defined the U.S. as "predatory democracy" because of the "unduly large proportion of the world's resources which it consumes, the social inequality it maintains, the discrimination it practices against minority groups, and the foreign policy it maintains, especially in Indochina" (Janowitz, 1974: 1324). Some designate U.S. capitalism as "jungle capitalism" promoting intense competition among social actors. As for this, Lee S.-S. (2001: 87–88) points out that "it is a socio-economic system enabled to always exploit the labor class and disadvantaged class as an industrial reserve army by removing protections including social security for them," and adds that "it is never grace or fortune to the world or to humankind that such a country having limitations on the socio-political horizon continues to maintain hegemony based on capitalist jungle features." Nederveen Pieterse (2008) suggests going beyond the "American bubble" of both U.S. capitalism and U.S. superpower syndrome.

4 In March 2008, Hillary Clinton in the Democratic Party race for presidential candidate argued about the U.S. invasion of Iraq that "we have given them the gift of freedom, the greatest gift you can give someone" (Gumble, 2008). As Blum (2000) points out, the superpower U.S. never apologizes for its "rogue" behavior.

5 In his congratulatory speech on the 72nd Independence Day of Korea on 15 August 2017, President Moon Jae-In declared that "it is only Korea that can decide any military action in the Korean Peninsula."

6 As Wendt (1995) notes, the Americans may feel more threatened by just two North Korean nuclear weapons than by 200 British nuclear weapons. In a similar vein, the North Koreans may feel more threatened by U.S. nuclear capacity around the Korean Peninsula than by hundreds of Chinese nuclear weapons. In this respect, "threat" is socially constructed rather than deriving from destructive physical power.

7 In regard to the U.S.-North Korea relationship, North Korea's primary goals are the "Peace Treaty" (currently the Korean Peninsula is in an armistice status) and the "establishment of U.S.-North Korea diplomacy." As for this, the U.S., the world's biggest possessor of nuclear weapons, has been asking North Korea to discard nuclear weapons as a prerequisite for negotiations. In this respect, the U.S. and North Korea are not equal counterparts at the negotiating table. The "security experts" in the U.S. and South Korea are supporting the hardline policy against North Korea, arguing in such a way that "North Korea is not trustworthy." The situation is that North Korea has been going its own way in response to the U.S. unilateral request sometimes accompanying the threat of "regime change" and a "preemptive attack."

8 The colonization of America brought about not only Europe's material change but also perceptual change. As Honour (1975: 34, 35) notes, "the sudden influx of birds, beasts, fishes, and plants unknown in the Old World stimulated [European] interest in those that were already familiar" and "there can be no doubt about the tonic effect the new flora and fauna, and the need to study and categorize them, had on the development of European science."

9 As for the materialistic and technological propensity of the West, the Indian politician Mahatma Gandhi pointed out that: "We notice that the mind is a restless bird; the more it gets the more it wants, and still remains unsatisfied … Our ancestors, therefore, set a limit to our indulgences. They saw that happiness is largely a mental condition … We have managed with the same kind of plough as existed thousands of years ago. We have retained the same kind of cottages that we had in former times and our indigenous education remains the same as before. We have had no system of life-corroding competition … It was not that we did not know how to invent machinery, but our forefathers knew that if we set our hearts after such things, we would become slaves and lose our moral fibres" (cited in McMichael, 2008: 39).

References

Adler, Emanuel. 1997. "Seizing the Middle Ground: Constructivism in World Politics." *European Journal of International Relations* 3(3): 319–363.

Ahn, Byeong-Jik. 2001. "Gyemong sasanggwa Europe-eui inyeom" [Enlightenment and the Idea of Europe]. *Seoyangsa yeongu* [*Western History Research*] 27: 1–18.

Alatas, Syed Farid. 2006. *Alternative Discourses in Asian Social Science: Responses to Eurocentrism*. New Delhi: Sage.

Amin, Samir. 1989. *Eurocentrism*. New York: Monthly Review Press.

Andreasson, Stefan. 2005. "Orientalism and African Development Studies: The 'Reductive Repetition' Motif in Theories of African Underdevelopment." *Third World Quarterly* 26(6): 971–986.

Apffel-Marglin, Frédérique and Stephen A. Marglin, eds. 1990. *Dominating Knowledge: Development, Culture, and Resistance*. New York: Oxford University Press.

Apffel-Marglin, Frédérique and Stephen A. Marglin, eds. 1996. *Decolonizing Knowledge: from Development to Dialogue*. New York: Oxford University Press.

Ashizawa, Kuniko. 2008. "When Identity Matters: State Identity, Regional Institution-Building, and Japanese Foreign Policy." *International Studies Review* 10: 571–598.

Baek, Dong-Hyun. 2003. "Gaehwagi eonron.jabji-e natanan seogugwan" [View on the West Reflected in Newspapers and Magazines in the Gaehwa Period]. Pp. 159–196 in *Gaehwagi hanguk-gwa segye-ui sangho ihae* [*Mutual Understanding of Korea and the World in the Gaehwa Period*], edited by the Academy of Asian Studies at Danguk University. Seoul: Gukhakjaryowon.

Beck, Ulrich. 1992. *Risk Society: Towards a New Modernity*. London: Sage.

Befu, Harumi. 2001. *Hegemony of Homogeneity: An Anthropological Analysis of Nihonjinron*. Melbourne: Trans Pacific Press.

Blaut, James M. 1993. *The Colonizer's Model of the World: Geographical Diffusionism and Eurocentric History*. New York: The Guilford Press.

Blum, William. 2000. *Rogue State: A Guide to the World's Only Superpower*. Monroe, M.E.: Common Courage Press.

Breslin, Shaun, Richard Higgott, and Ben Rosamond. 2002. "Regions in Comparative Perspective." Pp. 1–19 in *New Regionalisms in the Global Political Economy*, edited by Shaun Breslin, Christopher W. Hughes, Nicola Phillips, and Ben Rosamond. London: Routledge.

Brigg, Morgan. 2002. "Post-development, Foucault and the Colonisation Metaphor." *Third World Quarterly* 23(3): 421–436.

Brohman, John. 1995. "Universalism, Eurocentrism, and Ideological Bias in Development Studies: From Modernisation to Neoliberalism." *Third World Quarterly* 16(1): 121–140.

Carpentier, Nico. 2011. "The Ideological Model of War: Discursive Mediations of the Self and the Enemy." *At the Interface/Probing the Boundaries* 75: 13–38.

Chang, Ha-Joon. 2008. *Bad Samaritans: The Myth of Free Trade and the Secret History of Capitalism*. New York: Bloomsbury Press.

Cho, Hee-Yeon. 1998. *Hanguk-eui gukga•minjujueui•jeongchi byeondong* [*The State, Democracy, and Political Change of Korea*]. Seoul: Dangdae.

Cho, Hee-Yeon. 2000. "The Structure of the South Korean Developmental Regime and Its Transformation: Statist Mobilization and Authoritarian Integration in the Anticommunist Regimentation." *Inter-Asia Cultural Studies* 1(3): 408–426.

Cho, Hee-Yeon. 2002. "'Baljeon gukga'-eui byeonhwawa gukga-simin sahwoe, sahwoe undong-eui byeonhwa" [A Study on the Change in the State, Civil Society and Social Movements]. *Sahwoewa cheolhak* [*Korean Society for Social Philosophy*] 4: 293–351.

Cho, Hee-Yeon. 2003. "Jeongchi sahwoejeok damron-eui gujo byeonhwawa minjujueui eui donghak" [The Structural Change of Politico-Social Discourses and the Dynamics of Democracy]. Pp. 33–120 in *Hanguk-eui jeongchi sahwoejeok jibaedamrongwa minjujueui donghak (3)* [*Politico-social Dominant Discourse and Dynamics of Democracy in Korea (3)*], edited by Hee-Yeon Cho. Seoul: Hamgge ingneun chaek.

Cho, Hee-Yeon. 2004. "Park Chung-Hee sidae-eui gang-ab-gwa dong-eui" [The Opression and Consensus in the Park Chung-Hee Era]. *Yeoksa bipyeong* [*Critical Review of History*] 67: 135–190.

Cho, Seong-Woon. 2005. "Chongron" [Introduction]. Pp. 9–25 in *Ilje-eui sikminji jibae jeongchaekgwa maeil shinbo* [*Imperial Japan's Colonial Ruling Policies and the Maeil Shinbo*], edited by the Wednesday Research Group for History. Seoul: Duri media.

Cho, Young-Cheol. 2001. "Anglo American model-eui gieob jibae gujo-wa nosa gwangye" [The Corporate Governance Structure and Labor-Capital Relations of the Anglo-American Model]. Pp. 157–187 in *Miguk jabonjueui haebu* [*Anatomy of U.S. Capitalism*], edited by Jin-Bang Kim and Nak-Seon Seong. Seoul: Pulbit.

Choi, Jin-Woo. 2006. "Europe yeonhabeui munhwa jeongchaekgwa jeongcheseong-eui jeongchi" [EU Cultural Policy and Identity Politics in Europe]. *Gukje jeongchi nonchong* [*The Korean Journal of International Studies*] 46(4): 87–111.

Choi, Sang-Oh. 2003. "Rhee Syngman jeongbueui gyeongje jeongchaek-gwa gongeophwa jeonryak" [Korean Government`s Economic Policy and Industrialization Strategy in the 1950s]. *Gyeongje sahak* [*Journal of Economic History*] 35: 135–165.

Choi, Yeon-Sik. 2007. "Park Chung-Hee-eui 'minjok' changjowa dongwondeon gukmin tonghab" [Park Chung-Hee's Creation of "Nation" and Mobilized National Unity]. *Hanguk jeongchi oegyosa nonchong* [*Journal of Korean Political and Diplomatic History*] 28(2): 43–72.

Cowen, M.P. and R.W. Shenton. 1996. *Doctrines of Development*. London: Routledge.

Crotty, James and Kang-Kook Lee. 2007. "From East Asian 'Miracle' to Neoliberal 'Mediocrity': The Effects of Liberalization and Financial Opening on the Post-crisis Korean Economy." Pp. 73–94 in *Global Challenges and Local Responses: The East Asian Experience*, edited by Jang-Sup Shin. London: Routledge.

Curran, James. 2011. *Media and Democracy*. London: Routledge.

Dant, Tim. 1991. *Knowledge, Ideology and Discourse: A Sociological Perspective*. London: Routledge.

de Bary, Wm. Theodore and Richard Lufrano, eds. 2000. *Sources of Chinese Tradition*, vol. 2, 2nd edn. New York: Columbia University Press.

de Bary, Wm. Theodore, Carol Gluck and Arthur E. Tiedemann, eds. 2006. *Sources of Japanese Tradition: 1600 to 2000*, vol. 2 (abridged), part 2, 2nd edn. New York: Columbia University Press.

Denzin, Norman K. 2005. "Emancipatory Discourses and the Ethics and Politics of Interpretation." Pp. 933–958 in *The Sage Handbook of Qualitative Research*, edited by Norman K. Denzin and Yvonna S. Lincoln. 3rd edn. Thousand Oaks, C.A.: Sage.

Doty, Roxanne Lynn. 1993. "Foreign Policy as Social Construction: A Post-Positivist Analysis of U.S. Counterinsurgency Policy in the Philippines." *International Studies Quarterly* 37(3): 297–320.

Dudden, Alexis. 2005. *Japan's Colonization of Korea: Discourse and Power*. Honolulu, H.I.: University of Hawaii Press.

East Asia Institute of Korea. 2013. *Je 1hwoe hanil gukmin sangho insik josa bogoseo* [*Report of the First Survey on the Korean-Japanese Mutual Perceptions*].

Escobar, Arturo. 1995. *Encountering Development: The Making and Unmaking of the Third World*. Princeton, N.J.: Princeton University Press.

Esteva, Gustavo. 1992. "Development." Pp. 6–25 in *The Development Dictionary: A Guide to Knowledge as Power*, edited by Wolfgang Sachs. London: Zed Books.

Fairclough, Norman. 2003. *Analysing Discourse: Textual Analysis for Social Research*. London: Routledge.

Featherstone, Mike, Scott Lash, and Roland Robertson, eds. 1995. *Global Modernities*. London: Sage.

Forgacs, David, ed. 1988. *An Antonio Gramsci Reader: Selected Writings, 1916–1935*. New York: Schocken Books.

Foucault, Michel. 1972. *The Archaeology of Knowledge*, translated by A.M. Sheridan Smith. New York: Harper Colophon Books.

Foucault, Michel. 1977. *Discipline and Punish: The Birth of the Prison*, translated by Alan Sheridan. New York: Vintage Books.

Foucault, Michel. 1980. *Power/Knowledge: Selected Interviews and Other Writings 1972–1977*, edited by Colin Gordon, translated by Colin Gordon, Leo Marshall, John Mepham, and Kate Soper. New York: Pantheon Books.

Foucault, Michel. 2000. "The Subject and Power." Pp. 326–348 in *Power: Essential Works of Foucault 1954–1984*, volume 3, edited by James D. Faubion, translated by Robert Hurley and Others. London: Penguin Books.

Gil, Jin-Sook. 2004. "'Dongnip shinmun' 'maeil shinmune suyong-doen 'munmyeong/yaman' damron-eui euimi cheungwi" [The Semantic Hierarchy of the Discourse of "Civilization/Barbarism" Appearing in the "Dongnip Shinmun" and the "Maeil Shinmun"]. Pp. 59–95 in *Geundae gyemong-gi jisik gaenyeom-eui suyong-gwa geu byeonyong* [*The Acceptance and Transformation of Knowledge and Concepts in the Modern Enlightenment Period*], edited by the Research Institute of Korean Culture at Ehwa Women's University. Seoul: Somyeong chulpan.

Gramsci, Antonio. 1971. *Selections from the Prison Notebooks*, edited and translated by Quintin Hoare and Geoffrey Nowell Smith. New York: International Publishers.

Greig, Alastair, David Hulme, and Mark Turner. 2007. *Challenging Global Inequality: Development Theory and Practice in the 21st Century*. New York: Palgrave Macmillan.

Grosfoguel, Ramón. 2007. "The Epistemic Decolonial Turn: Beyond Political-Economy Paradigms." *Cultural Studies* 21(2–3): 211–223.

Gumble, Andrew. 2008. "Hillary Goes Orwellian on Iraq." *Huffington Post*, March 4, www.huffingtonpost.com.

Hahm, Dong-Ju. 2004. "Geundae ilboneui munmyeongron-gwa geu ijungseong" [Modern Japan's Ideas of Civilization and Their Duality]. Pp. 363–392 in *Geundae gyemong-gi jisik gaenyeom-eui suyong-gwa geu byeonyong [The Acceptance and Transformation of Knowledge and Concepts in the Modern Enlightenment Period*], edited by the Research Institute of Korean Culture at Ehwa Women's University. Seoul: Somyeong chulpan.

Hall, Stuart. 1996. "The West and the Rest: Discourse and Power." Pp. 184–227 in *Modernity: An Introduction to Modern Societies*, edited by Stuart Hall, David Held, Don Hubert, and Kenneth Thompson. Malden, M.A.: Blackwell.

Han, Sang-Il. 2005. "Dong-Asia gongdongcheron" [A Discourse of East Asian Community]. *Hanguk dongyang jeongchi sasangsa yeongu* [*The Review of Korean and Asian Political Thoughts*] 4(1): 7–34.

Heo, Eun. 2007. "1960nyeondae huban 'joguk geundaehwa' ideology jujowa damdang jisigin-eui insik" [The Formation of the "Modernization of the Fatherland" Ideology during the Late 1960s and the Perception of the Intellectuals Who Oversaw this Process]. *Sahak yeongu* [*The Review of Korean History*] 86: 247–291.

Heo, Eun. 2010. "Park Chung-Hee jeonggwonha sahwoe gaebal jeonryakgwa jaengjeom" [The Strategies of Social Development during the Pak Chung-Hee Government and Related Conflicts]. *Hanguk sahakbo* [*The Journal for the Studies of Korean History*] 38: 213–248.

Hettne, Björn. 1995. *Development Theory and the Three Worlds: Towards an International Political Economy of Development*, 2nd edn. Essex: Longman Scientific & Technical.

Hettne, Björn and Fredrik Söderbaum. 2002. "Theorising the Rise of Regionness." Pp. 33–47 in *New Regionalisms in the Global Political Economy*, edited by Shaun Breslin, Christopher W. Hughes, Nicola Phillips, and Ben Rosamond. London: Routledge.

Hobsbawm, E.J. 1975. *The Age of Capital 1848–1875*. New York: Charles Scribner's Sons.

Hobsbawm, E.J. 1987. *The Age of Empire 1875–1914*. New York: Pantheon Books.

Hong, Seok-Ryul. 2005. "1960nyeondae hanmi gwangyewa Park Chung-Hee gunsa jeonggwon" [The U.S. Policy Toward Korea and Park Chung-Hee Regime in the 1960s]. *Yeoksawa hyeonsil* [*Quarterly Review of Korean History*] 56: 269–302.

Honour, Hugh. 1975. *The New Golden Land: European Images of America from the Discoveries to the Present Time*. New York: Pantheon Books.

Howarth, David. 2000. *Discourse*. Buckingham: Open University Press.

Hyemin. 2012. *Meomchumyeon, biroso boineun geotdeul* [*Things that are Visible Eventually When We Stop*]. Seoul: Ssaem and pakeoseu.

Inkeles, Alex and David H. Smith. 1974. *Becoming Modern: Individual Change in Six Developing Countries*. Cambridge, M.A.: Harvard University Press.

International Forum on Globalization. 2004. "A Better World is Possible!" Pp. 438–448 in *The Globalization Reader*, edited by Frank J. Lechner and John Boli. 2nd edn. Malden, M.A.: Blackwell.

Jang, Se-Gil. 2011. "Duryeoumeyonseo, maeryeokjeok-imyeonseo, yaman-seureoun jungguk" [Fearful, Attractive, and Savage China]. *Bigyo munhwa yeongu* [*Comparative Cultural Research*] 17(1): 81–117.

Jang, Se-Jin. 2012. *Sangsang-doen America* [*Imagined America*]. Seoul: Pureun yeoksa.

Janowitz, Morris. 1974. "Review of 'Reflections on the Causes of Human Misery and Upon Certain Proposals to Eliminate Them' (by Barrington Moore)." *American Journal of Sociology* 79(5): 1321–1326.

Jayasuriya, Kanishka. 1994. "Singapore: The Politics of Regional Definition." *The Pacific Review* 7(4): 411–420.

Jeon, Je-Guk. 1999. "'Asia-jeok gachi' gwanryeon dongseo nonjaeng-eui jaejomyeong" [Review of Eastern and Western Debates over "Asian Values"]. *Hangukgwa gukje jeongchi* [*Korea and International Politics*] 15(1): 187–219.

Jeong, Hye-Gyeong. 2002. "'Maeil shinbo'-e bichin 1910nyeondae jaejo ilbonin" [The Japanese in Korea in the 1910s Reflected in the Maeil Shinbo]. Pp. 125–168 in *Sikminji Joseon-gwa maeil shinbo* [*Colonized Joseon and the Maeil Shinbo*], edited by the Wednesday Research Group for History. Seoul: Sinseowon.

Jeong, Il-Jun. 2009. "Hanmi gwangye-eui yeoksa sahwoehak" [Historical Sociology of ROK-U.S. Relations]. *Sahwoewa yeoksa* [*Society and History*] 84: 217–261.

Jeong, Il-Jun, Jeong-Hyeon Park, Jongtae Kim, and Byeong-Gwon Song. 2015. "Hanguk, jungguk, ilbon-eui baljeon damron soge natanan gukga jeongcheseong-gwa sangho insik bigyo" [A Comparative Study of National Identities and Mutual Perceptions in the Developmental Discourses of Korea, China, and Japan]. *Gyeongje•inmun sahwoe yeonguhwoe inmun jeongchaek yeongu chongseo* [*Report for the National Research Council for Economics, Humanities and Social Sciences*]. 2015–2022.

Jeong, Jin-Seok, ed. 1983. *Hanseong sunbo hanseong jubo* [*Hanseong Sunbo Hanseong Jubo*]. Seoul: Gwanhun keullup sinyeong yeongu gigeum.

Jeong, Mun-Sang. 2007. "Naengjeon sigi hangugineui jungguk insik" [Koreans' Perception of China during the Cold War Period]. *Asia munhwa yeongu* [*Asian Cultural Studies*] 13: 47–70.

Jeong, Mun-Sang. 2011. "'Junggong'gwa 'jungguk' saieseo" [Between "Communist China" and "China"]. *Dongbuga yeoksa nonchong* [*Journal of Northeast Asian History*] 33: 57–90.

Jeong, Mun-Sang. 2012. "Geunhyeondae hangugineui jungguk insik-eui gwejeok" [The Trajectory of Modern Koreans' Perceptions of China]. *Hanguk geundae munhak yeongu* [*Journal of Modern Korean Literature*] 25: 203–231.

Jeong, Seon-Tae. 2004. "Dongnip shinmun'-eui Joseon•Joseoninron" [Dongnip Shinmun's Discourse on Korea and the Koreans]. Pp. 167–191 in *Geundae gyemong-gi jisik gaenyeom-eui suyong-gwa geu byeonyong* [*The Acceptance and Transformation of Knowledge and Concepts in the Modern Enlightenment Period*], edited by the Research Institute of Korean Culture at Ehwa Women's University. Seoul: Somyeong chulpan.

Jeong, Yong-Hwa. 2004. "Hangugin-eui geundaejeok ja-a hyeongseong-gwa Orientalism" [Koreans' Formation of Modern Self and Orientalism]. *Jeongchi sasang yeongu* [*The Korean Review of Political Thought*] 10(1): 33–54.

Jeong, Yong-Hwa. 2006. "1920nyeondae cho gyemong damron-eui teukseong" [Characteristics of Enlightenment Discourse of the Early 1920s]. *Dongbang hakji* [*Journal of Oriental Studies*] 133: 173–198.

Jepperson, Ronald L., Alexander E. Wendt, and Peter J. Katzenstein. 1996. "Norms, Identity, and Culture in National Security." Pp. 33–75 in *The Culture of National Security: Norms and Identity in World Politics*, edited by Peter J. Katzenstein. New York: Columbia University Press.

Jin, Si-Won. 2003. "Sahwoe guseongjueui-reul tonghae bon Europe-eui jeongcheseong" [Social Constructivist Approach to European Identities]. *Gukje jeongchi nonchong* [*The Korean Journal of International Studies*] 43(3): 137–162.

Jiyul. 2004. *Jiyul, supeseo naoda* [*Jiyul Coming Out of the Forest*]. Sup chulpansa.

Kang, Jeong-In. 2003a. "Seogu jungsimjueui-eui ihae" [Understanding Eurocentrism]. *Gukje jeongchi nonchong* [*The Korean Journal of International Studies*] 43: 29–51.

Kang, Jeong-In. 2003b. "Jiguhwa•jeongbohwa sidae dong-a-munmyeong-eui munhwa jeongcheseong" [The Cultural Identities of East Asian Civilization in the Age of Globalization and Information]. *Jeongchi sasang yeongu* [*The Korean Review of Political Thought*] 9: 223–245.

Kang, Jeong-In 2004. *Seogu jungsimjueui-reul neomeoseo* [*Beyond Eurocentrism*]. Seoul: Acanet.

Kang, Jeong-In. 2013. *Jeongchihak-eui jeongcheseong* [*The Identity of Political Science*]. Seoul: Chaeksesang.

Kang, Jun-Man. 2007. *Hanguk daejung maechaesa* [*History of the Korean Mass Media*]. Seoul: Inmulgwa sasangsa.

Kang, Myung-Koo. 2000. "Discourse Politics Toward Neo-liberal Globalization." *Inter-Asia Cultural Studies* 1(3): 443–456.

Kang, Won-Taek and Hong-Shik Cho. 2009. *Hana-eui Europe* [*One Europe*]. Seoul: Pureungil.

Katzenstein, Peter F. 2002. "Regionalism and Asia." Pp. 104–118 in *New Regionalisms in the Global Political Economy*, edited by Shaun Breslin, Christopher W. Hughes, Nicola Phillips, and Ben Rosamond. London: Routledge.

Kim, Cheol-Gyu. 2002. "20segi baljeonjueui-eui hyeongseong-gwa hangye" [The Formation and Limitation of the Twentieth Century Developmentalism]. *Bigyo sahwoe* [*Comparative Society*] 4: 213–231.

Kim, Cheol-Gyu. 2003. *Hanguk-eui jhabonjueui baljeongwa sahwoe byeondong* [*Capitalist Development and Social Change in Korea*]. Seoul: Korea University Press.

Kim, Dae-Young. 2004. "Park Chung-Hee gukga dongwon mechanism-e gwanhan yeongu" [A Study on the Mechanism of Park Chung Hee Regime's State Mobilization]. *Gyeongjewa sahwoe* [*Economy and Society*] 61: 172–207.

Kim, Do-Jong. 2001. "Park Chung-Hee paradigm-eui deungjang-gwa jisoge gwanhan damronjeok jeobgeun" [A Discursive Approach to the Emergence and Continuance of Park Chung-Hee Paradigm]. *Hanguk jeongchi oegyosa nonchong* [*Journal of Korean Political and Diplomatic History*] 23(1): 127–150.

Kim, Dong-Chun. 2011. "Naengjeon, bangongjueui jilseowa hanguk-eui jeonjaeng jeongchi" [War-Politics in Korea under the Cold War and Anticommunist Order]. *Gyeongjewa sahwoe* [*Economy and Society*] 89: 333–366.

Kim, Dong-Noh. 2004. "Sikminji sigi ilsang saenghwal-eui geundaeseong-gwa sikminjiseong" [The Modernity and Coloniality of Everyday Life During the Colonial Period]. Pp. 13–36 in *Ilje-eui sikminjibaewa ilsang saenghwal* [*The Imperial Japan's Colonial Rule and Everyday Life*], edited by The Institute of Korean Studies at Yonsei University. Seoul: Hyean.

Kim, Geon-Woo. 2015. "Hanmal yuhakja-eui wigieuisik-gwa geundae munmyeong damron bipan" [The Sense of Crisis Felt by Confucian Scholars at the End of the Korean Empire and Their Criticism of the Discourse of Modern]. *Yugyo sasang munhwa yeongu* [*The Study of Confucianism*] 61: 95–128.

Kim, Gyeong-Mi. 2004. "Botong hakgyo jedoeui hwakribgwa hakgyo hunyook-eui hyeongseong" [The Establishment of the Primary School System and the Formation of Disciplining at School]. Pp. 485–530 in *Ilje-eui sikmin jibaewa ilsang saenghwal* [*Imperial Japan's Colonial Rule and Everyday Life*], edited by the Institute of Korean Studies at Yonsei University. Seoul: Hyean.

Kim, Hak-Noh. 2013. "Gukje jeongchi(gyeongje)hak-eui miguk euijonseong munje" [The Problem of the Political Economy's Dependency on the U.S.]. Pp. 298–337 in *Jeongchihak-eui jeongcheseong* [*The Identity of Political Science*], edited by Jeong-In Kang. Seoul: Chaeksesang.

Kim, Ho-Gi. 1998. "Park Chung-Hee sidaewa geundaeseong-eui myeong-am" [The Park Chung-Hee Era and the Bright and Dark Sides of Modernity]. *Changjak-gwa bipyeong* [*Creation & Criticism*] 99: 93–111.

Kim, In-Young. 2013. "Baljeon gukga-eseo post-baljeon gukgaro" [From the Developmental State to the Post-developmental State]. *Segye jiyeok yeongu nonchong* [*The Korean Journal of Area Studies*] 31(1): 29–53.

Kim, Jeok-Gyo. 2012. *Hanguk-eui gyeongje baljeon* [*The Economic Development of Korea*]. Seoul: Bagyoungsa.

Kim, Jeong-Hun and Hee-Yeon Cho. 2003. "Jibaedamron-euroseoeui bangongjueuiwa geu byeonhwa" [Anti-Communism as a Dominant Discourse and its Change]. Pp. 123–199 in *Hanguk-eui jeongchi sahwoejeok jibaedamrongwa minjujueui donghak (3)* [*Politico-social Dominant Discourse and Dynamics of Democracy in Korea (3)*], edited by Hee-Yeon Cho. Seoul: Hamgge ingneun chaek.

Kim, Jeong-Hyeon. 2005. "Orientalism-gwa dong-Asia" [Orientalism and East Asia]. *Jungguksa yeongu* [*The Journal of Chinese Historical Research*] 39: 159–192.

Kim, Jin-Ho. 2006. "Geunhyeondae hanguk-in-eui jungguk insik-gwa jungguk-in-eui hanguk insik byeonhwa" [The Understanding of Korean on China and Chinese on Korea]. *Jungguk munhwa yeongu* [*Journal of Chinese Cultural Research*] 8: 373–398.

Kim, Jong-Young. 2015. *Jibae batneun jibaeja* [*The Dominated Dominator*]. Paju: Dolbegae.

Kim, Jongtae. 2016. "The Discursive Constructions of North Korea and the United States: National Identities and Representations on Fox News." *The Journal of Korean Sociology* 50(3): 1–21.

Kim, Jongtae and Gi-Deok Han. 2013. "Hanguk daehaksaeng-eui oeiguk-in chabyeol euisik-eui geunwon" [The Sources of Korean University Students' Discriminative Consciousness Towards Foreigners]. *Damron 201* [*Discourse 201*] 16(3): 35–66.

Kim, Tae-Woo. 2013. *Pokgyeok* [*Bombing*]. Paju: Changbi.

Kim, Young-Beom. 2003. "'Gukje gyeongjaeng' jibae damron bunseok" [The Analysis of the Dominant Discourse of "International Competitiveness"]. Pp. 397–427 in *Hanguk-eui jeongchi sahwoejeok jibaedamrongwa minjujueui donghak (3)* [*Politico-social Dominant Discourse and Dynamics of Democracy in Korea (3)*], edited by Hee-Yeon Cho. Seoul: Hamgge ingneun chaek.

Kim, Yun-Tae. 1999a. "Baljeon gukga-eui giwon-gwa seongjang" [The Origins and Growth of the Developmental State]. *Sahwoe-wa yeoksa* [*Society and History*] 56: 145–177.

Kim, Yun-Tae. 1999b. "Neoliberalism and the Decline of the Developmental State." *Journal of Contemporary Asia* 29(4): 441–461.

Kim, Yun-Tae. 2007. "The Transformation of the East Asian States: From the Developmental State to the Market-oriented State." *Korean Social Science Journal* XXXIV(1): 49–78.

Laclau, Ernesto and Chantal Mouffe. 1987. "Post-Marxism without Apologies." *New Left Review* 11: 79–106.

Laclau, Ernesto and Chantal Mouffe. 2001. *Hegemony and Socialist Strategy: Towards a Radical Democratic Politics*, 2nd edn. London: Verso.

Latham, Michael E. 2000. *Modernization as Ideology: American Social Science and 'Nation Building' in the Kennedy Era*. Chapel Hill, N.C.: The University of North Carolina Press.

Lee, Byeong-Cheon. 1998. "Baljeon gukga jabonjueuiwa baljeon dilemma" [The Developmental State Capitalism and Development Dilemma]. Pp. 44–71 in *Wigi, geurigo daejeonhwan* [*Crisis and Great Transition*]. Seoul: Dangdae.

Lee, Byeong-Cheon. 1999. "Park Chung-Hee jeonggweon-gwa baljeon gukga mohyeong-eui hyeongseong" [The Park Chung-Hee Regime and the Formation of the Developmental State Model]. *Gyeongje baljeon yeongu* [*Economic Development Research*] 5(2): 141–187.

Lee, Byeong-Cheon. 2000. "Baljeon gukga chejewa baljeon dilemma" [The Developmental State System and Development Dilemma]. *Gyeongje sahak* [*Journal of Economic History*] 28: 105–138.

Lee, Deok-Jae. 2009. "Park Chung-Hee jeongbueui gyeongje jeongchaek" [The Economic Policies in the Era of Park Chung-Hee Government]. *Yeoksawa hyeonsil* [*Quarterly Review of Korean History*] 74: 79–112.

Lee, Gil-Sang. 2007. *20segi hanguk gyoyuksa* [*Korean Educational History in the 20th Century*]. Seoul: Jipmundang.

Lee, Gwang-Il. 2003. "Seongjang baljeonjueui jibae damron-eui sinhwa-wa dillema" [The Myth and Dilemma of the Dominant Discourse of Growth-oriented Developmentalism]. Pp. 201–236 in *Hanguk-eui jeongchi sahwoejeok jibaedamrongwa minjujueui donghak (3)* [*Politico-social Dominant Discourse and Dynamics of Democracy in Korea (3)*], edited by Hee-Yeon Cho. Seoul: Hamgge ingneun chaek.

Lee, Gyeong-Hun. 2004. "Yobo•mobo•gubo" [Life and Fashion in Colony]. Pp. 189–231 in *Iljeeui sikmin jibaewa ilsang saenghwal* [*Imperial Japan's Colonial Rule and Everyday Life*], edited by the Institute of Korean Studies at Yonsei University. Seoul: Hyean.

Lee, Jong-Min. 2004. "Gamok nae suhyeongja tongjereul tonghae bon sikminji gyuyul chegye" [Colonial Disciplining System Reflected in the Prisoner Control]. Pp. 445–484 *in Iljeeui sikmin jibaewa ilsang saenghwal* [*Imperial Japan's Colonial Rule and Everyday Life*], edited by the Institute of Korean Studies at Yonsei University. Seoul: Hyean.

Lee, Nam-Ju. 2013. "Bundan cheje ha-eseoeui pyeonghwa damron" [Peace Discourse in The Division System on the Korean Peninsula]. *Donghyanggwa jeonmang* [*Journal of Korean Social Trends and Perspectives*] 87: 76–104.

Lee, Ok-Soon. 2002. *Uri aneui Orientalism* [*Orientalism within Ourselves*]. Seoul: Pureun yeoksa.

Lee, Ok-Yeon. 2011. "Jonggyojeok jeongcheseong, jeongchijeok jeongcheseong, Europe-eui jeongcheseong" [Religious Identity, Political Identity, and European Identity]. *Hanguk jeongchi yeongu* [*Korean Politics Research*] 20(1): 121–154.

Lee, Sam-Seong. 2001. *Segyehwa-wa miguk* [*The World and the U.S.*]. Seoul: Hangilsa.

Lee, Seung-Hwan. 1997. "Nuga gamhi 'jeontong'-eul yokdoege haneunga?" [Who Dares to Humiliate Tradition?]. *Jeontonggwa hyeondae* [*Tradition and the Modern*] 1: 176–189.

Lee, Su-Hoon. 2004. *Segyecheje, dongbuga, hanbando* [*The World System, Northeast Asia, and the Korean Peninsula*]. Seoul: Arche.

Lee, Won-Gyeong. 2011. "Europe tonghabe isseoseo jiyeok jeongcheseong munje" [Subregional Identity in European Unification]. *Yeoksa munhwa yeongu* [*History and Culture Research*] 38: 225–262.

Lee, Won-Young. 1996. "Gaehwa sasanggwa munmyeong sagwan" [Gaehwa Thought and Civilizational Historical Perspective]. *Honam jeongchi hakhwoebo* [*Journal for Honam Political Science Association*] 8: 361–387.

Lee, Woo-Young. 1991. "Park Chung-Hee tongchi inyeomeui jisik sahwoehakjeok yeongu" [Knowledge Sociological Research on Park Chung-Hee's Ruling Ideology]. *Hanguk sahwoehakhwoe 1991nyeondo jeongi sahwoehak daehwoe balpyo nonmun yoyakjib* [*Presentation Book for the First 1991 Conference of the Korean Sociological Association*]: 62–69.

Lee, Wook-Yeon. 2004. "Dugae-eui hanryuwa hanjung munhwa gyoryu" [Two Hallyu and the Korea-China Cultural Exchange]. *Cheolhak-gwa hyeonsil* [*Philosophy and Reality*] 62: 58–68.

Leys, Colin. 1996. *The Rise and Fall of Development Theory.* London: James Currey.

Lim, Chun-Seong. 2009. "Hanguk daehak-eui migukhwawa jungguk insik" [The Americanization of Korean Universities and Their Perception of China]. *Hyeondae jungguk yeongu* [*Modern China Research*] 11(1): 290–320.

Lim, Hak-Soon. 2012. "Park Chung-Hee daetongryeong-eui munhwa jeongchaek insik yeongu" [Ex-president Park Chung-hee's Awareness of the Cultural Policy]. *Yesul gyeongyeong yeongu* [*Korean Association of Arts Management*] 21: 159–182.

Lim, Wun-Taek. 2012. "Europe tonghabgwa sahwoe ironeui gwaje" [European Union and Perspective of Social Theory]. *Sahwoewa iron* [*Society and Theory*] 21(1): 95–140.

Lin, Chun. 2006. *The Transformation of Chinese Socialism.* Durham, N.C.: Duke University Press.

Ma, Sang-Yoon. 2002. "Geundaewha ideology-wa miguk-eui daehan jeongchaek" [Modernization Ideology and U.S. Policy on Korea]. *Gukje jeongchi nonchong* [*The Korean Journal of International Studies*] 42(3): 225–247.

Mahathir, Mohamad. 1991. "The Way Forward." Office of the Prime Minister of Malaysia. Available at www.pmo.gov.my/?menu=page&page=1904.

McMichael, Philip. 2008. *Development and Social Change: A Global Perspective*, 4th edn. Thousand Oaks, C.A.: Pine Forge Press.

Mehmet, Ozay 1999. *Westernizing the Third World: the Eurocentricity of Economic Development Theories*, 2nd edn. London: Routledge.

Mills, Sara. 1997. *Discourse.* London: Routledge.

Miyaoka, Isao. 2011. "Japan's Dual Security Identity: A Non-combat Military Role as an Enabler of Coexistence." *International Studies* 48: 237–255.

Moore, Barrington. 1966. *Social Origins of Dictatorship and Democracy: Lord and Peasant in the Making of the Modern World.* Boston, M.A.: Beacon Press.

Moore, Barrington. 1972. *Reflection of the Causes of Human Misery and on Certain Proposals to Eliminate Them.* Boston, M.A.: Beacon Press.

Mora, Necla. 2009. "Orientalist Discourse in Media Texts." *International Journal of Human Sciences* [Online] 6(2): 418–428. Available at www.insanbilimleri.com/en.

Mun, Se-Young. 1938. *Joseoneo sajeon* [*Korean Dictionary*]. Seoul: Bakmun seogwan.

Ndlovu-Gatsheni, Sabelo J. 2012. "Coloniality of Power in Development Studies and the Impact of Global Imperial Designs on Africa." Inaugural lecture delivered at the University of South Africa.

Nederveen Pieterse, Jan. 1995. *White on Black: Images of Africa and Blacks in Western Popular Culture.* New Haven, C.T.: Yale University Press.

Nederveen Pieterse, Jan. 2001 [2009]. *Development Theory: Deconstructions/Reconstructions.* London: Sage.

Nederveen Pieterse, Jan. 2008. *Is There Hope for Uncle Sam? Beyond the American Bubble.* London and New York: Zed Books.

Nederveen Pieterse, Jan. 2017. *Multipolar Globalization: Emerging Economies and Development.* London: Routledge.

Nisbet, Robert A. 1969. *Social Change and History: Aspects of the Western Theory of Development.* New York: Oxford University Press.

Noh, Dae-Hwan. 2010a. "1890nyeondae huban munmyeong gaenyeomeui hwaksan-gwa munmyeong-roneui jeongae" [The Spread of the Concept of Munmyeong and the Unfolding of Munmyeong Thought in the Late 1890s]. Pp. 1–21 in *Hanguksa yeonguhwoe 276cha yeongu balpyohwoe jaryojib* [*The Presentation Book for the 276th Conference of the Research Association for Korean History*].

Noh, Dae-Hwan. 2010b. "1905–1910nyeon munmyeong-roneui jeongaewa saeroun munmyeonggwan mosaek" [The Development of Theory of Civilization and Search for New Directions from 1905 to 1910]. *Yuhak sasang yeongu* [*The Study of Confucianism*] 39: 347–386.

Ollapally, Deepa. 2011. "India: The Ambivalent Power in Asia." *International Studies* 48: 201–222.

Paek, Nak-Cheong. 1998. *Heundeulrineun bundancheje* [*The Shaking Division System*]. Seoul: Changjakgwa bipyeong.

Paek, Nak-Cheong. 2005. "Park Chung-Hee sidaereul eoddeokge saenggakhalgga" [How to Think About the Park Chung-Hee Period]. *Changjakgwa bipyeong* [*Creation and Criticism*] 128: 287–297.

Park, Eun-Hee and Hae-Jun Seong. 2008. "Hanguk daehaksaeng-eui ilboneo hakseub donggiwa ilbon insik-e gwanhan yeongu" [A Study of Japanese Studying Motive and Japan and Japanese Recognition of Korean College Students]. *Dongbuk-a munhwa yeongu* [*Journal of Northeast Asian Cultures*] 17: 517–534.

Park, Jeong-Hwa and Do-Hee Kim. 1997. "Hanil yangguk-in-eui sangho insik-e gwanhan yeongu" [Research on Mutual Perceptions between the Koreans and the Japanese]. *Dong-il eomun yeongu* [*Dongguk Japanese Language Research*] 12: 93–133.

Park, Jeong-Hyeon and Jongtae Kim. 2015. "Jungguk-eui baljeon damron-gwa gukga jeongcheseong-eui dilemma" [China's Development Discourse and National Identity Dilemma]. *Asia yeongu* [*The Journal of Asiatic Studies*] 58(4): 134–173.

Park, Jung-Hyeon. 2008. "'Mujiwa mugwansim'eseo 'seoro bogi'ro" [From "Ignorance and Indifference" to "Mutual Perception"]. *Yeoksawa yeoksagyoyuk* [*History and Historical Education*] 15: 61–80.

Park, Noh-Ja. 2005. "Dokjejaga hanminjok jeontong-eul naljohanda" [The Dictator Distorts Korean Tradition]. *Inmulgwa sasang* [*People and Thought*] 86: 158–172.

Park, Sang-Young. 2012. "Hanguk 'post-baljeon gukgaron'-eui baljeongwa jeongae" [Exploring Korea's Emerging "Post-Developmental" State]. *Hyundae jeongchi yeongu* [*Journal of Contemporary Politics*] 5(1): 63–90.

Park, Seung-Woo. 2011. "Dong Asia gongdongche damron review" [Review of the Discourses on East Asian Community]. *Asia Review* 1: 61–110.

Park, Tae-Gyun. 1997. "1950nyeondae mal miguk-eui daehan gyeongje jeongchaek byeonhwawa Rostow-eui geundaehwaron" [The Change of U.S. Economic Policy on Korea in the 1950s and Rostow's Modernization Theory]. *Hanguksaron* [*Theories on Korean History*] 37: 253–317.

Park, Tae-Gyun. 2004. "Rostow je 3segye geundaehwaron-gwa hanguk" [Rostow's Modernization Theory of the Third World and Korea]. *Yeoksa bipyeong* [*Critical Review of History*] 66: 136–166.

Park, Tae-Gyun. 2005. "Different Roads, Common Destination: Economic Discourses in South Korea during the 1950s." *Modern Asian Studies* 39(3): 661–682.

Park, Tae-Gyun. 2009. "Park Chung-Hee jeongbu sigireul tonghae bon baljeon gukga damrone daehan bipanjeok siron" [Reassessing the Developmental State Theory through Park Era]. *Yeoksawa hyeonsil* [*Quarterly Review of Korean History*] 74: 15–43.

Park, Yang-Shin. 2008. "Geundae chogi ilboneui munmyeong gaenyeom suyong-gwa geu sesokhwa" [The Acceptance of the Concept of Civilization in the Early Phase of Modernization and Secularization in Japan]. *Gaenyeomgwa sotong* [*Concept and Communication*] 1(2): 33–74.

Parsons, Talcott. 1971. *The System of Modern Societies.* Englewood Cliffs, N.J.: Prentice-Hall.

Passerini, Luisa. 2002. "From the Ironies of Identity to the Identities of Irony." Pp. 191–207 in *The Idea of Europe: From Antiquity to the European Union*, edited by Anthony Pagden. Cambridge: Cambridge University Press.

Patterson, Thomas C. 1997. *Inventing Western Civilization.* New York: Monthly Review Press.

Quijano, Anibal. 2000. "Coloniality of Power and Eurocentrism in Latin America." *International Sociology* 15(2): 215–232.

Rahnema, Majid and Victoria Bawtree, eds. 1997. *The Postdevelopment Reader.* London: Zed Books.

Rist, Gilbert. 1997. *The History of Development: From Western Origins to Global Faith*, translated by P. Camiller. London: Zed Books.

Rivero, Oswaldo De. 2001. *The Myth of Development: The Non-viable Economics of the 21st Century*, translated by Claudia Encinas and Janet Herrick Encinas, New York: Zed Books.

Rostow, Walt W. 1960. *The Stages of Economic Growth: A Non-Communist Manifesto.* Cambridge: Cambridge University Press.

Ryu, Sang-Young. 1996. "Park Chung-Hee jeonggwon-eui saneophwa jeonryak seon-taek-gwa gukje jeongchi gyeongjejeok maekrak" [Between World System and State: Park Chung-Hee's Choice of Industrialization Strategy]. *Hanguk jeongchi hakhwoebo* [*Korean Political Science Review*] 30(1): 151–179.

Sachs, Wolfgang, ed., 1992. *The Development Dictionary: A Guide to Knowledge as Power.* London: Zed Books.

Said, Edward W. 1979. *Orientalism.* New York: Vintage Books.

Sakai, Naoki. 1989. "Modernity and its Critique: The Problem of Universalism and Particularism." Pp. 93–122 in *Postmodernism and Japan*, edited by Masao Miyoshi and H.D. Harootunian. Durham, N.C.: Duke University Press.

Schmid, Andre. 2002. *Korea Between Empires, 1895–1919.* New York: Columbia University Press.

Seo, Jae-Jin. 1991. *Hanguk-eui jabonga gyegeup* [*Korea's Capitalist Class*]. Seoul: Nanam.

Seong, Nak-Seon. 2001. "Sinjayujueui-wa miguk-eui jeongchi gyeongje" [Neoliberalism and the Political Economy of the U.S.]. Pp. 55–85 in *Miguk jabonjueui haebu* [*Anatomy of U.S. Capitalism*], edited by Jin-Bang Kim and Nak-Seon Seong. Seoul: Pulbit.

Shim, Jae-Wook. 2002. "1910nyeondae maeil shinbo-eui sikminji jibaeron" [The Idea of Colonial Rule in the 1910s Maeil Shinbo]. Pp. 203–241 *in Sikminji joseon-gwa maeil shinbo* [*Colonized Joseon and the Maeil Shinbo*], edited by the Wednesday Research Group for History. Seoul: Sinseowon.

Shin, Jong-Hun. 2014. "Europe jeongcheseong-gwa dong Asia gongdongche damron" [The Identity of Europe and the Discourse of East Asian Community]. *Yeoksa hakbo* [*The Korean Historical Review*] 221: 235–260.

Shin, Myeong-Jik. 2004. "Sikminji geundae dosieui ilsanggwa manmun manhwa" [The Everyday Life and Causeries Cartoons of the Colonized Modern City]. Pp. 277–335 in *Iljeeui sikmin jibaewa ilsang saenghwal* [*Imperial Japan's Colonial Rule and Everyday Life*], edited by the Institute of Korean Studies at Yonsei University. Seoul: Hyean.

Shohat, Ella and Robert Stam. 1994. *Unthinking Eurocentrism*. New York: Routledge.

Sigal, Leon V. 2002. "North Korea is No Iraq: Pyongyang's Negotiating Strategy." *Arms Control Today*, December: 8–12.

Sikkink, Kathryn. 1991. *Ideas and Institutions: Developmentalism in Brazil and Argentina*. Ithaca, N.Y.: Cornell University Press.

Simon, Roger. 1991. *Gramsci's Political Thought: An Introduction*. London: Lawrence & Wishart.

Swale, Alistair. 1998. "America: 15 January–6 August 1872: The First Stage in the Quest for Enlightenment." Pp. 7–23 in *The Iwakura Mission in America and Europe: A New Assessment*, edited by Ian Nish. Surrey: Japan Library.

Tanaka, Stefan. 1993. *Japan's Orient: Rendering Pasts into History*. Berkeley, C.A.: University of California Press.

Tikhonov, Vladimir. 2010. *Social Darwinism and Nationalism in Korea: The Beginnings (1880s–1910s): "Survival" as an Ideology of Korean Modernity*. Leiden: Brill.

Tripathy, Jyotirmaya and Dharmabrata Mohapatra. 2011. "Does Development Exist Outside Representation?" *Journal of Developing Societies* 27(2): 93–118.

Tsoukala, Anastassia. 2008. "Boundary-Creating Processes and the Social Construction of Threat." *Alternatives* 33: 137–152.

Tucker, Vincent. 1999. "The Myth of Development: a Critique of a Eurocentric Discourse." Pp. 1–26 in *Critical Development Theory: Contributions to a New Paradigm*, edited by Ronaldo Munck and Denis O'Hearn. London: Zed Books.

Turner, Jonathan H. 2003. *The Structure of Sociological Theory*, 7th edn. Belmont, C. A.: Wadsworth/Thomson.

Wallerstein, Immanuel. 2000. "Globalization or the Age of Transition? A Long-term View of the Trajectory of the World System." *International Sociology* 15(2): 251–267.

Wallerstein, Immanuel. 2004. *World-Systems Analysis: An Introduction*. Durham, N.C.: Duke University Press.

Wallerstein, Immanuel. 2006. *European Universalism: The Rhetoric of Power*. New York: The New Press.

Wendt, Alexander. 1994. "Collective Identity Formation and the International State." *American Political Science Review* 88(2): 384–396.

Wendt, Alexander. 1995. "Constructing International Politics." *International Security* 20: 71–81.

Wiegersma, Nan and Joseph E. Medley. 2000. *US Economic Development Policies Towards the Pacific Rim: Successes and Failures of US Aid*. New York: St. Martin's Press.

Wodak, Ruth, ed. 1989. *Language, Power and Ideology: Studies in Political Discourse.* Philadelphia, P.A.: John Benjamins Publishing Company.

Yi, Hae Gyung. 2011. "Changes in the Concept of Yulli During the Enlightenment Period in Korea." *Seoul Journal of Korean Studies* 24(2): 219–239.

Yoon, Sang-Woo. 2005. *Dong-Asia baljeoneui sahwoehak* [*The Sociology of Development in East Asia*]. Paju: Nanam.

Yoon, Sang-Woo. 2006. "Hanguk baljeon gukga-eui hyeongseong•byeondong-gwa segyechejejeok jogeon, 1960–1990" [The Rise and Decline of the Korean Developmental State in the Context of World-system Conditions, 1960~1990]. *Gyeongjewa sahwoe* [*Economy and Society*] 72: 69–94.

Yoon, Sang-Woo. 2009. "Oehwan wigi ihu hanguk-eui baljeonjueuijeok sinjayu-jueuihwa" [Internalizing Neoliberal Globalization in Korea]. *Gyeongjewa sahwoe* [*Economy and Society*] 83: 40–68.

Yoon, Tae-Won. 2014. "Europe-gwa Europe yeonhabeui jeongcheseong gochal" [A Review of Europe's and the European Union's Identity]. *Dogileo munhak* [*German Literature*] 67: 239–256.

Yu, Bul-Lan. 2013. "'Wuyeonhan donglib'-eui bujeong-eseo munmyeonghwa-eui mosundoen geungjeong-euro" [From the Negation of "Independence by Luck" to the Conflicting Affirmation of Civilization]. *Jeongchi sasang yeongu* [*The Korean Review of Political Thought*] 19(1): 85–108.

Yu, Gil-Jun. 2004 [1895]. *Seoyu gyeonmun* [*A Travel Essay on the West*], translated by Gyeong-Jin Heo. Seoul: Seohae munjip.

Zhao, Suisheng. 1997. "Chinese Intellectuals' Quest for National Greatness and Nationalistic Writing in the 1990s." *The China Quarterly* 152: 725–745.

Newspapers: 1890s–1930s

Chosun Ilbo. 1921. "Daejeon hueui guju-munmyeong-eui singyeonghyang" [New Trend in European Civilization after the Big War]. 30 April, p. 1.

Chosun Ilbo. 1921. "Munmyeong-gwa yaman" [Civilization and Barbarism]. 20 June, p. 1.

Chosun Ilbo. 1921. "Gwahak munmyeong-gwa dodeok munmyeong-eui gachiwa sojang" [The Values, and Rise and Fall of the Civilizations of Science, and of Tao and Virtues]. 26 July, p. 1.

Chosun Ilbo. 1923. "Munmyeong-han sabeobgwa gyeongchaledo gomuni muhanira" [There is No Torture in Civilized Judicial and Police Systems]. 9 March, p. 1.

Chosun Ilbo. 1924. "Gyeongchal-eul munmyeonghwa hara" [Civilize the Police]. 12 July, p. 1.

Chosun Ilbo. 1924. "Jhoseon-eui gyeongchalgwa ilbon-eui munmyeong" [The Police in Korea and the Japanese Civilization]. 9 September, p. 1.

Chosun Ilbo. 1925. "Chimnyak munmyeong-e yurindoen joseon cheongnyeona gweol-gihara. Bonbo sajang Lee Sangje-ssi gangyeon" [Rise, the Youth of Korea, Who are Infringed by the Civilization of Invasion: The President of Our Newspaper Lee Sangje's Address]. 13 November, p. 1.

Daehan Maeil Shinbo. 1907. "Nonseol" [Editorial]. 21 August, p. 1.

Daehan Maeil Shinbo. 1908. "Nonseol" [Editorial]. 13 August, p. 1.

Daehan Maeil Shinbo. 1908. "Nonseol" [Editorial]. 6 October, p. 1.

Daehan Maeil Shinbo. 1909. "Nonseol" [Editorial]. 27 March, p. 1.

Daehan Maeil Shinbo. 1910. "Nonseol" [Editorial]. 7 January, p. 1.

Dong-a Ilbo. 1921. "Munmyeong-in-gwa yamanin-eui chai" [Difference between the Civilized and the Barbarian]. 27 June, p. 3.
Dong-a Ilbo. 1925. "Munmyeong-eui wonjil" [Nature of Civilization]. 15 September, p. 1.
Dong-a Ilbo. 1926. "Yeong-ung-gwa ko, munmyeong-in-ilsurok koga keugo nopda" [The Hero and Nose: The More Civilized, the Higher and Bigger their Noses]. 16 July, p. 3.
Dong-a Ilbo. 1929. "Munmyeong-in egeneun sarangniga eobda" [There is No Wisdom Tooth with Civilized People]. 26 June, p. 3.
Dong-a Ilbo. 1936. "Munmyeong-in deuleun ibi ppareuda" [Civilized People Talk Fast]. 8 August, p. 3.
Dong-a Ilbo. 1939. "Munmyeonghan sarameun eolgul-i dunggeul-eojyeo" [The Faces of Civilized People Become Round]. 11 February, p. 4.
Dongnip Shinmun. 1896. "Nonseol" [Editorial]. 30 June, p. 1.
Dongnip Shinmun. 1897. "Nonseol" [Editorial]. 6 April, p. 1.
Dongnip Shinmun. 1898. "Guhwanghal gyechaek" [Strategy for Famine Relief]. 25 August, p. 1.
Dongnip Shinmun. 1899. "Injong-gwa naraeui bunbyeol" [Difference in Races and Nations]. 11 September, p. 1–2.
Dongnip Shinmun. 1899. "Nonseol" [Editorial]. 20 September, p. 1.
Dongnip Shinmun. 1899. "Nonseol" [Editorial]. 14 October, p. 1.
Dongnip Shinmun. 1899. "Nonseol" [Editorial]. 2 November, p. 1.
Dongnip Shinmun. 1899. "Nonseol" [Editorial]. 9 November, p. 1.
Maeil Shinbo. 1912. "Hamchanggun-eui hamchang" [Hamchang town]. 17 July, p. 3.
Maeil Shinbo. 1912. "Saseol: Munmyeong-gwa hyoyeol" [Editorial: Civilization, and Filial Piety and Chastity]. 19 March, p. 1.
Maeil Shinbo. 1912. "Chungbuk-eui wango pabyeok" [Rejecting the Stubborn in the Chungbuk Province]. 27 March, p. 3.
Maeil Shinbo. 1912. "Hyeongje jaepan haneun yaman" [Barbarism of the Lawsuit between Siblings]. 25 June, p. 3.
Maeil Shinbo. 1913. "Shinmun-eun munmyeong wonin" [Newspaper is the Source of Civilization]. 20 March, p. 1.
Maeil Shinbo. 1913. "Je jibe bul notneun yaman" [Barbarism of Setting Fire on his Own House]. 18 June, p. 5.
Maeil Shinbo. 1914. "Inmul yuin haneun ddujaeng-i" [Matchmaker Alluring People]. 1 March, p. 3.
Maeil Shinbo. 1914. "Munmyeong-eui seonjinja doeneun cheongnyeon sinsa" [A Young Gentleman to be a Pioneer of Civilization]. 23 March, p. 3.
Maeil Shinbo. 1914. "Park Young-Hyo-eui paeso" [Park Young-Hyo's Defeat in Lawsuit]. 31 March, p. 3.
Maeil Shinbo. 1914. "Saseol: Munmyeong-guk-eui pisangman moseupham-i bulga" [Editorial: Not to Superficially Imitate Civilized Countries]. 2 July, p. 1.
Maeil Shinbo. 1916. "Sinim chongdok-eul hwanyoung haneun norae" [Song for Welcoming New Government-General of Korea]. 15 December, p. 3.
Maeil Shinbo. 1918. "Bonsareul bangmunhan hunchun sachaldan" [Visitors from Hunchun to Our Company]. 14 May, p. 3.
Maeil Shinbo. 1918. "Youngmun joseon chongdokbu sijeong yeonbo oejashinmun bipyeong" [Review in the English Newspaper of the Government-General of Korea]. 25 May, p. 1.

Maeil Shinbo. 1919. "Munmyeong-guk-eui gyeolhonsik" [Marriage in Civilized Countries]. 21 November, p. 3.

Maeil Shinbo. 1919. "Honhyeoljok-eui jangryeo" [Recommending Interracial Marriage]. 6 December, p. 1.

Maeil Shinbo. 1920. "Buingwa gajeong-e gwangye" [Relationship between Women and Family]. 21 July, p. 3.

Maeil Shinbo. 1920. "Joseon-eul wihayeo sokhi joeundero indo hayeoyagetso" [We are to Rapidly Guide Korea to the Good Place]. 19 November, p. 3.

Maeil Shinbo. 1921. "Manpil: Munmyeong-gwa buneob" [Stray Note: Civilization and the Division of Labor]. 25 February, p. 1.

Maeil Shinbo. 1921. "Miguk taehyeong gaesi" [The U.S. to Begin Corporal Punishment]. 21 March, p. 3.

Maeil Shinbo. 1921. "Ilbon-gwa segye-eui gamjeongjeok yeoron" [Emotional Public Opinions of Japan and the World]. 5 June, p. 1.

Maeil Shinbo. 1921. "Banhi gyeoknoreul yeohan hunyu" [Address to Have Contrarily Instigated Fury]. 7 June, p. 3.

Maeil Shinbo. 1921. "Manpil: Yamanseong-eui haebu" [Stray Note: The Anatomy of Barbarism]. 16 July, p. 1.

Maeil Shinbo. 1921. "Joseon-eui yeoksajeok gwanchal" [Historical Observation of Korea]. 23 September, p. 1.

Maeil Shinbo. 1921. "Joseon gugyeong" [Sightseeing of Korea]. 12 November, p. 3.

Maeil Shinbo. 1922. "Miguk-eui silhwang-eul geohayeo joseoneui hyeonsang-eul bipan hanora" [Criticizing Korea's Phenomena by the Situation of the U.S.]. 8 January, p. 1.

Maeil Shinbo. 1922. "Soeuigyo maenghyu-eui wonin" [The Cause of the Soeui School's Students' Strike]. 16 July, p. 3.

Maeil Shinbo. 1922. "Hyeondae munhwa saenghwal-gwa sein-eui ohae" [Modern Cultural Life and People's Misunderstanding]. 7 November, p. 1.

Maeil Shinbo. 1923. "Hyeondae munmyeong-gwa dongyang dodeok-eui gwangye" [The Relationship between Modern Civilization and Eastern Ethics]. 9 April, p. 1.

Maeil Shinbo. 1923. "1man 5cheon geon-eui geomgeo jung-e choedasuga paryeomchijoe" [The Largest Number is the Infamous Crime among 15,000 Criminal Cases]. 12 May, p. 3.

Maeil Shinbo. 1924. "Dobak haneun munmyeong-guk-in" [Gambling Civilized People]. 10 December, p. 5.

Maeil Shinbo. 1925. "Munmyeong-eun uri-eui jeomyumul-ida" [Civilization is Our Property]. 26 October, p. 3.

Maeil Shinbo. 1927. "Gakguk-eui sikmin jeongchaek" [The Colonial Policies of Each Country]. 7 February, p. 1.

Maeil Shinbo. 1927. "Sikmin jeongchaek-eui jeongsin" [The Spirit of Colonial Policies]. 14 February, p. 1.

Maeil Shinbo. 1927. "Joseon-eun yamanida gyojang sileoni wonin" [The Cause is the Principal's Slip of the Tongue that Korea is Barbarism]. 8 December, p. 2.

Maeil Shinbo. 1928. "Nonseol: Guanchi malla" [Editorial: Not to Be Complacent]. 7 January, p. 1.

Magazines: 1950s–1960s

Beobryulgwa Gyeongje. 1954. "Hanguk gyeongje jaegeon-eui silchejeok gicho" [The Real Base for Korea's Economic Recovery]. 1 February, pp. 44–47.

Beobryulgwa Gyeongje. 1954. "Hujinguk-eui gyeongje-jeok teukjing-gwa geu gaebal munje" [The Economic Characteristics of Hujinguk and its Development Problem]. 25 November, pp. 22–25.

Chojeom. 1956. "Asia gyeongje-eui gomin" [Agony of the Asian Economy]. 25 January, pp. 55–60.

Digest. 1950. "Soryeon gyeongje-neun gwayeon buheung haetna" [Has the Soviet Economy Been Recovered?]. 1 January, pp. 58–61.

Gyeongje Gongron. 1957. "Teukjib: Seodok gyeongje-eui buheung-e baewoora" [Special Article: Learn from the Rehabilitation of the West German Economy]. 10 May, pp. 20–26.

Gyoyukgwa Hunryeon. 1963. "Gyeongje baljeon 5 gaenyeon gyehyeok-eun we pilyo hanga?" [Why is the Five-Year Economic Plan Needed?]. 20 July, pp. 17–23.

Hyeondae. 1957. "Teukjib: Hujinseong-eui je munje: Hangukjeok hujinseong-eui je yangsang" [Special Article: General Problems of Backwardness: General Features of Korean Backwardness]. 1 December, pp. 68–74.

Hyeondae. 1957. "Teukjib: Hujinseong-eui je munje: Hujinguk gyeongje yeongu" [Special Article: General Problems of Backwardness: Research on Hujinguk's Economy]. 1 December, pp. 75–79.

Jaejeong. 1955. "Advertisement." 1 September. Cover pages.

Jayugongron. 1958. "Hanguk buheung gyehoek-eui hyeonjae-wa jangrae" [The Present and Future of Korea's Recovery Plan]. 1 December, pp. 51–57.

Jayusegye. 1952. "Hanguk gyeongje-eui buheungchaek" [Method for Rehabilitating the Korean Economy]. 25 January, pp. 111–115.

Jeonggye Jaegye. 1959. "Hujingukga-eui bosu hyeoksin jeongdang hyeonhwang" [The Status of Conservative Reformative Parties in Hujinguk]. 10 December, pp. 49–54.

Saebyeok. 1956. "Gyeongje jaegeon-eui gwageo•hyeonje•jangrye" [The Past, Present, and Future of Economic Reconstruction]. 1 November, pp. 76–79.

Saebyeok. 1959. "Hujinguk-gwa dokje" [Hujinguk and Dictatorship]. 15 October, pp. 62–67.

Sedae. 1963. "Heoyoung-eui sijang-gwa bingon-eui seongjang" [The Market of Vanity and the Growth of Poverty]. 1 June, pp. 120–123.

Shincheonji. 1953. "Unmyeong-eui guksanpum" [Domestic Products of Destiny]. 5 October, pp. 56–60.

Shinsegye. 1962a. "Dongmyeon-gwa ganan" [Hibernation and Poverty]. 1 January, pp. 101–102.

Shinsegye. 1962b. "Hasa jeongdo-neun doenda" [We are about Staff Sergeant]. 1 January, pp. 87–88.

Shintaeyang. 1958. "Teukjib 10nyeon hueui hanguk" [Special Article: Korea in Ten Years]. 1 April, pp. 90–93.

Shintaeyang. 1959. "Hyeondae sasang-gwa geu chogeuk" [Modern Thought and its Overcoming]. 1 March, pp. 34–42.

Shintaeyang. 1959. "1959nyeon haewoe hakgye joryu" [Trend in Foreign Academia in 1959]. 1 March, pp. 117–120.

Newspapers: 1950s

Chosun Ilbo. 1950. "Cheoeum boneun taeguk" [First Seeing Thailand]. 15 May, p. 2.

Chosun Ilbo. 1955. "Uri gyeongje-eui hujinseong(1)" [Backwardness of Our Economy (1)]. 8 September, p. 2.

Chosun Ilbo. 1955. "Uri gyeongje-eui hujinseong(2)" [Backwardness of Our Economy (2)]. 9 September, p. 2.

Chosun Ilbo. 1957. "Gyeongje jaegeon-eui chokjin bangbeob" [Methods for Facilitating Economic Reconstruction]. 19 June, p. 1.

Chosun Ilbo. 1958. "Hanguk gyeongje baljeon hyeonjeo … mi sangmuseong-seo jijeok" [Korea's Economic Development is Notable – the U.S. Department of Commerce Points Out]. 6 April, p. 2.

Chosun Ilbo. 1958. "59–60nyeoneui gyeongje gaebal gyehoek sulib" [The Establishment of 1959–1960 Economic Development Plan]. 22 June, p. 2.

Chosun Ilbo. 1958. "New York Times 6•25 ginyeom saseol" [*The New York Times*' Editorial Commemorating 6•25]. 27 June, p. 2.

Chosun Ilbo. 1958. "Gokga jeongchaek-gwa gyeongje baljeon-eui goeri" [Discrepancy between Grain Price Policy and Economic Development]. 11 November, p. 1.

Chosun Ilbo. 1958. "Janggi gyeongje gaebal gyehoek-eui mokpyowa yoryeong" [The Goal and Method of Long-term Economic Development Plan]. 7 December, p. 1.

Chosun Ilbo. 1959. "Gwahak munmyeong-eui jeoljeong-e seoseo" [At the Peak of the Civilization of Science]. 1 January, p. 7.

Chosun Ilbo. 1959. "Segye ingu giwon 2cheonnyeonen 60eok: Munmyeong-guk-boda hujinguk-i deo paengchang" [World Population Will Be 6 Billion in 2000 AD: Hujinguk is Expanding More than Munmyeong-guk]. 5 April, p. 3.

Chosun Ilbo. 1959. "Hujinguk-iran mueosinga" [What is Hujinguk?]. 12 June, p. 2.

Newspapers: 1960s–1970s

Chosun Ilbo. 1968. "Seon-hujinguk hoeeui-e jungyongjido-reul jikyeo" [Keep the Virtue of Moderation in the Seonjinguk-Hujinguk Meeting]. 14 January, p. 1.

Chosun Ilbo. 1968. "Hujinguk sajeoldan apjang ohaebadeulkkabwa sayang" [Having Refused It Not to Get Misunderstood as a Leader of the Group of Hujinguk]. 21 January, p. 2.

Chosun Ilbo. 1969. "Seonjinguk-eui jalmot" [The Wrongdoings of Seonjinguk]. 4 November, p. 5.

Chosun Ilbo. 1972. "Seonjinguk-eui hanguk-jeok euimi" [The Korean Meaning of Seonjinguk]. 9 March, p. 4.

Chosun Ilbo. 1972. "U.N. ingan hwangyeong hoeeui-eui euieuiwa seonjinguk-eui chaekmu" [The Meaning of the U.N. Conference on Human Environment and the Responsibility of Seonjinguk]. 7 June, p. 2.

Chosun Ilbo. 1973. "80 yeondaeen seonjinguk daeyeol-e" [Getting into the Rank of Seonjinguk in the 1980s]. 4 July, p. 1.

Chosun Ilbo. 1975. "Hanguk gyeongje jiwi hyangsang. Imi seonjingukgweon jinip" [The Status of the Korean Economy has Improved to Already Get into the Range of Seonjinguk]. 12 December, p. 2.

Chosun Ilbo. 1975. "Hanguk, 10nyeonnae seonjinguk-euro" [Korea Expected to Become Seonjinguk in Ten Years]. 26 December, p. 2.

Chosun Ilbo. 1977. "Seonjinguk-e igineun gileun tujiwa noryeok" [The Way to Win Seonjinguk is Fighting Spirit and Hard Effort]. 1 January, p. 11.

Chosun Ilbo. 1978. "Samangyul seonjinguk-eui 44bae" [The Mortality Rate 44 Times that of Seonjinguk]. 24 January, p. 3.

Chosun Ilbo. 1978. "Imsanbu samang seonjinguk-eui 10bae" [The Maternal Mortality Rate Ten Times that of Seonjinguk]. 27 January, p. 5.

Chosun Ilbo. 1978. "Hanguk, seonjinguk daeyeol-e mi gukmuseong bogoseoseo gonggae" [Korea in the Rank of Seonjinguk, Made Public in the U.S. State Department Report]. 22 June, p. 1.

Newspapers: 1980s–1990s

Chosun Ilbo. 1983. "Seonjinguk munmul, gwayeon geugeoseun modu joeun geosinga" [Are the Material and Culture of Seonjinguk All Good?]. 1 January, p. 14.
Chosun Ilbo. 1983. "Seonjinguk-haeng" [Bound for Seonjinguk]. 16 November, p. 7.
Chosun Ilbo. 1984. "Seonjinguk-eui singyeong gwamin" [Seonjinguk's Hypersensitivity]. 11 March, p. 3.
Chosun Ilbo. 1984. "Seonjinguk-eui jogeon" [Conditions for Seonjinguk]. 11 November, p. 6.
Chosun Ilbo. 1984. "Seonjinguk gonghae saneop gaedoguk goeui ijeon" [Seonjinguk's Intentional Transferring of Pollution Industries to Developing Countries]. 7 December, p. 4.
Chosun Ilbo. 1985. "Yangjaetmul anmasigi. Seonjinguk gonghaemuljil suip eopseoya" [Not to Drink Lye; We Should Not Import Seonjinguk's Polluting Materials]. 12 January, p. 5.
Chosun Ilbo. 1985. "Seobang 7guk jeongsanghoedam oneul gaemak" [The G-7 Summit Opens Today]. 2 May, p. 4.
Chosun Ilbo. 1985. "Gaebangman hamyeon seonjinguk inga" [Is it Seonjinguk Only if Open?]. 1 November, p. 2.
Chosun Ilbo. 1986. "Golchodeul yeon baekman myeong sumjyeo – je 3segye" [One Million Heavy Smokers Dying per Year in the Third World]. 19 January, p. 4.
Chosun Ilbo. 1986. "Jeontong munhwa mani gajin naraga seonjinguk" [A Country Having a Lot of Traditional Cultures is Seonjinguk]. 11 March, p. 5.
Chosun Ilbo. 1987. "Chun daetongnyeong 'seonjinguk jinip mungori jabatta'" [President Chun Said, "We Have Grabbed the Door Handle of the Entrance to Seonjinguk"]. 5 March, p. 2.
Chosun Ilbo. 1987. "Chun daetongnyeong 'urineun seonjinguk doenda' gangjo" [President Chun Emphasized, "We Will Become Seonjinguk"]. 6 March, p. 2.
Chosun Ilbo. 1987. "Chun daetongnyeong 'seonjinguk hyanghae gal junbi kkeutnatta'" [President Chun Said, "We are Ready for Seonjinguk"]. 13 March, p. 2.
Chosun Ilbo. 1987. "'Venetia gyeongje seoneon' soksem" [The Hidden Intention of the Venetian Economic Declaration]. 17 June, p. 3.
Chosun Ilbo. 1991. "'Seonjinguk-hyeong tupyo seonghyang natanaetta'" [It Demonstrated Seonjinguk-type Voting Tendency"]. 21 June, p. 2.
Chosun Ilbo. 1993. "4mari yong jung seongjangyul kkoljji–in hanguk" [Korea at the Bottom in Economic Growth among the Four Asian Dragons]. 11 March, p. 10.
Chosun Ilbo. 1993. "Kkeut-eob-neun gyeongje suleong hyeonhwang-gwa daechaek" [The Situation of the Endless Economic Slump and Measures Against it]. 4 April, p. 7.
Chosun Ilbo. 1995. "OECD gaiphamyeon gukje heureum yecheuk seonjinguk" [If Joining the OECD, it is Seonjinguk of Predicting World Trend]. 29 March, p. 9.
Chosun Ilbo. 1995. "Gukmin sodeuk manbul sidae" [The Era of the Per Capita Income of $10,000]. 6 June, p. 9.
Chosun Ilbo. 1995. "Seonjinguk-eui gil" [The Way to Seonjinguk]. 24 July, p. 5.
Chosun Ilbo. 1995. "Gukminseong-gwa seonjinguk" [National Character and Seonjinguk]. 20 December, p. 5.

Chosun Ilbo. 1997. "Seonjin simini doepsida (1)" [Let's Become Seonjin Citizen (1)]. 1 January, p. 47.
Chosun Ilbo. 1997. "Bangsongdo seonjinguk-euro" [Towards Seonjinguk in the Field of Broadcasting Too]. 24 November, p. 23.

Newspapers: 2000s

Chosun Ilbo. 2001. "Hujinguk-hyeong jeonyeombyeong nadoneun hanguk" [Korea in Which Hujinguk-style Epidemics are Rampant]. 8 January, p. 2.
Chosun Ilbo. 2001. "I 'sseuregi'-ga uri sujun" [This "Garbage" is Our Level]. 7 August, p. 2.
Chosun Ilbo. 2001. "World cup gaechoegukga-e wen ijil?" [Is Dysentery in the World Cup Host Country?]. 17 December, p. 2.
Chosun Ilbo. 2003. "Segyeeui geoul-e bichin oneul-eui hanguk" [Today's Korea Reflected in the World's Mirror]. 16 October, p. A31.
Chosun Ilbo. 2005. "Simpan ttokbaro bolkkayo?" [Would We Referee the Game Correctly?]. 13 April, p. A31.
Chosun Ilbo. 2005. "Eotteoke ollaon seonjinguk munteok-inde ireoke jujeo anna" [How Could We Collapse in Front of Seonjinguk, to which We Have Ascended that Hard?]. 1 July, p. A35.
Chosun Ilbo. 2005. "Daetongnyeong 'seonjinguk-i mokpyo', biseosiljang 'imi seonjinguk'" [President is Saying "The Goal is Seonjinguk," While the Chief Presidential Secretary is Saying "Already Seonjinguk"]. 26 November, p. A31.
Chosun Ilbo. 2007. "Gieop jeonmang, segyeneun balkgo hanguk-eun eodubgo" [The World is Bright While Korea is Dark in the Prospect for Corporations]. 22 February, p. A35.
Chosun Ilbo. 2007. "'Gyoyukbu-ga jugeoya gyoyugi sanda'-go jeungmyeonghan gyogwamok gaepyeon" [The Curriculum Reform that has Proved "Education Would Live if the Department of Education Died"]. 24 February, p. A31.
Chosun Ilbo. 2007. "Gyeongje gyumo 12 deung, daeoe wonjoneun OECD kkolchi" [The Economic Scale is 12th, While Foreign Aid is the Last in the OECD]. 26 February, p. A35.
Chosun Ilbo. 2007. "Kim hoejang-i boyeojun 'noblesse oblige'-eui hyeonjuso" [The Current Status of "Noblesse Oblige" Shown by Chairman Kim]. 2 May, p. A31.
Chosun Ilbo. 2007. "Dang-i saerowueo jiryeomyeon Lee hubo meonjeo saerowueo jyeoya" [Candidate Lee Should Become New First Should the Party Become New]. 22 August, p. A35.
Chosun Ilbo. 2007. "Geonbo, mujakjeong insang malgo mirae cheongsajin naenoaya" [It Should Present a Future Plan, Rather than Blindly Raising Health Insurance Fee]. 16 November, p. A35.
Dong-a Ilbo. 2003. "Ilboeui yangsigeun eodiro gatna" [Where is Japan's Common Sense?]. 3 November, p. 2.
Dong-a Ilbo. 2006. "Jayuwa sijang-eul jikigesseumnida" [We Will Defend Freedom and Market]. 1 April, p. 39.
Dong-a Ilbo. 2006. "Hanguk-eseon oemyeondanghan '2006 seonjinguk trend'" ["2006 Seonjinguk Trend" Ignored in Korea]. 26 December, p. 35.
Dong-a Ilbo. 2007. "Gieop hagi nappeunde salgi joeun narado inna" [Is There Any Country in Which Living Conditions are Good Even if its Business Condition is Bad?]. 21 March, p. 35.

Dong-a Ilbo. 2008. "Anjeon euisik-gwa bangjae system hujinguk-eui chamgeuk" [Tragedy of the Hujinguk of Safety Awareness and Disaster Prevention System]. 9 January, p. 35.

Dong-a Ilbo. 2008. "'Siktak anjeon eopsi seonjinguk motdoenda'" [We Can't Be Seonjinguk Without Food Safety]. 25 March, p. 31.

Dong-a Ilbo. 2008. "'Yeoksi jeongchi hujinguk' ipjeunghan 17dae gukhoe" [The 17th National Assembly that has Proved "Hujinguk of Politics After All"]. 9 May, p. 35.

Dong-a Ilbo. 2008. "Amnesty, hanguk-eui beopjilseo heundeul seminga" [Amnesty, Are You Going to Shake the Korean Law Order?]. 21 July, p. 27.

Dong-a Ilbo. 2008. "Jeongbu surip 60nyeon, gwangbok 63nyeon daehanminguk-eui gil" [The Way for Korea in the 60th Anniversary of the Government Establishment and the 63th Anniversary of Independence]. 15 August, p. 27.

Dong-a Ilbo. 2008. "Danil minjok-eul neomeoseo damunhwa sahoereul saenggakha-neun gaecheonjeol" [The National Foundation Day to Think about a Multicultural Society beyond the Unified People]. 4 October, p. 27.

Dong-a Ilbo. 2008. "'Gukga seoyeol' jeonjininya hutoenya gallimgil-e seotda" [Our "National Rank" on a Forked Road to Progress or Retreat]. 22 October, p. 31.

Dong-a Ilbo. 2008. "Daetongnyeong toeim 9 gaeweol maneui 'hyeongnim' geomchal chuldu" [The Appearance of the "Elder Brother" in the Public Prosecutor Office Nine Months after President's Retirement]. 2 December, p. 31.

Dong-a Ilbo. 2008. "Saeroun suchul drive model changchulhal ttaeda" [It is Time to Create a New Model for Export Drive]. 9 December, p. 31.

Dong-a Ilbo. 2010. "Hanjung, bada sseuregi oyeom hujinguk-euro nameul geonga" [Are Korea and China Going to Remain as Hujinguk of Polluted Sea Wastes?]. 11 January, p. 35.

Dong-a Ilbo. 2010. "Yu Myung-Hwan janggwan ddal teukchae bujeokjeol haetda" [Minister Yu's Daughter's Special Employment Was Inappropriate]. 4 September, p. 27.

Dong-a Ilbo. 2010. "'Sobang mubangbi' hohwa gocheung geonmul, ireon ge hujinguk-ida" [This is Hujinguk, Luxurious High-rise Buildings without Fire Prevention System]. 4 October, p. 35.

Dong-a Ilbo. 2012. "Ileun seongeogu julineunde urineun neulligetdaneun geonga" [Are We Going to Increase Election Precincts While Japan is Reducing Them?]. 30 January, p. 27.

Hankyoreh. 2006. "Saneop yeonsusaengje pyeji, mirul iyu eoptta" [There is No Reason to Put off the Abolition of Industrial Trainee System]. 12 January, p. 27.

Hankyoreh. 2008. "Bijeonggyujik euijon hamyeon hakgyo patan nanda" [School Education Will Be Ruined if Depending on Temporary Workers]. 1 May, p. 27.

Kukmin Ilbo. 2011. "Boheom beomjoe geunjeol, ibeonen gidaehaedo doegetna" [Can We Expect the Eradication of Insurance Crime This Time?]. 27 January, p. 22.

Kyunghyang Shinmun. 2003. "Gyeongje teukgu, seonjinguk didimdolro" [Let's Make the Special Economic Zone Be a Step Stone for Seonjinguk]. 7 August, p. 7.

Kyunghyang Shinmun. 2010. "Jungguk, ingwon hujinguk beoseonaya daeguk-ida" [China Will Be a Great Country if it Escapes from Human Right Hujinguk]. 12 October, p. 35.

Segye Ilbo. 2012. "Sae euiwon hoegwan, teukgwon euisik jeonsijang doeji ankireul" [We Hope the New Congressperson Hall Not to Become an Exhibition Place for Privileged Sense]. 23 May, p. 31.

Segye Ilbo. 2013. "Sebi insang geobuhan mi euihoe, yeongeum chaenggin han gukhoe" [The U.S. Congress Has Refused to Increase Salary, While the Korean Congress Has Taken Pension]. 5 January, p. 23.

Seoul Shinmun. 2004. "Il anbori sangim isaguk jagyok inna" [Is Japan Qualified for the Permanent Member of the U.N. Security Council?]. 23 September, p. 31.

Presidential Addresses: Rhee Syngman

Kim Gu seonsaeng geubseo-e tongtan bulgeum [Deploring Kim Gu's Sudden Death]. 28 June 1949.

Soegukjueui-reul baejeham [Rejecting Isolationism]. 10 August 1949.

Nambuk dongponeun hyeobjo hara [Cooperate, the South and North Koreans]. 1950.

Sinsegye-e sal gachi itneun sarameul mandeulja [Let's Make People Deserve to Live in a New World]. 1950.

Gyeongje jalibchaek-e daehayeo [About the Policy for Economic Self-reliance]. 9 September 1952.

Chinil chingong bunjareul eopge hara [Make Sure that There are No Pro-Japanese and Pro-Communist People]. 13 May 1954.

Nabseneun munhwa gukmineui euimu [Paying Tax is Civilized People's Obligation]. 3 June 1954.

Jeonguk sileopga-e bonaem [Sending to Businesspeople in the Country]. 2 July 1954.

Yugyoeui gyohuneul jikyeo lyeeuijiguk baekseong-i doera [Be a People of the Country of Courtesy by Abiding by the Lessons of Confucianism]. 1 October 1954.

Jung-ang jeonhwaguk seoguk sinseoleul chiha [Congratulating on the Establishment of the West Branch of the Telephone Office]. 3 July 1957.

Wusuhan guksanpumeul saengsan hayeo haeoe sijang-eul gaecheok hara [Pioneer Foreign Market by Producing High-quality National Products]. 15 July 1957.

Dongseong dongbon honine daehayeo [About the Marriage between Persons with the Same Family Name]. 18 November 1957.

Gukmieun samgang oryuneul jikyora [Abide by the Three Fundamental Principles and the Five Moral Disciplines]. 30 December 1957.

Naraeui wisin-gwa jiwireul bojeontorok hara [Protect the Nation's Pride and Status]. 25 March 1958.

Urinara younghwa-eui baljeoneul chiha [Congratulating on the Development of Our Country's Movie]. 2 January 1959.

Presidential Addresses: Park Chung-Hee

Dongbu jiyeok gonggong haengjeong gigu je 3cha chonghwoe gaehwoesik chuksa [Congratulatory Message on the Third General Meeting of the Eastern Area Public Administrations]. 1964.

Bisang gyeeomryeong seonpo-e jeueumhan damhwamun [Statement on the Proclamation of the Emergency Martial Rule]. 3 June 1964.

8•15 je 19junyeon gyeongchuksa [Congratulatory Message on the 19th Anniversary of 8•15]. 15 August 1964.

Je 46hwoe 3•1jeol gyeongchuksa [Congratulatory Message on the 46th 3•1 Day]. 1 March 1965.

Jinhae je 4 biryo gongjang gigongsik chisa [Congratulatory Message on the Ground Breaking of the Fourth Fertilizer Factory in Jinhae]. 2 May 1965.

5•16 hyeokmyeong je 4junyeon ginyeom chisa [Congratulatory Message on the Fourth Anniversary of 5•16]. 16 May 1965.

Sesu hwakbo-e daehan seosin [Letter about Securing Tax Revenue]. 11 June 1965.

Jeheonjeol je 17junyeon gyeongchuksa [Congratulatory Message on the 17th Anniversary of the National Constitution Day]. 17 July 1965.

Je 2 Youngweol hwaryok baljeonso jungongsik chisa [Congratulatory Message on the Completion of the Second Youngweol Thermal Power Plant]. 15 September 1965.

Je 4298junyeon gaecheonjeol gyeongchuksa [Congratulatory Message on the 4298th Anniversary of the National Foundation Day]. 3 October 1965.

Hangeulnal-e jeueumhan damhwamun [Statement on the Hangeul Day]. 9 October 1965.

Paldang suyeok baljeonso gigongsik chisa [Congratulatory Message on the Ground Breaking of Paldang Water Power Plant]. 9 June 1966.

Busan joseon gongsa jonghab gigongsik chisa [Congratulatory Message on the Ground Breaking of Busan Shipbuilding Public Company]. 6 July 1966.

Je 3hwoe jeochuk-eui nal damhwamun [Statement on the Third Saving Day]. 25 September 1966.

Daetongryeong jimyeong surak yeonseol [Acceptance Speech for the Designation of Presidential Candidate]. 2 February 1967.

Daejeon yuse yeonseol [Campaign Speech in Daejeon]. 17 April 1967.

Jeonju yuse yeonseol [Campaign Speech in Jeonju]. 18 April 1967.

Je 22hwoe gwangbokjeol gyeongchuksa [Congratulatory Message on the 22nd National Independence Day]. 15 August 1967.

Busan yeonhab cheolgeum gongjang jungongsik chisa [Congratulatory Message on the Completion of the Busan Ferrous Metal Factory]. 29 September 1967.

Je 4hwoe suchul-eui nal ginyeomsik chisa [Congratulatory Message on the Fourth Export Day]. 30 November 1967.

Gonghwadang dangwon dongji-ege bonaeneun teukbyeol damhwa [Special Statement to the Comrades of the Republican Party]. 15 August 1968.

Je 2 gyeongje undong silcheon gukmin gwolgi daehwoe chisa [Congratulatory Message on the Rally for the Second Economy Movement]. 28 September 1968.

Jejudo pododang gongjang jungongsik chisa [Congratulatory Message on the Completion of the Glucose Factory in Jeju Island]. 1 November 1968.

Hanguk gijahyubhwoe changlib je 5junyeon ginyeomsik message [Congratulatory Message on the Fifth Anniversary of the Journalist Association of Korea]. 18 August 1969.

Gukmin tupyo silsi-e jeueumhan teukbyeol damhwamun [Special Statement on the Referendum]. 10 October 1969.

4•27 daetongryeong seongeo Daejeon yuse yeonseol [Campaign Speech in Daejeon for 4•27 Presidential Election]. 10 April 1971.

4•27 daetongryeong seongeo Chuncheon yuse yeonseol [Campaign Speech in Chuncheon for 4•27 Presidential Election]. 15 April 1971.

4•27 daetongryeong seongeo Daegu yuse yeonseol [Campaign Speech in Daegu for 4•27 Presidential Election]. 17 April 1971.

4•27 daetongryeong seongeo Seoul yuse yeonseol [Campaign Speech in Seoul for 4•27 Presidential Election]. 1971.

Hyundai geonseol Ulsan joseonso gigongsik chisa [Congratulatory Message on the Ground Breaking of the Ulsan Dockyard of the Hyundai Construction Company]. 23 March 1972.

Gyeongje-eui anjeong-gwa seongjang-e gwanhan gingeub myeongryeong-eui gongpo sihaeng-e ddareuneun teukbyeol damhwamun [Special Statement on the Emergency Order for Economic Stability and Growth]. 2 August 1972.

Pohang jonghab jecheol gongjang jungongsik chisa [Congratulatory Message on the Completion of the Pohang Iron and Steel Factory]. 3 July 1973.

Je 13hwoe suchul-eui nal chisa [Congratulatory Message on the 13th Export Day]. 30 November 1976.

Jeonguk saemaeul jidoja daehwoe yusi [Message for the National Meeting of Saemaeul Leaders]. 10 December 1976.

Hawaii imin 75junyeon ginyeom message [Congratulatory Message on the 75th Anniversary of the Immigration to Hawaii]. 13 January 1978.

Minju gonghwadang changdang je 16junyeon chisa [Congratulatory Message on the 16th Anniversary of the Democratic Republican Party]. 26 February 1979.

Je 10hwoe gukhwoe gaewonsik chisa [Congratulatory Message on the Tenth Opening of the National Assembly]. 15 March 1979.

Sobi jeolyak chujin beomgukmin daehwoe chisa [Congratulatory Message on the National Meeting for Frugality in Consumption]. 27 March 1979.

Presidential Addresses: Kim Young-Sam

Yeoeuido club hwoewoneui nal yeonseol [Speech for the Day of Yeoeuido Club Members]. 17 June 1993.

6•25 Chamjeon yongsa wiroyeon yeonseol [Speech for the Korean War Veterans]. 25 June 1993.

Je 165hwoe jeonggi gukhwoe yeonseol [Speech for the 165th Regular Session of the National Assembly]. 21 September 1993.

yeondu gija hwoegyeonmun [Statement for the 1994 New Year Press Conference]. 6 January 1994.

yeondu gija hwoegyeon [Statement for the 1995 New Year Press Conference]. 6 January 1995.

Segye ilbo teukbyeol hwoegyon [Special Interview with the Segye Ilbo]. 27 February 1995.

Je 32hwoe muyeok-eui nal yeonseol [Speech for the 32nd Trade Day]. 30 November 1995.

12•12 satae balsaeng 16nyenjjae doeneun naleul maja gukminege deurineun malsseum [Speech to the People on the 16th Anniversary of the 12•12 Incident]. 12 December 1995.

Je 28hwoe gukga jochan gidohwoe yeonseol [Speech for the 28th Breakfast Prayer Meeting for the Nation]. 30 April 1996.

Daejeon jihacheol 1hoseon gigongsik yeonseol [Speech on the Ground Breaking of Line 1 of the Daejeon Subway]. 30 October 1996.

Gyeongje salligireul wihae gukminege deurineun malsseum [Speech to the People for the Sustaining of the Economy]. 11 December 1997.

Presidential Addresses: Lee Myung-Bak

Je 28junyeon 5•18 minjuhwa undong ginyeomsa [Congratulatory Message on the 28th Anniversary of the 5•18 Democratic Movement]. 18 May 2008.

Daegu seongseo 5cha cheomdan saneop danji gigongsik chuksa [Congratulatory Message on the Ground Breaking of the Fifth High-tech Industrial Complex in Seongseo, Daegu]. 21 May 2008.

Gukminege deurineun malsseum [Message to the People]. 22 May 2008.

Je 18dae gukhwoe gaewon yeonseol [Speech for the Opening of the 18th National Assembly]. 11 July 2008.

Gukmin seonggong silcheon yeonhab vision seonposik chuksa [Congratulatory Message on the Proclamation of the Vision for the National Success Movement]. 12 July 2008.

Wonju-Gangreung cheoldo geonseol gigongsik chisa [Congratulatory Message on the Ground Breaking of the Railway between Wonju and Gangreung]. 1 June 2012.

Je 19dae gukhwoe gaewon yeonseol [Speech for the Opening of the 19th National Assembly]. 2 July 2012.

Index

Notes: 'n' indicates chapter notes; bold indicates tables; italics indicate figures.

www.ingramcontent.com/pod-product-compliance
Ingram Content Group UK Ltd.
Pitfield, Milton Keynes, MK11 3LW, UK
UKHW011003180926
475701UK00004B/534
9780367359942